Happy Birthday
to
Donald; from
08.08.08

SCOTTISH ISLAND VET

Scottish Island Vet

ROBERT SILLARS M.R.C.V.S

SERENDIPITY

First published in 2008 by
Serendipity Publishers, Darlington, UK

ISBN 978-1-84394-221-4

Printed and bound in Great Britain by
Biddles Ltd, King's Lynn, Norfolk

I wish to dedicate my father's book to my mother who passed away on 31 October 2005, without whose support this book would never have been written.

To Malcolm Goodsall for the photography.

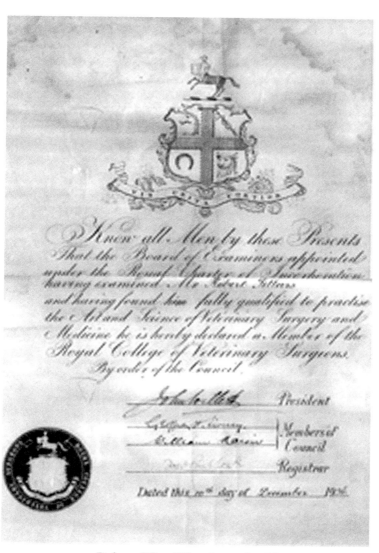

Robert Sillars' Veterinary Certificate

CHAPTER 1

I think I had better explain right at the outset that the title, *Scottish Island Vet*, whatever impression it may convey to the passing eye, refers only to one island, the Isle of Arran in the south-west and some of the islands right up in the north-east, namely that part of Orkney which is generally called the North Isles. The North Isles, not to be confused with the Northern Isles, a term which includes all the islands in the Orkney and Shetland plus some tiny, isolated ones like Fair Isle, are a group of something like ten inhabited islands to the north and east of the main island or 'Mainland' of Orkney. But before I got there, I had spent a good many years in Arran and other parts of Britain.

Arran it was which had the inestimable privilege of receiving me into this world in the early part of the 20th century. There I landed, right in the middle of the small valley of Shiskine, which extends south-west from an area where two small glens join to form Glen Loig, for roughly four miles to Blackwaterfoot, the only village on the south-west shore.

I was relatively old when I started school, mainly because our mother did not believe in starting us early, and she probably had a good point there. She maintained that age six was quite young enough for a child to begin to lose any of that early freedom which ideally it should have, and I must have been nearing seven years old when I first set off for school on that beautiful morning in May. Until then, despite the elder members of our family, I was most of each day on my own. At a very early age, so I was told, I spent some part of most days in a clothes basket on an old chest between the kitchen table and the window where the ground was level with the window sill. There I had long talks with the hens when they gathered there for sun and shelter. They were probably a lot older than I was.

From talking to the hens I progressed, as I became more mobile, to exploring my environment. The feu, the plot of land on which the house stood, was open to the public road, thus giving me access to it and to the banks and hedges at the roadside. I distinctly remember there was a blackie's nest just three or four yards from the end of the hedge and another few yards from it a navie's, i.e. a navis or thrush's nest. Across the road, which was maybe twelve feet wide in those days, and through the other hedge at a place where the bank was high, was a wren's nest, a dainty, tiny thing with an entry hole maybe a inch wide. But I did not discover that one. Someone else had learned of it and showed it to me. I took a close interest in the progress of the nests, with my frequent inspections, probably far too frequent. I don't think I caused any of the birds to desert their nests though I probably got some dirty looks from those indignant prospective mothers.

Like most children I had artistic proclivities too and in mine I have no doubt a child expert seeing them would have detected a strong leaning towards veterinary or at least equine affairs. There was for example my first attempt to draw a horse, an attempt which was very likely the same as that done by millions of other very young children. I managed his top line all right, a long, fairly straight line from left to right with nothing much in it to suggest a neck nor withers nor saddle nor quarters. At the left hand side I drew what was recognisably a head. At the other end a few pencil strokes made what was clearly a tail. Four perpendiculars dropped from the top line, with loops on the ends of them, made legs and feet. Ah, but even at early age there must have been a critical though quite embryonic veterinary eye at work. I soon saw that my horse had no middle. None at all. Surely a serious fault in any horse, no matter for what purpose he was intended. I think then there followed quite a long time before I solved the problem of how to give my horse a middle and some substance to his neck and legs.

There were other indications of my early interest in animals. Several of our closer relatives were crofters or farmers, each with at least one horse, or more than one. All had cattle, some had sheep as well and maybe a pig or two. Everybody had dogs and cats and hens. But we had a cat and some hens at home, and hens were just things that made a lot of noise and got into the scullery and stole things.

For seeing more horses and some of the things that could be done with them there was the smithy, or smiddy, as it is called in Scotland. In fact there were two, the nearer one two or three hundred yards up the road, not too far for small legs to reach. On a calm day when the wind was right we could easily hear the hammers in the anvil and maybe also see a horse standing outside the smiddy. When one or more horses came in to be shod or to have their shoes 'shifted' (the shoes taken off, the hooves trimmed down and the same shoes put back on again) the smiddy was a fascinating place of bright, rearing flames, dark corners and the pungent smell of singeing horn on the feet of what seemed to me big, big Clydesdale horses. We were not allowed to get very near them, but near enough to see plenty and hear at close range the clang of hammers on the anvil and their thudding into the red hot iron of shoes in the making. I wonder how many blacksmiths today, starting with the proper bar of iron and the right equipment, could make a set of horseshoes and fit them to any given horse presented for shoeing? Not many, I would guess.

These were some of the joys of my earliest days. Another joy was in some of the reading material I found from time to time. Animal stories: I don't believe there was another kid for miles around who was so daft about animal stories. Some of the more easily identified include one about an Old English sheepdog, one about a mongoose, one about a Rocky Mountain ram and one, perhaps most famous of all, about an English carriage horse. There were lots of other similar stories.

If on occasion we could not go as near as we would have like to the horses in the smiddy there was at least one other occasion, again involving a specimen of the Equidae, when I had no wish to get any nearer. I would be about three or four years old when nearly the whole family of us were visiting one day one house among several visits that day in Lochranza. As a diversion for the children it was suggested that they all go and see the donkey. The donkey lived in his own small stable, up a steep path at the back of the house. Off we went, the elder ones in front, I happily pegging along behind. Halfway up the path the air was suddenly torn with the most appalling noise that had ever assailed my young ears.

Of course I knew right away what had happened. A large piece of the sky had fallen; that's what it was. Somewhere over near the pier, not far away, and more likely to fall at any moment right on top of me. I waited neither to hear any more of it nor for any explanation of it but turned tail and fled precipitately down that path and into the house before anyone fairly knew what I was doing.

I had never before heard a donkey braying, so how was I to know that the horrendous sound I had just heard was only his welcome to visitors who, he very likely anticipated, were probably bringing him something nice to eat? Only long afterwards was I persuaded that the sound I heard came from a donkey.

Fifty to sixty years ago that same three hundred yards of road served, besides the smiddy, about a dozen different households representing as many different occupations. There was the doctor who served the west half of the island, there was a busy licensed hotel, a big farm, a meal mill, an active grocery and general store, a post office, a passenger transport and carrier business, a painter and decorator, two firms of joiners, a busy tailor's workshop and a much less busy police station. So quiet was the police station, so law-abiding were the people of Shiskine and neighbouring districts that between fifty and sixty years ago the police station was closed and its business transferred to the Lochranza station which the authorities (no doubt very wisely) decided should be kept going. However the Lochranza people must have quietened down a lot since then because that office too has been closed for a long time now. As for the occupations in that part of Shiskine, nearly all of them and in one or two cases even the buildings which housed them, have long since gone. Of the meal mill, for example, which once stood three storeys high, there is not now one stone left standing on another.

Right through primary and secondary school this literary appetite for nature stories continued. It abated only with my entry to Glasgow Veterinary College and closer acquaintance with real animals, or rather, their carcases in the much less romantic setting represented by the anatomy lab.

Veterinary work was not quite my first choice but it was a close second, which is why, when I was advised by a University Adviser of Studies against following my first choice, I quickly fell back on my second. But that is another story which may emerge sometime later. What happened then was that either that same day or the next one I was enrolled at Glasgow Vet. College, as it then was, for the four-year course for the diploma MRCVS, three weeks late in starting it and probably one of the last students in the country to embark on that curriculum.

Five years and one term later, Glasgow Vet. College and the Royal College examiners combined to release my devilishly destructive energies on a wholly unprepared, unsuspecting and defenceless British Public. That was on 10 December 1936, one reason why I can always remember the date of the Abdication.

A dialogue such as could be imagined as passing between two young men, college friends and both qualifying at that time, might have gone something like what I here venture to suggest:

'Hullo there, George. Congratulations. Good man. Any word of a job yet?'

'No, Tammas, my ancient, trusty, drouthy crony, not a thing. Congratulations to yourself. So we've finally made it. You fixed up with anything yourself yet or not?'

'Final, final, George, you great callous brute, don't even suggest the sound of that word to me; not for years and years to come. No I haven't got anything yet.'

'Anything decent in the *Veterinary Record* this week?'

'Decent, uh, there never is anything decent in it, not in the way of assistantships, if that is what you are thinking of. There might be something that's just bearable and paying enough to buy our crust of bread and rags to cover our shivering bones, our emaciated frames, but I doubt it.'

'I saw a chap as I came in here with a copy of it, probably taken from the library. I'll see if I can find him and borrow it.'

About two minutes later the dialogue is resumed.

'There are four or five here, all pretty much the same: 'Reply stating salary required and enclosing three recent references, (copies please). All information with first letter please: Box No ...' Here's another one. 'State salary required, live in, sign usual bond. Box No ...' And so on and so on). Where in all blue hell do they think I'm going to get three recent references recent or old or middle aged? What do they think they –'

George's slightly inflammable comments would have continued in full flow but that Tammas interrupted.

'Exactly, Just the usual form and likely all the same old advertisers. Living in is no good anyway.'

'I know it all too well. I had it with the bloke who usually had me to see practice with him. A helluva nice chap himself, mind you, but...'

'Absolutely. Beautiful expressed and your eloquence does you credit. Attend to his dogs, sit in with his kids, be all things all times and I bet if you asked him for more than a fiver a week inclusive he would start talking as if you were trying to ruin him.'

'It might not be as bad as that, but some of them are not far short of it. Some of these cranky old beggars in practice for ten or fifteen years before they could afford to get married want an awful lot for their money.'

'George, me boy it's me that kens it. Ungrammatical but emphatical.'

'There's no such word as emphatical.'

'There is, as from now on. I've just invented it.'

At this point there might been a brief silence, crammed with thought, before either of them spoke again.

'Nothing doing with the Min. of Ag., is there? Any firms with laboratory jobs going, or sales reps, wanted or anything like that?'

'Don't see anything. In any case you need outside experience first.'

'Och well, let's leave it at that in the meantime. Are you doing anything special tonight?

'I hadn't thought of anything in particular; maybe the modest noggin and a half pint, either to celebrate or drown my sorrows, depending on how things went.'

'OK. Two or three of us are meeting here tonight about seven o'clock if you feel like turning up. There's nothing arranged so far. We'll think of something when we get here then.'

In my own case there was just such a meeting and from it we set off on a pub crawl. I was quite unaccustomed to strong drink of any kind and as the evening progressed my intake became less and less cautious. With embarrassingly brief warning I began to show symptoms of marked overdosage followed by summary rejection of part of my evening intake. But never mind; I had done, as had the others with me, what we had started out years ago to do. I had qualified as a vet. I was now a member of the Royal College of Veterinary Surgeons.

By the time I qualified I had failed twice in Physiology and Histology (treated as one subject) and once in Surgery. It was not that I disliked those subjects, nor did I dislike Pathology and Bacteriology (one subject), also failed, but rather that I had always tended to read and remember better the sort of information I thought I might find most useful as a vet for the farm animals, which was the kind of vet I had always intended to be. Such information seemed to take precedence with me over the more technical data which might better have helped me through the next professional exam. Consequently I arrived as a member a little bit late and perhaps a little too intent on marrying theory to practice, but in any case, and like a good few others, unemployed and looking for a job. Even with all the practice a student could cram into the years in which he was at college he was, when newly qualified and entitled to practice, still woefully inexperienced, a fact of which no one was more aware than himself. Consequently the usual and probably wisest plan for anyone intending to practise was to get a job as an assistant with an experienced practitioner in whatever type of practice was selected, who could steer the young graduate clear of most of the mistakes he would otherwise make.

New graduates on the old four-year course, in Glasgow at least, especially if they were not country bred, generally left college with a lot of little gaps in their knowledge which they were only too anxious to fill as soon as possible. For that reason among others, they were prepared to work long hours, indeed any hours at all, and for low wages, politely called salaries.

I remember hearing, many years ago, of on example of this sort of gap in basic knowledge. A certain farmer, finding his yearling Clydesdale colt showing signs of colic, sent for the vet he usually had. The vet had gone from home for a few days, leaving in his place a young man who was not then qualified but who was in his final year. It may be said here that while, strictly speaking, employing students was illegal it was commonly done all over the country in those days. The patient need not have fared any the worse on that account and might in fact got better treatment from an undergraduate with some of the right kind of experience than in the hands of a graduate who had none. What got the farmer worried was that the student, in the course of his examination of the colt, asked the farmer if he had it in the cart much lately.

The farmer of course saw immediately that no vet who was anywhere near having the necessary experience of farm horses would have dreamt of asking if a yearling colt had been carting much. That one question from the young veterinarian was a big factor in the farmer's deciding to look for another vet who was less unfamiliar with farm horses.

Only long afterwards did I hear that little story from the farmer concerned, and to me it illustrated vividly one of the differences between a country, not necessarily farm, boy and one with an urban upbringing.

CHAPTER 2

Finding a job was for me made less easy by the fact that I had, ever since early days, a certain difficulty in speaking which began to appear gradually when I was about six and which varied in degree from time to time being anything from nil to a complete 'block'. And when I 'blocked' as it is called, on a word, the hold-up was complete. It was not a stutter; it was not exactly a stammer either; just a dead stop for which I never did find a reliable remedy. Now that I am older and can take a more detached view of it I can see pretty clearly how the 'blocking' mechanism works and what I can do about it, but until that stage was reached the trouble remained quite baffling.

For the first few decades of my life there seemed to be little understanding of my case by anyone. Despite the endless introspective hours I spent on it, the innumerable consultations with therapists and a good many psychiatrists, none of them was ever any real help. All were much better at asking questions, listening to everything I could tell them and making superficial comment than at giving any information of any real value. Now, I really do not think they had any to give. About the only thing of which I could be fairly sure was that the more important the word or phrases the more meaning it conveyed the more likely I was to block on it. This difficulty made speaking to strangers a thing which I for a long time tended to avoid though, when I had to do it, I could generally say something, often in a quite natural way, before they could begin to think that that I could neither speak nor hear. Among those times when I took too long to speak I know there were a few, a very few, when the stranger rushed to that conclusion, with somewhat embarrassing results, but we always got things straightened out.

One noticeable consequence to the speaking trouble was that while the new graduate without any disability might not have great luck in finding a job, I had less. Quite understandably most employers wanted a better speaker and I never could blame any of them for that, but it left me searching among the residue, the left-overs of jobs available, that was if I could get any job at all, which was not always the case.

I did eventually get one. In the earlier-mentioned, imaginary conversation between two new graduates in the college there are a few remarks about assistantships. The job I got was simply that part of that conversation acted out. There was the care of the household dogs, the occasional charge of the children, liability for duty at any hour in the week, even weeding the garden when all else failed; all for £2 10s. (now £2.50) per week and my keep. I stuck it for only a short time, keen as I might be to keep my first job, then, when I got the latest arrears of pay (for which I always had to ask), I gave notice. When, as a parting act, he gave me the references I had asked of him, his conscience was such that he felt he had to mention in it his criticism of me, or so he pretended to me. I then wondered if this was the same person I had heard some weeks earlier tell me, in something like these words:

'If you are ever out on a round and you get a message to go to a milk fever case when you have already used your calcium, don't hesitate to fill your bottle at the first clear spring or burn you come to, and inject that. Remember, inflating the udder at the same time will get them up as good as, or better, than the calcium.' I accepted his rotten reference and hoped he was not a typical practitioner yet I feared he was.

After making my way by easy stages back to Arran again I found I had little to do there beyond giving a helping hand here and there while looking in all directions for another job. Occasionally I reflected on the nature and quality of the profession of which I had become a member after prolonged, laborious effort, and sometimes speculated lightly on how a vet might fare in certain circumstances in this very island of Arran. Somehow I do not seem now to have found either line of thought very cheering.

True I would not have lacked for scenery. There were the blue, or usually blue, mountains to the north: Ben Nuis, Ben Bharrain (pron. Varen), Goat Fell and others, all between two and three thousand feet. There was the fertile valley of Shiskine with its level to level floor; there was the view of Brodick Bay from the top of the String Road, the road which traverses the middle of the island east to west and rises to a height exceeding 750 feet. There were the glens and the burns, an expanse of forestry here and there, the whole surrounded by the waters of Kilbrannan Sound and the Firth of Clyde. But scenery did not provide veterinary work nor pay the bills for that work. For that matter I had often heard there were a few clients who did not seem too keen on that bit either.

In any case I still lacked experience enough for independent practice and so, when in late October 1937 I was accepted for the post of second assistant in a practice in the East End of London I was off again, surely this time, I thought, to broaden my experience and acquire a useful and growing bank balance.

The practice in which I arrived consisted almost entirely of heavy draught horses and small animals. The principal, who was a tall, voluble gentleman, had also acquired the goodwill of at least two, probably three or four, other practices adjoining or not too far away, with surgeries (so called) as central points for them. Of these 'surgeries' the sole, salient feature was the almost total lack of any equipment whatsoever: medicines, instruments, dressings, utensils, hot water anything.

I remember attending a 'surgery' in Bethnal Green, the only one I ever did there and probably the last one ever to be done in that place before some drastic, long overdue change was made to it. During that visit I had but one client, a girl who brought in a dog which had a few wart-type growths, all quite small, on its skin. I could find but one solitary pharmaceutical product in the whole place, a crude, liquid, arsenical preparation of uncertain age. I also found one bottle, a 10 oz. size, far too big for the purpose in hand. I filled the bottle, labelled it with some stray label found about the place and gave it to the girl. There was in me at that time a vague belief that arsenic did have some sort of caustic action on the skin when applied externally, apart from its well known action on the skin in general when taken as a course of medicine at a correct dosage. She said she had not brought any money; could she take the bottle and she would come back with it later? To that idea I, reckoning that the money she would bring would be about the same in value as the treatment she had got for the dog, gave my approval. Of course I never saw her nor the dog again, nor the money, which would have been about three shillings at that time, so what became of the dog, the warts and the half pint of arsenic preparation I never heard nor had I any wish to hear.

Probably not the least valuable part of my London experience was what I got in driving to and from those places in a Ford 8 car. I am not happy driving in traffic of that density now. I was no happier then. If there was scope anywhere for making a driving error I made it. It was just no trouble at all to me to miss a NO ENTRY sign and enter. I once caused a policeman to leave his position on point duty and tell me to move my car back a bit from a busy junction. Why? Because I was on a pedestrian crossing, that was why.

Another time, having got part way up the Strand from Trafalgar Square and seeing people waving at me I immediately thought: 'what nice, friendly people the English are.' It was true enough then that they were rather more oncoming that the Scots who were generally acknowledged to be a little dour. One would never expect such friendly gesture in, say, a main street in Glasgow, even if one did catch a few of the pedestrians' eyes. I daresay I also considered the possibility that there was some trivial thing out of order about the car, but I would see to that when I stopped. A few yards further on, however, a young man stopped me and then revealed the scandalous truth that I was driving the wrong way in a one-way street.

Certainly my employer had retained the vestiges of a practice in Grays Inn Road. I had probably been there and might have been doing a visit to a client as the follow-up of a message left there for one of us, as happened once or twice. It matters not now and it did not matter then. I was in the Strand and on a drive to the east when every other driver was going west. Could I get off it immediately or sooner if possible, before they clapped me into the Tower or I suffered whatever other fate happened to people who did that sort of thing? I could and did. Right speedily I answered my own question.

But that episode was one more little piece of the picture which was slowly assembling the message that London and I were not exactly for each other. The same could have been said for the type of practice I encountered in London's East End. By 'practice' here I mean the work done for clients, not the claim that one is practitioner to a number of clients, few or many.

Nearly all the horse work was done by the principal and the senior assistant. Not that I was unfamiliar with the handling of a heavy draught horse; far from it. In fact I was probably better experienced in that respect than either the principal or the senior assistant, for had I not spent my entire summer vacation of 1931, between school and college, carting stones off a very stony beach at Machrie in the Isle of Arran up to the roadside, to the stone-crusher then in use on the local road improvement scheme.

More than that, the mare which I worked suffered from the effects of cystic ovaries though I, at that time, had little idea of the exact nature of her trouble. The one other horse on the job had to be – of all kinds of horse a 'rig', i.e. a monorchid. The word 'rig' is known to horsemen and means, in this context, that of the two testicles which are formed in the abdomen before descending into the scrotum some time before birth, one does not so descend. (Where both fail to descend the animal is known as a cryptorchid.) Such animals have a reputation for being vicious and treacherous although this poor beast never seemed to be fed well enough to show much spirit of any kind perhaps just as well for those of us who had to get close to him. Anyway, against him the mare maintained a permanent vendetta and, in warm weather, she, who was entirely the agressor, behaved worse. Out of all this this came one development. If it could have been said that I was not too expert in the handling of a carthorse when I started at the beginning of that July I was no novice when I stopped, early in the following October.

In that job in London I was sent out one day, travelling probably on foot, to find a certain stable and rasp a certain horse's teeth. The place was, I think, in the Isle of Dogs, certainly somewhere off Commercial Road. I duly found the place and the men and prepared to start work. This horse was a big Shire gelding, well fed and fresh. I had rasped horses' teeth before, though not very many, but though I had four carters helping by restraining the patient and the London carters of that day certainly knew their way about a horse he did not get a lot of rasping.

Very likely his mouth was tender in at least one place and I was too poorly equipped and too inexperienced to examine his mouth before I used the tooth rasp. He got no sedative beforehand whereas the same case today would have got a very effective intravenous injection to keep him calm. I would also have had a gag, or mouth speculum as it is properly called, or a cheek wedge, and with either of these a suitable torch. No doubt the carters saw that I was doing my best but they also saw that the job called for more resources than I had. So, when with the horse reversed in the stall and a high corn chest placed across it he placed both forefeet firmly on top of it and looked as if he might not stop at that, he being big and lively, we stopped. I do not know who rasped his teeth, or if they were ever rasped. I never heard another word about him.

One of our commonest jobs on the small animal side of the practice was to a police call to attend a dog or a cat hit in a street accident, usually to put them down as quickly as humanely as possible. The spectators who instantly began to gather at that particular spot on the pavement soon began to show hostility if they thought the animal was being left in pain a moment longer that necessary, supposedly because of lack of adequate veterinary skill. This, I soon learned, could be embarrassing for the police officers, who were usually young. So, on the instructions of the senior assistant I used the same method as he used. The chosen agent was prussic acid (Scheele's), injected into the rib cage. Not an ideal nor a pretty way to do the job but still not as unpleasant, used in that way, as it was on one occasion when I had to find some method of euthanasia for a monkey.

Again it was in the Isle of Dogs area, the sort of job and journey in connection with it which one does not readily forget. The monkey, a fairly small specimen, had become vicious, or was said to be so. It was kept in a cage among other cages in an outbuilding. The lady, the only person I saw during my visit to the house, having shown me the monkey, clearly regarded her duty as having ended there and declined to have anything more to do with the case. Here was a puzzle: if nobody was prepared to handle him and if, as I was told, he was a biter, how was I to get the lethal dose into him? What was the next move? Dash it all, I had not even got a pair of leather gloves for some protection against a bite. However, I soon saw that the monkey, when offered things through the wire mesh of his cage would nibble at them with his teeth. Right, there was the method made obvious to me. Draw three c.c. Scheele's into the 5 cc syringe, present the nozzle at the wire mesh, then, when he nibbles the nozzle I press the plunger. He did, I did and, poor little thing, he got the lot. In a few seconds he thudded to the floor with hardly any of the usual loud cry in such cases: dead. I do not say I felt exactly like a murderer or anything quite like that, but I did not feel good. It was as if I had invited his trust and then betrayed him. Horrid.

For a visit at that sort of distance, where we supplied something or did something, or both, we could charge and were expected to collect five shillings. In such a case this sum was generally paid readily enough. Where it was not so readily forthcoming was in those cases where service or material were obviously quite useless because nothing could avert a fatal outcome to the case.

'Why should we pay you? You haven't done anything for it. We can get advice from other people for nothing.' That was the core of their argument, but there was usually much more of that kind of talk.

At these times some hard talking would have been needed to persuade them that the vet had had the trouble of getting to the case instead of having the case brought to him as would have had to be done if they had made use of any of the charitable services for animal welfare, and that he had spent a good many years acquiring the sound training and experience which enabled him to give them a competent opinion and treatment wherever treatment could be of any value. Against that harder-shelled type of client I was neither able nor willing to contend and could not really blame my employer when, as he gently put it to me one day, 'You can see for yourself the work's not there.'

Looking back now I do not think that the work I did in a week could have paid for my board and my salary, which was three guineas per week. I had then been two months in London: an interesting and eye-opening experience, but just not my scene. As I found I could not stay on in that job I was lucky to get myself fixed up with another one at short notice, this time in Cornwall, so to Cornwall I would go. I arrived in Bodmin early January 1938.

CHAPTER 3

Whatever might or might not be said of Cornwall it was a change, for me a very welcome change from the East End of London. Whereas in London I had on at least one occasion stood below a street nameplate about twelve to fifteen feet above the pavement and been unable to read it because of the fog between it and me, here in Cornwall the air was mostly very clear, though of a temperature not really very suggestive of a Riviera.

Practice was or the type with which was most familiar and was fairly leisurely though it had its moments too, those moments being usually in the early hours of the morning. The cold on Bodmin Moor either in a small, unheated car or lying, stripped to the waist, on a cowshed floor was something not soon forgotten. But there was one calving in particular which made me forget the cold.

The presentation of the calf was, so far as I remember, if not normal a least not requiring a great deal to be done to it to correct it. So I got a cord on the head and one on each forefoot in the usual way and we pulled, but without much success. The cow was standing opposite a doorway so, after a time, seeing that our unaided efforts lacked success we placed a spar across the doorway and got a light pulley (often a very important item among the vet's calving tackle) rigged between the spar and the calving lines. After a fairly hard pull we got the calf, which emerged with more the usual rush at the end. The, horror of horrors, what do I see extending from a point under the calf to somewhere inside the cow but yards of what appeared to be her own small intestine.

'Dear oh dear': so ran my feelings at that moment. At once I thought, 'This has been the cause of the obstruction. Her uterus has somehow been ruptured before I got here; it's been full of her own small intestine, that's what was holding back the calf and I am going to lose my patient. With all that contamination, peritonitis and death are certain, even if the intestine is not ruptured.'

There were no sulfa compounds nor antibiotics in general use at that time for treatment of the sort of case I envisaged. Some of my gloom was probably conveyed to the farmer as I gingerly lifted the exposed intestine which then slid clear of any contact with the cow. What the devil was this?

Suffering cats; all the same, not suffering anything like as such as I. So ran my thoughts. It's not the small intestine of the cow, it's the large intestine of the calf. I see now it emerges from the calf at the navel, which means either that the calf has had a very big, congenital, umbilical hernia which was ruptured by our pulling or else the calf itself is a case of a recognised type of monstrosity in which the intestine are not enclosed in the abdominal cavity as the embryo develops.

In that freezing cold and dim light in which the large intestine of the calf looked much the same as the small intestine of the cow the calf got the briefest of looks. It did not matter any more. The cow was going to be all right and could safely be left. There seemed to be for us no prospect of a hot drink, nor any other kind of warmth there at the time. The next move was, along with the chap who had come along with me as usual to act as pilot and general helper, to head back for the town and our beds.

I reached mine about half past three or four o'clock, with feet like lumps of ice, to waken about eight o'clock with feet just as cold as when I went to sleep. I could not remember ever before having that happen to them.

The days slipped into weeks, the daylight grew longer, the weather a little rainier. The Cornish landscape, apart from a few huge mounds of waste from the china clay workings, was a pleasure to behold. It did not have wild, towering mountains nor deep, dark glens and lochs just thereabouts. Surely not; and to the devil with them anyway. Had I not got a plentiful supply and more than plenty of that sort of scenery in Scotland?

What Cornwall did have was field upon field of good grass, separated by the 'banks' which were a feature of that countryside. I had opportunities to see them when we drove to place such as Wadebridge, St. Austell, St Blasey, Lostwithiel, Fowey, East Looe, West Looe and their environs though, of those places, I remember almost nothing now.

One thing I do remember is the dog show in Bodmin, at which I officiated as the sole veterinary surgeon in attendance. I daresay the other people in attendance, officials and exhibitors alike, were not very pleased with my performance. That was all right with me. Come to that, I was not very pleased to be there.

I had never been to a dog show anywhere in my life before, let alone work at one. No one had told me at all clearly what to expect, nor what was expected of me in the way of examination of the animal to be shown for fitness, and on that sort of thing my own ideas were somewhat limited. I knew, for example, from one of those little bits of physiology which did not help me to get a pass in that interesting subject at college, that travel and excitement could send up the temperature of a perfectly healthy dog several degrees and make his pulse largely meaningless. That being so, I probably showed a degree of seeming casualness in my dealing with the exhibits which was far from pleasing to their owners.

I probably rinsed my hand in warm antiseptic before I started to examine the procession of dogs which were placed onand removed from the examination table, but I did not rinse my hands between dogs as I ought to have done. I took the view that, milling around on the main floor as they were doing, they had every chance of exchanging any pathogenic germs they might be carrying, but I should not have enhanced such opportunity by omitting an antiseptic hand-rinse between each exhibit I handled.

What I did was to take a quick look at the buccal mucosa, commonly called the lining of the mouth, and the teeth for any appearance of coating, the conjunctiva for any congestion of, after which I palpated the prescapular lymph glands for detection of possible enlargement. If those, the earliest signs of distemper or allied disease, were absent, the absence of any other disqualifying ailment was taken on trust and the dog got a quick go-ahead. As well as my unspoken resentment at being pushed into what I felt was a fairly pointless exercise I probably harboured some unspoken disapproval of the bases on which such shows were judged. The show points on which exhibits were judged and prizes awarded seemed to me to have been based almost wholly on aesthetic values and hardly at all on practical considerations and, at that, by judges and breeders who were not veterinarians. There would seem to be reasonable grounds for the belief that if selective breeding were to be carried out more on the advice of vets who practise on small animals and less on the fanciful notions of the breeders, the vets would gradually find a reduction in the incidence of those troubles which have arisen out of unwise selection.

To take what is perhaps the most commonly cited example, a spaniel might be awarded more points for having a greater length of ear than a rival in the same competition, ignoring the fact that the longer the ear flap the more tightly it presses over the opening of the ear, the less ventilation there is and so the more moisture is retained, In short, the more favourable are the conditions for causing a smelly, unhealthy condition of the ear called by whatever name one may apply to the condition arising.

Then there is the problem of the size of the head of the unborn bulldog pup, something which has too often been the cause of difficult birth, besides other problems caused mainly by irrational, selective breeding.

As if that were not enough, man, having started with the wolf-like ancestry of the present-day dog and produced in the course of the centuries descendants as diversified as the great Dane and the chihuahua, Irish wolfhound and Yorkshire terrier, borzoi and bulldog, left some of his products with the whole of their tails while others, on the slightest pretext or none at all, suffered the loss of nearly the whole of theirs. And if some dogs' ears could hardly be got long enough, others in bygone days were cropped. Yet we are said to be, and I believe genuinely are, a nation of animal lovers.

To get back to the show, if only for a moment, I think I looked at everything I was asked to inspect and I left on good terms with everyone, to all outward appearances anyway. But I rather suspect, now looking back, that what most probably underlay my low level of co-operation was a disinclination to aid and encourage what I saw as being a largely nonsensical procedure with dogs. I suppose it could be argued, not that I am going to argue, that someone holding that sort of view has more real respect, and in some cases more real liking, for dogs than has the most assiduous exhibitor. And if, for saying so, I find any heavy artillery turned on me I shall merely retreat into my assault-proof shell and make faces at my attackers.

Whether the dog show had anything to do with it or not, there was not a great deal of small-animal work in that practice, that spring. It also happened, probably due to a spell of milder weather, that there was a lull in the usual springtime spate of troubles connected with breeding and rearing in cattle. It was quite temporary, but before the work picked up again my boss had decided to let me go. Soon I was on the move again, heading for a job in the next county which of course had to be Devon.

As things turned out I had not been there many days when there came an urgent message from Bodmin asking me if I could go back again immediately as my former employer had gone off sick or injured. I think now, so far as I can remember, the trouble was a not too serious injury. Unfortunately I couldn't or did not choose to go. Had I done so things might have panned out better for me later on, but I probably felt too strongly that I had not enough experience to take on full responsibility in a practice.

That is how I came to be in Devon at the beginning of April 1939. 'Devon, sunny Devon where it rains six days in seven', according to some of the residents there, meant for me a change in one important respect. For the first time in my undistinguished career since leaving college I had a job in which I was living out. That is to say, for those unacquainted with the term, I was living in lodgings, not in my employer's home. Under that arrangement sometimes one paid one's own lodgings and received what was supposed to be a commensurately higher salary, sometimes the employer settled directly with the landlord or landlady. The new employer seemed to pay more attention than any other I had ever had to my speech difficulty. Mainly on that account he obtained my services which, besides normal working hours, were to be on call at any hour of any day, all for a salary of four pounds per week. Though four pounds may seem an absurdly low figure now, many vets who were recently qualified about that time could testify that five pounds per week, live out, or three pounds ten shillings, live in, was a pay commonly offered to, and accepted by, ordinarily capable veterinary assistants.

In due course there was an 'agreement', sometimes called a 'bond'. Such agreements, I learned, were commonly drawn up by one form of solicitors, one partner or the principal acting for the principal of the veterinary practice, another partner or an assistant solicitor acting for the assistant vet. I had no experience of such matters and knew nothing about them. I knew only that when everything was completed and signed I seemed to have conceded a great deal and gained little or nothing.

I was not to start practice on my own nor with anyone else within twenty-five miles of my present (then) employment nor within ten years of leaving it. (These were quite usual provisions of the 'bonds' of those days.)

How about time off for myself. Oh, I would probably do better, actually, by not insisting on any hard and fast hours off.

Believe me or not, I fell for that one and I did *not* do better by not insisting. I know because I could not have done worse.

I could be called out of the local cinema, and often was, or from a private entertainment somewhere, go up to the boss' house and find him sprawled in an armchair, but full of advice about some new case he had never seen. Where possible I gave the patient his suggested treatment. Mine would have been wrong, whatever

I did, favourable outcomes got no comment from him; bad ones of course came up for dishonourable mention.

Praise from him? No fear. Never. Give the assistant any praise and, sure as fate, he'll be asking for a rise the very next day. That, I strongly suspect, was the underlying philosophy. I was never once offered even the price of my cinema seat.

The precious 'bond' did not in fact mean anything, though neither I nor anyone else, including the lawyers, knew that at that time. Some years later, evidently, learned counsel in the course of pursuing a case of a violated agreement which was taken so court, discovered that such agreements have no force in law.

There came the occasion, late one afternoon, when I told him that the promised increase in pay was due, along with that month's pay.(I always had to ask for my pay, no matter how long I let it stand.) Oh. I should go and have my tea and he would have the cheque ready for me when I came back. And so he had a cheque for £16.10s. I was completely taken aback and could only stammer that I expected a bit more than that. My response was probably exactly what he sought because instantly came his riposte:

'Oh, and how much did you expect?'

I, as simple a fish as ever rose to a bait, thinking that if half a crown (12 1/2p) per week was his idea of a rise, there was little to be gained by starting an argument I could ill maintain, by claiming a rise to five pounds per week as mentioned when I started with him a year earlier, said I had expected at least £4.10s.'Oh, let me see, Ah yes, I've made a mistake. Four pounds ten did you say?' Then after a moment and handing me a cheque for eighteen pounds: 'There, is that right, now?'

What could I say? It was as slick and neat a performance as I had ever encountered anywhere. It may have represented, indeed I think it did represent, a new low in my recollections of LPDT(long-planned dirt tricks) but by gosh it was slick. I must admit I was hopelessly outgeneralled from the start. Of course I was taken by surprise an important military principle here demonstrated and I had so much lighter guns. I have sometimes since then wondered if he planned that little tactic all by himself!

Still, I am not sure that the poor chap was altogether to be condemned. He did not belong to those parts and did not seem to be in great demand as an agricultural vet. He never seemed to me to be close enough either to the livestock or to the soil. I doubt if he really had the means to maintain the lifestyle he would fain have displayed. Apart from keeping one fairly good hunter, which he seldom rode, and I do not know how it performed at the hunt if it ever saw one, he gave no other sign of affluence. He quite possibly employed an assistant more for health reasons than for any volume of work he had, though he never complained nor explained about any possible bad health he might have had. Practice, even with with all the extra work there should have been in the spring time was never at a very high pressure. He died a good many years ago.

CHAPTER 4

With the arrival of April 1940 I would by then have put in a solid two years' work in that practice for a total remuneration of not more than £460, a sum which was really not quite reached at the end of twenty-five months there.

One of the big jokes of that period was that anyone earning that kind of money, say £4 per week with no more than minimal allowance against income tax, paid it. Great fun, if one could see the joke. Did anyone think they were going to get the whole £4 to pay their digs and squander the rest on clothes and a hundred cigarettes a week and riotous living in general? Or did they think to begin building up with it a vast, head-turning fortune in the bank? Good lord, man; wasn't there the country to be run, and it with a war on its hands. Hadn't we seen the masses of soldiers in the street, all of them to be supplied with the sinews of war and paid their two shillings per day, or whatever it was at that time? Were there not munutions manufacturers and contractors and all sorts of other people to be paid?

I was on £4 10s. per week when war broke out. That was the position and these were some of my thoughts. Age twenty-seven, engaged in a reserved occupation, tucked always in a quiet corner of England, all set to vegetate like the best, most intelligent vegetable that ever existed, right through the war, more like 72 than 27. There I was, a redhead with temperament to match, fit as a flea and rarin' to go. I do think I would have gone too, but for the blasted speech problem. But then, but for the existence of that, goodness knew where I would have been at that time.

I turned again to the idea of doing something more about it, to see if a prolonged, all-out effort in diagnosis and therapy would eradicate the trouble once and for all. I had heard from an authoritative source of a reputedly good course in speech therapy. My savings, all the money I had, totalled nearly £160. At ten guineas per week and keeping some cash reserve I could afford twelve weeks whole-time therapy, which might just do the trick. And if it were to do that, I saw I could be off to a fresh start, this time on equal terms with other people. Then, I believed, I would hold my own or at least not come last in the race.

The gamble seemed worth taking. I stood to gain a great deal and lose nothing but a little money and a very unsatisfactory job. So little pleased with it was I that when my employer offered to keep the job open for me for three months of my absence, as he did several times, I declined the offer each time. My reckoning was that if I could do the job well enough to satisfy him and his clients, of whom some had begun to ask for me in preference to him, I should be able to do do the same for some other employer who customarily paid a more attractive salary. So I worked my month's notice which I had carefully tendered in writing (all according to the agreement), had two or three days breathing space and left.

I had my twelve weeks of therapy and they did not change anything. That, in fact, is the usual outcome of a great many speech therapy courses. The trouble seems to be that the causes of the complaint are already deep-seated when treatment is sought, and, having launched on a course of therapy, diagnosis and treatment are so superficial, so empirical that they never get anywhere near the root cause and so fail to show any lasting improvement. In any case I soon discovered that while lodging in that house was a full-time arrangement, therapy was very far from being that, and what we got of it not very good anyway.

It may not be out of place here to remind some of the younger folk that in 1940 a sum of £160, or any comparable sum, was worth anything between ten and twenty or more times what it is worth at the time of writing this. For example, the 25 to 30 shillings ton of coal then is now the £40 to £50 or more in some parts of the country for a ton of coal. There may be still around and lively some few stalwarts who will claim that that thirty shillings then was just as hard to earn as is the sixty pounds now. That argument is here being carefully not pursued.

The single, detached bungalow, a good one for £500, a very good one for £600, is now a 200-250 thousand pound bungalow, with prices still rising and the buildings only doubtfully as durable as their pre-war ancestors. Those two examples may be startling, or they may not, but there are many, too many others no less so. From all of this then it may be seen that the pound or the hundred pounds in 1940 or earlier had a vastly different purchasing power than what it has today. However that may be, I had the earnings of my little money and I had the spending of it, and that was that.

Those twelve weeks, May, June and July 1949, I spent in a quiet little spot in Buckinghamshire, not too far from the Thames. For much of that time I had the pleasure of the company of three young ladies all pretty, all pleasant. Several times we went on intrepid voyages up the Thames (fearless sailors, with me anyway) in a punt. I had been well acquainted with the rowing boats since childhood but though I soon got the knack of paddling a punt, I did not know much about it at the outset. Neither did any of the girls. But I soon discovered that the ship's company consisted of three captains and a crew of one. The crew also served as the main engine, which in this case had three occasional auxiliaries, all engines defiantly low-revving.

I knew the captains did not really mean to be bossy and the crew did not mind receiving orders, so long as he was not clapped in irons for mutiny, for only by mutinous disregard of captains' orders could he avoid the undesirable attention of other river users. It was all new and interesting to me, all very pleasant but it could not last.

I arrived back in Arran about the end of July with practically no money, still with the old problems as bad as ever and, as things more and more seemed to me, virtually no prospects.

Discovering gradually and uncheerfully that re-employment as an assistant was more elusive than ever, I got myself de-reserved and in due course arrived at the appropriate centre for a medical examination to see if I could enlist. Dammitall: even the forces did not want me. How then could I expect the principal of a busy practice, the only kind likely to need an assistant, to want me? To that question I had no answer.

In Robert Browning's work 'The Pied Piper of Hamelin' there is a couplet in which he avers of the civic dignitaries of Hamelin: "One thousand guilders', the mayor looked blue. So did the corporation too.' Possibly. But I bet they did not look more blue nor feel even half as blue as did I when, after some months, I still had not got a job.

However, it has been well said that Nature abhors a vacuum. The existing veterinary services for the island were said by some of the people at any rate in the part in which I lived to be inadequate. (Was there ever, I wonder, one such service not said by some of its clients to be inadequate?) Thus it happened that though I had neither the proper medicines nor other veterinary equipment of any kind, I began to be called out to the odd case which lay within whatever distance I could contrive to travel. This development represented at least a gleam on the horizon.

As my transport at first was a bicycle my range was very limited, more by the strength of the winds and the gradients of the roads than by any other consideration. When all I could usually hope to do, unless it was a case for manual interference, was to diagnose the trouble, prescribe something from the chemist and improvise desperately for anything else required, the hire of a car did not often seem justified, though sometimes the owner did hire one to take me to and from a case.

The bag I brought into the service to carry my medical stuff was a small, brown Gladstone, given to me as a gift while I was still at school. It was then nearly forty years old, the donor told me, but it served me for a good many years after that. Many a little mild amusement my clients had with their reference to 'Doctor MacGreegor and his wee, black bag' as in the well-known old music-hall ditty, all blithely ignoring the fact that by bag was brown. That of course gave me a chance to be very superior about their defective powers of observation.

While at first my main problem with the bag was to find suitable things to put in it to make it look full, that problem soon changed to one of deciding what I might leave out. From the small bottle of Lysol, one of tincture of iodine, cotton wool, lint, bandages, 10 cc syringe, a few things for injection, scalpels, forceps, etc., the few thing gradually became a good many things for injection. The problem, as I have indicated, was to find space.

CHAPTER 5

Before I had gathered much in the way of equipment there happened one of the first cases I ever remember being asked to attend, a colic in a young Clydesdale filly. As to what I was to get to treat her I had no idea, but about the colic itself I did have some knowledge. I had it because in 1936 I had had the rare good fortune to spend the first four months of that year working as a student in the practice of an eminent veterinary surgeon, Henry Caulton Reeks of Lincolnshire. About him I would here to explain a little.

He was the author of a book, *The Common Colics of a Horse* and I not only learned from it a little of the differential diagnosis of equine colics but also received from him a presentation copy of that book, autographed in the green ink which he mostly used. Another autograph I received from him was on a substantial cheque which his secretary handed to me on the morning when I was leaving to go back to Glasgow and which just about floored me by its total unexpectedness. Clearly do I remember as I staggered from an upstairs room down the stair towards his office to thank him, having blundered into practically everything on the way down, seeing him walking rapidly out of the office and down the yard, laughing hard.

Where some practitioners in his position might have wanted payment for being bothered with students it was not so with H.C.R. Another and rarer gift from him was one of the microscopes which had been used in the practice until only a year or two before then.

Henry Caulton Reeks was for some years a member of the board of external examiners who twice yearly went around the five colleges (properly called schools) then in existence, examining the students in each year by oral examination plus, in some cases, a certain amount of practical. Each year had its own group of examiners and each subject in that year its own two or three members of that group. Caulton Reeks was one of the men for the final year, but whether he examined in medicine or in surgery I cannot remember.

The case I now had on my hands was, as far as I remember, an impaction of the small colon. The usual treatment of such a case in the adult horse would have been two to three gallons of warm saline given by stomach tube and containing about a certain proprietary purgative together with measured doses of bowel stimulant, carminative and antizymotic agents, far in excess of the recommended doses or those stated in the relevant textbooks. One then gave instructions for gentle walking, on grass if possible in case the patient lay down, water to drink if it was wanted, with plenty of long rests between the walks, and one generally got the desired result. There were other colic cases which walking was definately not wanted.

An odd and interesting feature about equine purgatives, at least those using aloes or aloes derivatives, as many and old vet in a northern agricultural practice could confirm, was that while the recommended textbook dose was effective for horses in, say, the south of England, the further north one went the less effective such a dose would be. In those regions of the British Isles far to the north and the north-west, to have given the textbook dose of two or three drachms of such a purgative to a heavy draught horse with an uncomplicated impaction would have been a culpable waste of precious time. I have never heard of any theory offered as a possible explanation of this regional variation in the pharmacology of that medicament.

No such deliberations, however, entered into my treatment of that case because, for one reason, I did not have such a thing as a stomach tube and, for another reason, I had nothing to send through it if I had one. I used cold water enemata, the same as I had seen H. Caulton Reeks use in selected cases though it was hard to see what good they did. The only possibility was that by some rather improbable action they stimulated some part or parts of the upper bowel. But at least it showed I was trying – I was doing something. Goodness knows what was in the draught given to that unlucky young horse (a 'draught' here means, in veterinary terms, a quantity of liquid administered by mouth) but most probably it was linseed oil containing ol. Terebinthinae and other nauseous, noxious nostrums. Whatever it contained, the patient survived.

Some time about then, during the periods when I was, so to speak, high and dry without either an assistantship or means of independent practice, I had at least two surgical cases, both in horses, which taxed my slender experience beyond its limits.

The first was a horse which, while in the cart, had trodden on an upward pointing nail and walked on with the nail penetrating deeper at every step until he could go no further in the cart. I think he must have got back to the stable on three legs. This was one of the cases to which I was called and with I had no success. My failure, as I saw in retrospect, was quite predictable.

In those days I was, if I say it myself, pretty sound on the anatomy of the horse's foot. I knew it because I had spent most of one morning going over it in the Anatomy Department of the veterinary college just before my professional oral examination in anatomy and in that exam had the luck to be taken for questioning on that very subject. On that account I had a pretty clear idea of what the nail had done, what would be the minimum requirements in treatment and what were the chances of a good recovery. But in the face of all that and, I suppose, hoping where there was no hope, I advised the owner to try a long period of tubbing, that is, keeping the foot for long periods in a tub or bucket or warm antiseptic fluid. But, as was only to be expected, the patient rapidly lost flesh and soon had to be destroyed.

The nail had almost certainly penetrated not only the frog but the planter cushion, the deep flexor tendon insertion and the os pedis (or the phalanx, as Sisson's *Anatomy* calls it). Contamination and trauma were likely to be gross and probably insurmountable. What I see now as having been weakness and unwarrantable optimism on my part were the joint causes of my failure to tell the owner at the very outset: 'It's a hopeless case. There is nothing I can do that will be any real help. Your best plan is to shoot it now.'

A young vet, intent on gaining and keeping clients, had to be very brave to give that kind of advice.

It is conceivable that had I obtained the help of the blacksmith, anaesthetised and simultaneously cast the horse, got his hoof pared down, opened it and dug down to the os pedis, packed the cavity with dry dressing such as iodoforn-sulfa compound mixture with dry packing and kept a cover on the wound I might have got healing from the bottom by granulation. On the other hand I might have got necrosis of the bone, chronic discharge and just an awful mess with a fatal ending.

There was another time when I was called to another case, broadly similar to the above, where the same first advice should have been given. Again it was a horse, lame in a hind leg by gross injury. This one was not in the foot but in the hock. The horse, presumably in the act of scratching the leg against a fence post, had got the leg over a single strand of barbed wire. In his attempts from time to time to release the leg he had made the whole front of the hock a dreadful sight, even for a vet accustomed to seeing such things.

Again a faint heart and over-optimism prevailed over better judgement. Treatment was attempted and again a fatal outcome ensued. I believe now that nothing short of the best resources of a first class veterinary hospital would have won that case.

Happily, practice on my own and for so long under-equipped was not always nor even very often a matter for self-doubt and self-criticism. I had, if I say it myself, my odd clever touches here and there too, and they, however few in number they be, are liable to break cover and flaunt themselves herein from time to time, later on.

All the practice I had, however, the unusual, the ordinary and the deadly dull all put together were not enough to provide adequate occupation and reward. I had the work of some of the herds which were already attested as being tubercle-free in the island, but while the annual renewal tests provided probably the bulk of my income, they occupied little of my working time in the year. Most of the herds in the island were already attested by the time war broke out, when the attested Herds Scheme for the whole country was suspended. But there were still a good few herds to be brought into the scheme when it reopened in 1944 and, of them, the herds with which I was concerned were all distributed up the west side and in the north end of the island.

CHAPTER 6

If I write about the merit of the Attested Herd Scheme and the inter-relationship of bovine and human tuberculosis I am on well trodden ground. I am not 'starting to blaze a trail by ploughing a lonely furrow to pitch my tent in the wilderness, leaving no stone unturned in my quest for truth'. In short, it has all been said before. Here I shall merely recapitulate a little, adding only a few remarks of my own.

There was for many years, and perhaps still is, a lively variance of opinion between proponents of human medicine and those of veterinary medicine, and even within the ranks of the vets themselves, as to the value of eradication of bovine tuberculosis as an aid towards the bigger aim, the eradication of human tuberculosis. This proposition is placed opposite the supposed immunising properties of milk from tuberculosis cows, pasteurised and consumed by human beings, with special reference to children, they being if anything more susceptible than adults to infection by the tubercle bacillus.

Scotland's greater incidence of human tuberculosis as compared some years ago with that of England was held by some to be directly connected with the reduced incidence of bovine tuberculosis in Scotland, consequent upon the greater progress of attestation there. Demonstration of the passage of tubercle germ antigen or antibody from the cow, via the milk, to the human being, was apparently not considered a necessary support for that argument. That was rather lucky, as demonstration was impossible, and the supposed process not demonstrated was highly improbable in any case.

The lower, overall standard of housing and, it is feared, very often a low standard of hygiene too, were again ignored in debate. Highland cattle had a very low incidence of tuberculosis and Scottish sanatoria drew a large proportion of their patients from the Highlands: so ran the old argument. Less often mentioned was the fact that the old 'black houses' hardly to be found nowadays unless specially preserved of the Highlands and Islands while being very weatherproof were very nearly ventilation proof as well. So one person with 'open' tuberculosis of a lung or both lungs, lungs being among the commonest seats of such infection, resident in such a dwelling and discharging live tubercle germs with every cough, exposed the other occupants to very high risk of similar infection by inhalation.

What is not in dispute and not forgotten is that the bovine strain of the tubercle germ can and does invade the human body, gaining entry very often through the human being's drinking of milk taken from a tuberculosis udder before anyone suspects any disease in it. A cow will secrete tuberculosis milk only if she has active tuberculosis in her udder. The trouble is that the cow can have that and be excreting virulent tubercle germs long before the tuberculous udder is detectable by palpitation, i.e. manipulation by hand to detect the first sign, a very hard lump, sometimes described as a 'stone in the udder'.

With the above considerations in mind, my own rationale, which may be different form the official one – if there is a official one – of the Attested Herds Scheme is as follows:

- Human Beings, especially children, can contract tuberculosis from drinking tuberculous milk.
- Tuberculous milk comes from tuberculous udders.
- We can be sure that tuberculosis is not in the udder by making sure it is not anywhere in the cow.
- We can make sure it is not in the cow, or having gained entry into her but of too recent arrival to make her sensitive to the tuberculin test, only by ensuring as far as possible that is not in the herd.
- We can reasonably assume it is not in the herd when the herd has passed successive tests at appropriate intervals and has not been exposed at any time to possible infection by the mammalian strain of the germ.

This last condition involves, among other attesting all in-contact herds, which in turn means attending the attestation process in a selected area right out to the natural boundaries of that area. These natural boundaries which are so desirable if not absolutely necessary for this purpose, give an island area in the process of becoming attested a natural advantage, one which must have helped a lot in the case of an area covered by the term Scotland-England-Wales, a well-known, large island which became all attested a good few years ago now.

There is one point specially to be noted in applying the tuberculin test. The test may fail to detect the advanced case of tuberculosis, e.g. the cow that has got generalised tuberculosis has got it in her lungs, her abdomen, her udder etc., because such a case is already so saturated with her own tuberculin, the product of her own germs and antibodies, that the single drop of each of the two tuberculins, mammalian and avian, which are injected into the thickness of her skin, do not evoke any significant reactions to them, or, if they do, show less to mammalian than to avian tuberculin. So she passes the test. But such a case should be, and usually is, readily detectable by the clinical symptoms she shows.

More than once I have seen just such a cow, though not in Arran, not even skinny nor showing a hard coat, pass the test comfortably while the cows on either side of her went down. Madam herself would not be giving anything away except that, if one happened to be standing around long enough after the test, perhaps discussing the result with the owner, one became aware of a rather frequent cough which was soon located as coming from madam. Brief auscultation of the lungs then gave sufficient supporting evidence.

When I first put an ear to that kind of cow's chest I realised that, in Scotland at any rate, the term 'a kiat o' whistles' could be applied to other things besides an early and derogatory description of the earliest type of church organ. Here we had a chest and it certainly contained whistles among sundry other sounds. The squeaks, the hissing, the little piping sounds etc., all to be heard coming from one bovine lung, were astonishing to one who until then had heard only normal lung sounds.

How much havoc a case like that, discharging active tubercle bacilli into the air with every cough, could do in a byre of cows would depend largely on the efficiency of the ventilation, among other things. Things such as hygiene, or the lack of it, probably counted for less among cattle than among human beings in a comparable situation, but such speculation is in any case futile.

It is still not very many years since there was living memory of the days when, at times like cutting the corn and later on bringing it in, or at the potato gathering on the big farm of a crofting district, there would be a big turn-out of hands from the crofts and smallholdings round about. When at the end of the day's work they gathered in the big kitchen for supper, which no doubt would be as cheerful as ever any poet described, the main course was placed in a large bowl or basin in the middle of the table and the company helped themselves. Second helpings would sometimes be by self service, the diner using his or her own spoon. Nobody would of thought twice about contamination or, if they did, would have kept quiet about it and either risked it or done with one helping. But, of those present, anyone with tuberculosis of the lung and, most likely, an open and undiagnosed case of it, was very unlikely to keep his or her bacilli to him- or herself. And as a further hazard, some if not all of those folk would have come from cottages with windows which did not open. In those circumstances, if the bacillus whether of human or bovine origin set up infection in any individual, such infection got every chance to produce its worst effects, whether or not a tuberculous cow's milk could ever contain protective antigens or antibodies. We do know that a tuberculous cow's milk could and did produce infection, sometimes of very serious extent, in the human subject.

Possibly because I had been used to hearing of tuberculosis in one form or another form my earliest days in Arran I was always interested in the subject and, when it came up for study in the pathology and bacteriology classes in the college it seemed to have a special interest for me. So when the Attested Herds Scheme re-opened in 1944 I was all the more interested to get going at the point where it had been stopped in Arran.

Arran, that part of it at any rate which I brought forward through two clear tests to await the official tests, came out strikingly well. Whereas the average incidence over the whole country was about 33 per cent or one in three, in the part of Arran which I tested the incidence was not higher than 8.5 per cent and, in some parts of the area I worked, even lower than that, down to two or three per cent and at that closely comparable with Shetland. Shetland, as I seem to remember clearly, was at one stage neck and neck with Arran in what looked to me rather like a race to see which was going to be the first wholly self-contained, 100 per cent attested area in Scotland. Shetland won in a canter, but Arran, I think, was second.

An interesting little piece of evidence supporting the figure for average incidence was turned up when, a short time before the AHS was reopened in general, one small area containing three herds was admitted by itself. One, a herd of twelve, had one reactor, the second with twenty-four had two and the third with thirty-seven head had three. That was just on 8.5 per cent all round. The west and north of Arran I divided into three districts under the headings, Machrie, Pirnmill, Lochranza. Each contained something like 120-150 head, scattered through possibly eight or ten herds varying in numbers from one to forty thereabouts. Now I know some rural vets might regard 150 head as a good start to a morning's work but no more than that. Yes, and I myself once, far away from Arran, tested a herd of just under two hundred head and finished, both days, before 10.15 a.m. Just an average herd, neither very difficult not very easy, but the owner and his men had to be clear by 10.15 a.m. I was not loitering.

Of some of the places I had to reach when I started those tests, yes and before I even got started to them – well, there were places like 'The Craw' which, one might think on reaching it, must originally have been named 'The Craw's Nest' but which, fortunately for me, got rid of its solitary specimen of the bovine race before testing started. That disposal saved me several climbs of something like three hundred feet each, irrespective of what the weather might be, and all for quite minute recompense. Let us now, as we are on the Lochranza round, leave 'The Craw' undisturbed, do another two or three calls and herds, then we head for North Newton, but, of it, later.

I usually drove as near to each place as I could make the little car go, then walked and climbed the rest of the way, and wearing wellingtons. The tracks were usually narrow, rutted, twisted, steep and rough, all in varying degrees and by permutations and combinations. There were all meant to be usable for cars, but after any prolonged downpour, such as Arran got in plenty, the tracks were more like the beds of burns. They called for some nice judgement as to whether should I try taking the car up them and then risk sticking and having to back all the way down, or at best, manage an uncomplicated turn somewhere, or take the extra time and effort required from the very start to walk it all, and not even get footpath mileage for it. No doubt this made life more interesting if also more strenuous.

Having done the mountaineering part, I would find on arrival that there was seldom more than one person and that one person not always a man, to help me. And where there were only a very few cattle, perhaps only one or two, they would be used to one person only, which was no help at all to any outsider having to do with them, especially when the only person they knew was a woman.

There seems to be little doubt that the animal behaviour here, as an example of something that happens all the time, was governed by an animal sense of smell. This is something which varies in degree, according to the situation. There is a saying: 'a dog lives by its nose', and in that saying there is a great deal of truth, I think. The more one considers that proposition the more apt the saying seems to be. Domestic animals are still very much creatures of instinct, domestication seeming to lie very lightly on most of them.

Everybody knows, for example, the two-way function of the sense of smell as between a predator and its prey, but there are other examples which are less easily understood. Many people among those accustomed to working with horses must have seen, at some time or other, a perfectly normal horse on catching suddenly the smell of a pig, go seemingly stone mad and head for that quantity of pig, singular or plural, with intent to destroy it, or else head for the skyline. It can happen with horses of both sexes, young and old, and it happens so quickly as to give little time for countermeasures. At one moment the horse is with you, the next he is not. Consequences of this part of behaviour have often taken the form of some very nasty accidents.

Is it instinct? Racial memory of some unsettled business, going back for countless thousands of years between the wild stallion and the wild boar, the hooves of one versus the tusks of the other, or something like that? I have never heard any explanation and know of none. But I do know I did not need any explanation of some of the things I had to settle in some of the byres I entered.

No description of the hazards and highlights or tuberculin testing on the west side of Arran in the nineteen forties would be adequate without some mention of High Dougarie.

High Dougarie or, as I believe it is named in Ministry records, Dougarie Farmnow: there we had a memorable occasion, in fact six memorable occasions, two for each of three tests, not to mention a test once a year thereafter. Those cattle: in setting out to describe them even after several decades I am still as might be a cub reporter describing a tidal wave, only with less exaggeration.

The basis of the herd was eighteen pure-bred Galloway heifers. In due course they all calved before the first test, a fact which gave us not simply eighteen big lots of high explosive but many small lots of explosive too. Those calves: maybe they were wee but by gosh they were lively. When they were roped and I looked them in the eye and they looked me in the eye they plainly said "maybe we're wee and we're roped but by golly we'll fight you all, you crowd of --------s" and fight they did.

In addition we had some Highland cattle blood, pure, as in the old bull himself and from him, mixed in varying degrees with shorthorn and others. Despite the number of Galloways which might have been there, the herd despite its adjuncts of Highland and shorthorn never totalled more than thirty-seven or thereabouts. That was the greatest number I remember testing there, and what tests they were.

The adult Galloways were the real tartars, some of them worse than others. They were not Belted Galloways; we were the ones who got belted if they got the slightest chance at us. One unfortunate animal, unfortunately for herself, could be tested only by pulling her up to the railings tightly enough that she got short of breath then, when she was swaying and sufficiently subdued, nipping into the pen beside her and doing what had to be done. Her coat was the deepest black of them all and she had what I think was the proudest eye I ever saw in any cattle beast. She would not have been easily defeated by circumstances. Alas, she and some others succumbed apparently from lack of food during one hard winter. I was not consulted. I saw them often as I passed them in their field beside the road.

The calves were of various colours and earned for themselves names such as Red Pepper, Black Pepper, Yellow Peril, Dynamite, Mustard, Jumper, etc. None was called Kicker. They all kicked, i.e. whenever they thought they might get us. The first test charts of cattle given the preliminary test asked for 'names if any'.I supplied the names for most of the calves.

An ordinary herd had the man in charge and perhaps one other hand to help me. This herd had four good men to help with the job. Our fame or notoriety must have spread, or so it seemed, for one day the Arran Estate factor came to see for himself how we were coping with the herd, which was owned by Arran Estate. He did not stay long.

But after a very few years there was a change of management, the herd was dispersed and I was not sorry. I learned afterwards that when the old Highland bull was being removed, so violent was his resistance to the move that, having somehow got his head and shoulders under the back end of the lorry which was to convey him, he lifted it clean off the ground. The lorry was probably of a size to take a three-ton load.

What was really sad was that the old Highland bull died in the lorry, somewhere between Dougarie and Brodick. Whether his resistance had proved too much for his old heart or whether he had succumbed to sheer terror, which itself would have affected his heart, terror of something he had probably never seen before, was a question I was not at all keen to pursue. But I sometimes felt, whenever I thought about it afterwards, that had I been called in beforehand to help with sedatives and advice I could probably have made things easier for him.

We always managed through the preliminary tests somehow. Many of the smaller herds and even some not so small had no reactors nor doubtfuls at first test, which meant that that test was automatically their qualifying one. Whenever a herd passed its qualifying test it was then supposed to be inspected by a whole-time inspector of the Animal Health Branch of the Ministry who then did a PIR – Preliminary Investigation – and Report, generally called a PR.

The PR took account of premises, boundaries, movements of animals, neighbours' livestock etc. and asked some fairly searching questions. In the west side and the north end or Arran the making of these reports was left with me who, as a local veterinary inspector and private practitioner, should, strictly speaking, have had nothing to do with them. I knew the boundary fences (and their absences), I knew about common hill grazings and other things pertinent. Now I claim and would be very hard to shift from that claim, that while I did not actually depart from the truth, my replies to the questions showed a degree of inventiveness which has never since been equalled.

Still, if that part of my work was costly in time and effort for seemingly little reward it had its occasional compensations too. There was, for instance one particular morning when, in the course of my work in the Lochranza district I was going round to an isolated croft called North Newton. One could go to North Newton by several permutations of route and transport, the choices depending mainly on the weather prevailing at the time.

One could walk from the mouth of the loch, where the road ended, round between the cliff and the shore until one climbed the cliff at a part from which it was easy to reach the house. Or one could again walk but use a cart track which started at the head of the loch and got up on to the ground above the cliff, thence round the hill and above the hill to the destination. Alternatively, given a dry spell beforehand one could risk taking the little car up that way and turning at the end or the track on a firmly steep grassy slope, which just had to be dry. In none of the few times I had the car up there I did ever start a rapid, unusual and quite unplanned descent to the shore, but it was a strong possibility.

On this particular sunny morning I was walking along the high route, not the faintest breath of wind and the sea like a sheet of glass stretching over to Kintyre, when I heard a sound like the barking of dog. Nothing remarkable about that, except that this sound seemd to be coming from somewhere out at sea. So I stopped and listened. Yes, there it was again: definitely a dog and definitely coming from somewhere out across the sea. North Kintyre, its nearest point three and a half to four miles from the shore below me, was very clear that morning and had there been so much as a rowing boat on the water I would have seen it. There was nothing. Could I be hearing a dog barking at a distance of three and a half to four miles away? When I got to the house, where I had five or six cattle to test, I would ask Johnny.

Johnny was the man of the house and, according to him, it was entirely possible to have heard the dog barking on Kintyre. Not only that, he added, but in years gone by, when farm carts had iron-shod wheels, if the Kintyre farmers of that part had their carts down on the shore on a very calm day, the North Newton folk would commonly hear the wheels rattling on the stones. (As I myself in the distant past many a time had a horse in just such a cart, on a shore closely set with stones large and small, I knew just what an infernal racket such movements can make, but to be heard at a range of four miles was astonishing).

I have since been told that at Lenimore, which is also in the north end of the island (there is another one in the south end), much the same thing happened in reverse. At that place in the north end there is a long, level stretch of grass on which once stood a church. The minister, on certain occasions when congregation was too large for the church, would sometimes hold the service outside, at the foot of the steep hill which rose from the level greensward. On certain of those occasions, when the weather was calm enough, the people in Kintyre directly opposite Lenimore could hear the old Scottish psalms being sung. Not only that, but they could tell, afterwards, which tunes had been used. The people would be about a hundred yards from the shore and the distance to the nearest point of Kintyre nearly three and a half miles.

A rare walk like that one round the hill could compensate for an awful lot of drudgery. On the other hand, a day of east wind or, come to that, any direction of wind with rain whistling round the hillside or along the shore, could make me wish I had no errand to North Newton just on that particular day.

Johnny had but one good arm. He was all too literally single-handed. His little byre needed repairs it just could not have, and his cattle were a law unto themselves. But we managed.

CHAPTER 7

It was in Lochanza too that I encountered a case which although by no means unique in this country was uncommon, and the only one of its kind I had ever seen. The owner of the herd phoned me one afternoon, I think it was a Sunday, asking if I could go and see a heifer, about six and a quarter years old, which seemed to have something wrong with a hind leg and perhaps its back as well.

When I got there I found the patient showing some rise in temperature, loss of appetite and emphysema that was roughly defined as a collection of gas or gases in some enclosed space within the body. This condition however was seen only in the biceps femoris of the right leg and one segment in the lumbar part of the longissimus dorsi, the great long muscle, the biggest in the body, which runs the whole length of the spine.

The case, I had to admit, was a new one to me. Blackquarter of the usual kind I had seem many a time in Devon where in some areas it was almost a scourge. In those cases the carcases one saw, for they were nearly all carcases when we were called to them and then only if there was a question of insurance cover, were swollen and gassy, generally in one large area only. It was blackquarter alias blackleg, caused by *Clostridium chauvoei*, the beast was dead and that was that, all nice and tidy.

Here in this particular situation in Arran I had a young beast with gassy musculature not in one place but in two, she had other symptoms of clostridial infection and she was still alive. What could we do? Clearly nothing I had in the car nor anything at home would be of the slightest help. Serum, even if I had ever thought of keeping any against the possibility of having to treat an unforeseeable case like this, would most likely have been date-expired several times over.

Serum? But wait a moment: years earlier, in Lincolnshire, I had seen those good folk who ran the practice in which I was accepted as a student, when they urgently needed some serum they had not got, get on the phone to the International Serum Company in London. The required serum would be sent off by the very next train and soon after that was in H. C. Reeks' office, if not taken straight from the station to the case to be treated.

There was a phone in the house where I was. The owner and I between us made known our purpose to the operator, whoever it was, that Sunday afternoon on Brodick exchange. Here I would like just to say in passing that whatever other people may have to say, or have said in the past, about telephone exchange operators, I speaking for myself have nearly always found them very helpful. And to that small averment, Brodick was no exception, especially on this occasion. Maybe I was just lucky. I don't think so. Within a very short time I was speaking to someone at International Serum. Yes, they had what I wanted and yes, they would put it on a train right away. It reached us, so far as I remember, the following day, something which, with a twelve mile sea crossing as part of the journey, I reckon was pretty good going.

I injected the serum copiously into the affected area, but without much hope of success. A good few days later when I was in the same byre for another purpose I saw my patient again. One of the muscle parts had become quite necrotic and was easily removed. The patient seemed to be nearly normal and likely to recover well enough, though I never did hear what was the final outcome of that case.

I gathered from the information I read, years later, that the causal agent in such cases is not likely to be *Ci. Chauvoei*, the bacterium which is the usual causal agent in blackleg, but one or more of the other *Clostridia*. At any rate I reckon I laid the little blighter out.

A few years after that I had another case of clostridial infection in a young bovine, but this time it had all the appearances of a typical case of blackquarter, exactly like those seen in the old days in Devon. I sent off a chunk of muscle from it to a laboratory and in due course got a report on my specimen. I forgot now exactly what the report said, though I believe it confirmed *Ci. chauvoei* infection, but the case was interesting because no one could recall a similar case on that farm, which carried a comparatively large herd, nor on any other place around, and I never saw another such case in Arran.

It was all the more interesting because if I had, on the strength of one typical case, advised prompt, wholesale vaccination of the herd and my advice had been acted upon, the vaccine there would have acquired a reputation as a one hundred per cent efficient immunising agent. And the cost would have been no less impressive.

Blackquarter, blackleg, whichever one of the half a score of names for it one uses, simply did not enter into our reckoning in practice. Neither did several other well known complaints such as redwater (except for one small area of my practice) nor grass sickness in horses nor sundry other complaints which commonly occur in many mainland practices. But we did not all the worst scourges, for, as well as redwater in cattle in one area, we had red worm in horses in several others. Infestation with these parasites could be a very serious matter because they are probably the most vicious of all the equine bowel worms. Where present in sufficient numbers and given sufficient time, which may be no more than a week from the time symptoms are first seen and reported, they can cause the death of the horse, especially a young one, despite all efforts toward the contrary.

How many practitioners today remember the use, with much caution, of *Oleum henopodii*, generally called chenopodium, by the practitioner? *Ol. Chenop.* together with *ol. Terebinthinae*, commonly called turpentine, linseed oil and other ingredients, all in a strong salt solution, probably about a pound to three gallons of water, made a fairly hellish mixture, to be given only by stomach tube.

Yes it worked well, though never one hundred per cent efficient. No worm dose in those days was that efficient, but gradually the horse came into better condition, its coat took on some gloss and the owner was pleased. Unfortunately, things did not always work like that. The problem of heavily contaminated pastures remained a problem and in due instance provided a case which caused owner and vet alike considerable chagrin.

On this particular farm where, I think, there had not been any horse breeding for many years, there was born a Clydesdale foal which in due course became an attractive yearling. I was called in to see him because he was loose in the bowel and obviously not doing at all well.

The rest of the story is short and sad. He had been on the same grazing as were several adult horses at the same time. He had a heavy infestation of red worms and was severely anaemic. A worm medicine which was then fairly new, phenothiazine, which like many another good new product was perhaps over-praised on first appearance, was given to the patient and he passed a lot of red worms, but a few days later he was still scouring without any sign of drying up. Rectal examination produced live, red worms on my arm as I withdrew it, a common feature of this type of infestation, showing that the parasites were being expelled, but not nearly completely nor quickly enough.

By that time our poor little horse was too weak to have much interest in anything. We tried plenty of strong oatmeal gruel which was really simply slightly watery porridge, by stomach tube. We used it by the gallon and frequently, but we lost him. Perhaps continued mini-dosing with worm medicine would have won the day for us, or perhaps we should have risked one stiff dose with one of the older worm medicines. I do not know, but I do not think so. My opinion is that the saving of that colt's life, if it could have been saved, rested on spotting the trouble sooner than was done. By the time his condition was noticed, damage of lethal extent had almost certainly already been done by the worm larvae in the bowel wall and the arteries supplying it.

What could I say to the owner more than to tell him never, never to put a very young horse to graze on the same pasture as adult horses whenever there is any suspicion of worm infestation of the adults and therefore contamination of the pastures. Had such a thought ever entered his mind beforehand I am pretty sure he would have been asking his vet what to do about it, for he was a keen and careful stockman and I was not consulted beforehand.

There were not many foals altogether born in that locality though for those that were, nearly all managed to grow up without any serious mishap, apart from the few that somehow got joint-ill from somewhere, with the usual mixed sequelae. In such cases, vet and attendant between them would combine medication with nursing and generally, if the foal would stand long enough to feed and the mare had plenty of milk, prognosis was good.

But if foal ailments were not a prominent feature of practice, the same could hardly be said of calves. When I think of them, ah, the wee rascals: that, at any rate is the strongest description I care to put on paper. Some of them started making trouble before they were born and they or others kept it up for long afterwards. Even if they got born naturally they often left behind them their foetal membranes. Once they were born they often developed scours of varying colours, the odd case of joint-ill, parasitic gastritis later on arriving because, like some other ailments, it took more to develop.

Speaking of being born, I remember one calf which never did get born though its mother was a big, strong, black and white heifer, apparently in perfect health. I was on the place for quite some other purpose, talking with the owner about something else when he mentioned her. 'I have a quey here' (a quey is a heifer) 'she should have calved by now or showing signs; you know, when they're getting ready to calf, but she doesna' seem to be showing anything at all. Would you have a look at her and see what she's like?.'

I readily agreed; we proceeded round to the other byre where I saw my patient standing cudding and not showing any noticeable unease. Here was a chance for me to demonstrate a quick and easy calving by which I would produce a fine, healthy calf for only a moderate display of skill and strength. That was what I thought. So I soon had an arm well washed and lubricated and inside her. I explored as far as I could – and that was all I did. At that particular time because it was all I could do.

Oedema: I had never before and have never since known a case like it. Head and shoulders were in what seemed to be the normal presentation but grossly oedematous and the vagina was somewhat swollen too. I pushed in as far as I could reach and found that my hand ran along what seemed to be an endless expanse in all directions of tightly stretched skin. So after I had grasped the situation and explained it to the owner we settled on a plan. I would go home (this was in the late forenoon) and come back in the afternoon with, in addition to the calving kit I normally carried, the embryotome, plus anything else I thought might be useful. And that was what I did.

All our preparations turned out to be but one more example of the fallibility of the best laid schemes o' mice and men.' There was no method by which I could have got that embryotome wire round the back of that head and kept it there if I had got it there. I then tried to take off one leg, for a start, or, if not at all of it, as much of it as I could get. What I have since then thought must have been the case was that both legs were bent at the elbows, but the true position was concealed by the gross oedema. I got the wire of the embryotome as far as I could get it, up and around one leg, knowing I was well short of the elbow but hoping to create a useful amount of space, made my cut and found that all I had got was about eight or nine inches of leg. I was then very little better off for space, worse off for a grip.

As my original plan of removing the head and then somehow collapsing the thorax simply did not stand a chance of success, I told the owner I did not think the heifer could be delivered by any means, by the usual route, and that, in my opinion there was nothing more to be done. He was quite philosophical about it and in no way perturbed by my news. We took her outside, regretfully ended her life and made an investigation.

To me, accustomed and all as I was to terminating lives in certain selected cases, to have to put down a fine, big, healthy or apparently healthy, heifer at calving like that represented some degree of shock, as it may have done as so to the owner. Yet it was the logical procedure, and one to which there was no alternative. Only after I had started the post mortem did the owner have another idea.

'Here,' he said, 'we could've ta'en it oot by the side. We never thought o' that.'

What he meant, I suppose, was that he himself had never thought of it. After all, it was hardly his job to think of such things, but it was mine, and I had thought of that idea while the heifer was still on her feet and strong to withstand a big operation. When he mentioned it I took the opportunity to draw his attention to what I thought he must already seen for himself, that the shape of the calf closely resembled that of a pear. Taking the head of the calf and the head was much swollen as being the top of the pear, the hindquarters made an amply proportioned base which, with the hind legs oedematous and set in a sitting position, gave a minimal diameter of something like fifteen inches, possibly more.

We did not try to remove the calf because what was apparent, even without removal, was that the length of incision required for such removal would have allowed too much spread of the viscera. But with a diameter of fifteen inches the length of incision needed for removal of the calf would have been not less than twenty-two inches, that is unless I was going to attempt some miracle of embryotomy through the abdominal wall. I never did at any time feel up to that. When I pointed out to the owner the length of incision which would have been required and the great post-operative risks, he immediately agreed.

Rightly or wrongly, that fine big heifer was one calving case about which I have never had any regrets except the very real one that there was no happier solution available for that problem. Probably if we had had any means of weighing the calf it would have been weighed and the weight recorded.

That is the story of one calf which did not get born. Among those which did and which survive the dietary and environmental hazards attendant on them, really not very many met with any other kind of setback. The chief instance that comes to mind is the case of one, a little Ayrshire heifer, about five or six months old, which received a severe injury to one leg.

This little lass, grazing in a field with a bunch of others, received on the inner face of her right radius and ulna a blow which not merely broke them but the skin as well, clear through to the periosteum. The owners, although they already knew what I had told them about such things, and although they knew beforehand that I would tell them that simple fractures, never mind compound ones, in grazing animals of that age or older were bad prospects for full recovery, yet nevertheless begged to me to have a go at treatment.

Inwardly I was not exactly relishing the prospect of having to order her very untimely slaughter, so, more with the idea of avoiding that, or at least postponing it until it might be more clearly indicated, than with any expectations of success, I agreed to try something. In fact even then as I was discussing the case I had a plan forming at the back of my mind.

From the case I went straight to the local joiners' shop and explained to my good friends there exactly what I wanted. What I wanted was a box splint for a calf. They had never seen nor heard of a box splint and therein I had the advantage of them, for

I had at least heard of such a thing. Not heard much, mind you, and only once, but heard. Anyway one of the joiners made, according to my instructions, a light box of half-inch white pine or similar wood measuring four inches square internally at one end and three, or was it three and a half, at the other, length fourteen or fifteen inches. The box was made with one side left open. The board which closed that side fitted the other two boards with bevelled faces but was never permanently attached to them. Having got my box with one detachable side I then cut notches at all four corners, top and bottom so that with wire, or hard cord like fishing line, pulled tight around the box, top and bottom, in the notches, I had a rigid case which I could pad with cottonwool to suit the leg. It was of course to suit the leg before fitting the fourth side.

The detachable side was, as might be guessed, the one directly over the wound and was removed as required to dress the injured part. It and the front and rear side stopped at the elbow joint. The whole box was held up with a sling over the calf's shoulder, for which purpose the outermost side of the box may have been left a little bit longer. The calf's foot was left clear for weight bearing. At that, with the job as complete as I could make it, the little heifer with the box applied round her foreleg and padded at all points of contact, seemed quite reasonably comfortable. She was then in her own stall in the calf byre and soon became expert at using her tie and her outstretched foreleg for the purpose of getting up.

Her particular accident happened sometime during the late nineteen forties when antibiotics were in full supply after the war. With them, good nursing and good luck the broken skin and the fracture healed without any bony or periosteal complications. She became quite famous within a radius of least a mile. The young, recently qualified veterinary surgeon and the veterinary student alike came from near and far to view the case and discuss it during its progress. You think I'm joking? Most certainly not. One came from a place very near at hand, the other came from Glasgow and they were on a visit to the farm. I do not know when she was returned to the field and the herd. No doubt it would have been sooner than I would have preferred, but in any event she made a complete recovery and became one of a small, select group of animals. perhaps the only one, to sustain a compound fracture while at summer grazing in Arran and make a complete recovery with the aid of a box splint – homemade at that.

CHAPTER 8

A little earlier I mentioned calf bowel disorders which resulted in scours of various colours. The most significant colour was white, and it may have been the commonest, but if so it was nothing like as common as it might have been. The reason for this, oddly enough, might be traced back to a certain man well known in Germany and elsewhere, by the name of Adolf Hitler. At any rate he, as leader of a great many like thinking people got blamed for staring a war which we know happened anyway, whoever started it.

One consequence of it was shortages of certain foods in Britain, among them a few for which increased milk supplies helped to compensate. One result of the shortages was that much of the milk which should have gone to the rearing of the British calves went instead for human consumption. The British calves might not have liked that, if they had ever known what they were missing, and if their mothers had understood the situation and had had the power of independent flight there is no saying what have might have happened.

As things were, however, the bowel disorders resulting in calf scours which were not noticeably white were usually accompanied by a history of feeding on artificial foods variously know as milk substitute, cream equivalent and so on, of which the main ingredient seemed to be linseed. They grew up to be apparently well-grown normal heifers, some of them a bit leggy and a bit slim about the hindquarters, but those features might have been more a matter of breeding than of rearing. What is not a matter for conjecture is that an unduly high proportion of them, when they reached the age at which they should have been displaying oestrus, failed to do so.

There were various theories expressed and so much was written about the problem, without such data on which to base the writing that really anyone concerned with it, no matter how little the material he had on which to base his opinions, was as ready as anyone else to express them. I could not avoid seeing much of the background of the problem; I read other practitioners' opinions about it and gradually formed my own.

Most dairy farmers, besides selling milk to the Milk Marketing Board also reared a few heifer calves, some to be replacements in their own herds, others to be sold as in-calf heifers near the calving. The trouble was that they so often did not even take even the first steps towards getting in calf. They were anoestrous and that was the stage at which the vet was called in.

Quite often the story was that two or three or more of them were persistently anoestrous, or it could even be that out of a bunch of ten or more of them all but two or three of them had failed to 'come in for the bull'. Observation and inquiry would bring out the fact that they were pail fed and had been from birth onwards, as one would anticipate in a dairy herd, and the admission that they had had very little milk altogether. Rectal examination generally revealed a reproductive tract underdeveloped, sometimes markedly so. I have palpated heifers of normal appearance externally, except perhaps for the rather slim hindquarters earlier mentioned, and found them to have one ovary about the size of a pea, with the other one not much bigger. The remainder of the tract would be correspondingly puny.

After two or three years of wartime conditions when the difference between an in-calf heifer and a barren heifer made it more important to have her in calf, the number of such cases for which veterinary advice was sought increased very noticeably. With the increase and the passage of a year or two it was also noticeable that the trouble seemed if anything to be more prevalent in those herds where least milk was kept at home for the calves.

Milk, I had read more than once, and as it is well know to physiologists, is akin to blood in its chemical composition. Did the similarity extend to the presence in the milk of the sexual hormones, indeed all the hormones of the female, taken from her blood and secreted into the milk by the mast cells of the udder?

As Nature arranged these things before Man ever interfered, the calf would start life with a bellyful of colostrums: just as much as the mother could supply and the calf had the energy to suckle from her. The colostrums besides being the natural laxative for the evacuation of the meconium and supplying antibodies for the immediate protection of the calf, may also contain either some of the sex hormones or the making of them. But if we do not know about that, we do know at least that the calf was intended to continue on its mother's milk while the mother returned to her normal sexual cycle and repeated it a number of times before the calf was weaned.

It did look as if the shortage or complete absence of the mother's milk in early calfhood as compared with a sufficiency of it then and even into late calfhood where rearing was under completely natural conditions, had something to do with the under-development of the developing, female reproductive organs. Such information if it was known to physiologists at that time was certainly not widely disseminated. But whatever the causes of anoestrus, the veterinary surgeon, having been consulted, was expected to rectify matters or explain why he could not do so.

It might not be out of place here to explain to those who may never have thought about the matter that while the dairy animal can go on producing milk through many lactations over many years, the beef animal produces but one item and only once itself when it is presented as a butcher's animal. But an out and out dairy animal such as a pure bred Jersey or an Ayrshire, if it fails to have a calf and produce milk, is of very little interest to the butcher as a carcase, or if it is, the interest is heavily concealed under a much reduced price.

The vet then has made his examination and if he has found anything much in the way of ovaries, has used either luteinising hormone or follicle-stimulating hormone or some other product, depending on the state of the ovaries, e.g. whether he thought the object he detected in one or the other, if he detected anything at all, was a corpus luteum or a Graafian follicle. I always hoped I was right, which I was not always, in my opinion of the state of the ovaries, for treatment of them based on a wrong decision could be near-disastrous. One possible sequel would be multiple pregnancy which could not go to full term because of the number of embryos engendered but would end in the multiple birth of premature, still-born foetuses, with little or no milk production to follow.

Then there was the heifer, but more commonly the cow, which would come into season but which would not hold services. I would be called in, get busy with a pre-service douche and quite often the animal would hold service after that, whether the animal had been going to hold service anyway that time or not. Whenever a pleased client gave me credit for clearing up the trouble I graciously accepted all such credit.

There was a lot of satisfaction in hearing that a cow or heifer previously infertile had settled to the bull after treatment, then later finding by rectal examination that she was in calf. A similar satisfaction was the feeling after a successful calving, when one was called in early, made a few, quick, strong, possibly skilful manoeuvres and produced a fine, healthy calf.

Having got that, what I always wanted to do next was to give the calf to the mother to lick dry. I would explain to the owner how very good was that procedure, both for the cow and for the calf, because the dairy substance on the calf contained hormones which helped the cow to cleanse, also because it dried the calf, thereby saving it the heavy loss of body heat which it would suffer if left to dry on its own, and that the licking dry improved the circulation and was in every way what nature intended. The person in charge however generally showed marked reluctance to follow my recommendations. He would mostly demur on the ground that allowing the dam access to the calf, especially if she got the calf sucking her (though I would mention the ecbolic effect of this as well) made her much more awkward to manage when the calf was removed from her.

No doubt there was some force in what he said, though not enough, I think, to justify total rejection to the whole procedure, so the calf just had to dry by gradual evaporation, probably in a draught and aided hardly at all by a few perfunctory wipes with a handful of dirty straw. It thus suffered all the ill effects of refrigeration caused by evaporation, hastened possibly by a cold wind, when the calving occurred out of doors. Later I would most likely have to attend the cow for removal of the afterbirth, if nothing worse, and the calf for something or other which need never have happened to it, but for its being stupidly deprived of the simple, vitally important thing nature intended it to have.

Thus would I think and talk; then I would think again. Dash it all, why should I, of all people, complain about that? If the stock-owners who were my clients got too good at animal husbandry I would go out of business. Couldn't I keep my mouth shut and tell them less? It began to look as if I had better, because more and more of them seemed to be paying more attention to what I said.

That represented a big change from things as they were when I first started going out to cases at home in Arran. Then I suppose I was the young graduate full of newfangled ideas, some seeming, in the opinions of my listeners, fairly ridiculous while I at the time battled against some quite inane or even dangerous folklore and old wives' tales which were mostly absurd. Just as some clients at times barely concealed their amusement at what I regarded as ordinary, everyday information and procedure, so I on my part sometimes had to suppress my irritation at them. The confident superiority of some small few of them was born out of an overwhelming, absolutely unassailable ignorance, aided a rare time by arrogance. As is so often the case, argument of that kind came from those persons least qualified to argue.

I remember one case in particular, probably the most obnoxious client I ever attended. Luckily my visits were for one case only and that one not in Arran. The case was a little heifer which had got the bull at age about ten months, lost her calf somewhere outdoors at seven months, retained the membranes – a common feature of such cases – and was not seen for at least four days after that. The owner did not seem to know how long she had been calved, or he may have been covering up his delay in calling me, but I knew by my examination of her what would be the minimum time since she calved. By that time, because of the natural contractions of the calfhood, manual removal of the membranes was impossible, even with a very slim hand which is, in those and similar cases, a great advantage. Here was clear indication for the use of pessaries, but those usually carried in the car had all been used and not replace. She was badly intoxicated in the literal sense of that word, i.e. poisoned with substances produced within herself, a process better called auto-intoxication.

I gave her a massive dose of mixed antibiotics, intramuscularly, gave advice on her feeding etc. and left. Visiting again some days later I saw, directly as I got near her, by her general bearing that she was feeling better. I was going to try again to remove the afterbirth when the owner dissented.

'Are you going to go into that beast again?' this in no very friendly tone.

I indicated that such was my intention.

'I don't think you should. You haven't done anything for her.'

'I gave her a big injection last time.'

'You haven't done anything I couldn't have done. I could have done anything you did. I think you'd better leave her.'

That to me was enough effectively to shut off my flow of talk. I did not, as I would fain have done, join verbal battle with him there and then, tell him what he was, which was what the Gaels would mocking describe as *duine northe,* big man (phon. pron. doonye nor). He really was full value for a brief, pungent address which, bad luck, he did not get.

'Oh indeed; so you knew what the trouble was, and how it would affect her. You knew all the time what to give her, how to give it and how much to give. No doubt you have a suitable syringe as well and know how to use that.'

Whatever might have been his reply, if he had found one, I should have continued my relentless and deadly destructive theme.

'You really don't need a vet, do you? I don't know why you called one in the first place. But your little heifer is going to make a full recovery this time, and you can thank me for that. Let's hope you are as lucky in finding a vet for your next case.'

I would then have collected everything pertaining to me which might have been there, and walked with great dignity out of the place.

The gentleman was lucky in two respects: one, that he got a recovery and, two, that he was not my client. Riposte was something of which I was seldom short. I usually had plenty of verbal ammunition, stockpiled for years and years back. What I needed was more fire power.

From one premature calving then to a few considerations, however random, of calving in general. On these I had, and still have, some strong feelings. One example of the sort of thing which used to send up my blood pressure was the treatment in the hands of some people, of cows immediately after calving,

In certain small herds, the cow would be running with others on field and hill grazing, so much at liberty that for her to calve at home rather than than outside would be partly by choice and partly by chance. On those rare occasions when I was present at such calvings I would advise, when the job was over, that the cow be given all the cold water she wanted to drink. Yes, they could warm it lightly if they pleased, though there was no need for that.

'We always give the cow a warm drink after she calves, with a handful of oatmeal in it, and not too much water to drink. I'm surprised at you, a vet, that you don't know ye shouldna give a cow cold water after she calves. You could give her a bad chill that way, if you do. Yes.'

'But what if she calved outside? When she finished calving she would just rise and walk to the nearest wee burn and fill herself up to what she wanted with cold water. A cow after calving is a gey thirsty beast and I never heard of anybody taking the chill off the burn, nor putting a handful of ...'

'Yes, yes, but she's used with that. All these cows run out on the hill every day. That drink out of the burn every day, do you see?'

I did not see. I would leave the vicinity of that cow possibly slightly cross-eyed, and she would be by no means a rare instance of such treatment and thinking, if thinking is the word.

CHAPTER 9

Practice was not all cattle, with the occasional equine case thrown in. I was gradually if not too eagerly acquiring a high and wholly unwarranted reputation as an expert on dogs. On one occasion I was standing near the roadside at my old home when a car pulled up beside me and a certain very great lady began to consult me about one of her dogs.

Amid the flow of her information she threw in the remark: 'I hear you are the Oracle on dogs.' Immediately I pleaded not guilty, admitted that I might possibly have a slightly oracular style of speaking, but otherwise maintained my innocence of the charge.

Ah me: likewise, oh woe, och no no! and much more in the same minor key. If the good lady had but known how very un-oracular I could be – worse, worse than that – if the usual oracle workers had heard that I was considered by some to be one of the regular Oracle staff, or even the whole Oracular cheese in one department (dogs), there would have been a strike right away about employment of non-union labour, then another on about demarcation of labour and a third one about pay differentials, for they were bound to be worth more than me, a non-union, non-oracle man.

Incidentally, the dog, an uncomplicated case of haematuria, made an easy recovery as a consequence of, or perhaps in spite of, the medicine I immediately dispensed for him, and I had not even seen the case. On hearing that report I immediately awarded myself five medals and seriously considered a glass of whisky.

It has been said in print, and I believe what was said, that eighty per cent of all clinical cases would recover by natural processes without treatment of any kind. It was an idea I did not disseminate too widely among my clients. The practice was quite little enough as it was, without my doing anything to diminish it. Though dog work made me slightly uneasy and I always saw cats as sleek, supercilious creatures somewhat tinged with hostility, I could not afford to do without what little work came from those two sources. Afford or not, I was sometimes the only veterinary aid available in the island and so could not avoid the case. Medical cases were seldom complicated and, if they had a prognosis at all favourable, generally responded to the good nursing they got, wherever they were, which was seldom in my hands. Two or three were, for short periods, but they come into other stories.

There was one type of case to which I never could find nor imagine any answer. That was the case of chronic constipation in the household dog. By chronic I mean not that it was habitual, though it may have been that, but that it was cumulative; where in each case the patient must have gone a matter of weeks before veterinary attention was sought. Just how long the condition had existed could be no more than a fairly broad guess since there was no reliable evidence as to when the patient had last had a bowel movement. Whether by coincidence or not I do not know, but each of the three cases I saw was of the same breed, which was one of the terriers.

The first case I saw of it happened before I was qualified and my view of it was only at the post mortem done by the vets in charge of it. It is remembered clearly because it was the only one of its kind I had seen and was not easily forgotten Not only the rectum but the lower colon also was distended with rock-like faeces to a diameter of something like one and a quarter inches. Clearly the patient had no hope of voiding such a mass unaided. Enemeta alone or with attempted purgation might not have killed the patient, though they jointly or singly stood a good chance of doing do, but they certainly would not have helped.

The next two, seen at intervals of several years between each, were exactly the same. There might be almost aphorism here in saying that as cases they had no history and no future. All three were of the same breed, but whether their common ailment was idiosyncratic to that breed or, more likely, due to chronic shortage of water in the dogs' water-bowls is something wholly unknown to me. I did not know and would certainly never have been told about water-bowls.

Treatment by a fore and aft approach was useless and a direct approach by laparotomy likely to be the same. If there was anything useful to be done I could not think what it was.

If I seem to have shied away from, or not even considered, laparotomy under those circumstances, I did not avoid it in a very different sort of case in which it was the obvious and only way, in this case, in a bitch there were pups unborn, and to them normal egress was denied.

In each case – I had three in all – the history was the same: the bitch seemed for a time to be preparing to have pups, nothing appeared, actively subsided and the owner, seeing no need for action, either did nothing or merely kept watch on the bitch for two or three days until discharge and odour from her compelled him to act. The vet, of whom action was expected, needed very little time to ascertain that delivery, however it was going to be done, was not going to be by the normal route.

It so happened that the first case of this kind occurred just one mile from my base and, in travelling home to prepare for the operation before I would take the dog, who should I meet but a colleague, the other vet on the island. That meeting saved me the trouble of trying to phone him when, clearly, had I done so I would not have got him. We discovered that although I had seen the operation but had never done it I was still ahead of him, for he had never seen it at all.

It may reasonably be asked at this point by the reader, how was it possible for a student to graduate from a veterinary school in Britain without having seen an operation as commonly required as that one? It was perfectly possible. Any difficulty arising lay not in contriving to see it.

The Glasgow school, in which we had both qualified about the same time, had had its Government grant withdrawn under the findings of those who, in their inscrutable wisdom, decided that four such schools were enough for the whole of

Britain and Ireland. Glasgow, however, although killed, refused to lie down dead. Somehow it contrived to carry on though, for many years, money was desperately short. This unjustified deprivation of funds meant that facilities for teaching and for practical demonstrators, etc., varied between the very sparse and the non-existent. That my colleague had not seen the operation now in hand was only one of innumerable instances of that kind of thing. In fact in those days it would have been less the exception than the rule. We agreed that we would meet again in two hours' time at my place of work. I needed that time to prepare for a major operation of that kind, and he needed it to do whatever he had to do. We had got all the technical details arranged; in due course we met as planned and I went back along the road and fetched the patient.

Having been the visiting physician, then the auxiliary theatre staff then ambulanceman I next became anaesthetist and surgeon. Later on, if the operation went right, I would be filling in as night nurse besides taking on the duties of stoker, charlady and general handyman. There was no other course open to me. If I was on an island situated twelve miles across salt water from the mainland then so be it. There was no question of conveying the patient into a veterinary hospital of any kind. Either we did the whole job from start to finish ourselves or we adopted the unhappy alternatives.

The time when we were ready to start was well into the evening, and the date must have been some time in the pre-mains electricity era, not post -1947, because our only light was a Tilley lamp. But, as many an old soldier might affirm, there has been many a good job done by the light of a Tilley lamp in a time of emergency and at other times too. The patient was anaesthetised with Nembutal and fixed in position. We gave the dope intraperitoneally, a technique no doubt fairly crude by modern standards, but it worked well. We then disinfected the site as best we could, clapped on our sterile drapes (oh yes, we were doing the thing in style), prepared our hands, hoped they were sterile and got started. I opened the abdomen, exposing the gravid uterus – and it certainly was gravid –which then bulged upwards. We tied off everything that was for tying and removed the mass.

The main trick really was in the treatment of the stump. I had already explained to my colleague how I would deal with it, or thought I would deal with it, for I had never before tried the plan I had in mind.

The plan began from a question which had been set in one of the exams, the professional exams at that, which went something like this: 'Describe at least three methods of dealing with the uterine stump in a canine hysterectomy.' Candidate No. 21 – or maybe that was my number in the next surgery exam, the one I passed – or whatever number it was, had heard, a good while before that, some talk about 'flyping' the stump, which meant inverting the cut end into the vagina by use of a pair of forceps passed along it and catching the stump with them. Awfully clever, if you can do it. There was another procedure called marsupialisation which, if I had got my information right, consisted of attaching the cut surface of the stump to the external abdominal wall, for drainage. Didn't sound good to me; still, it counted. The third method was ' peritonisation' which meant somehow covering the cut surface with peritoneum.

As I in that examination room had no clear idea of how either of the latter methods was performed, I, on the spot, invented a fourth one. With the calmness of desperation I wrote in my paper something like 'This writer sees no reason why the following method should not be successful...' I then described and illustrated with a diagram how, by making a long, V-shaped incision flat wise (in fact two incisions meeting at the apex of the V), in the body of the uterus, with the apex directed posteriorly and in the lumen of that body, the anterior part and the brancher would then be severed. The newly incised surfaces of the corpus uteri could then be brought into complete contact with each other and sutured together, thus closing the V shaped incision.

CORPUS UTERI   CORPUS UTERI
INCISION OPENED   INCISON CLOSED

It was a bold scheme and, if I say it myself, very neat and ingenious, a thorough credit to the nameless candidate who had suddenly dreamed it up. The only trouble was that he had never heard of it before, nor so far as he knew, had anyone else. Against that, it had the virtue that it filled a good part of one page of the exam paper and probably did not lose him any marks; or not many, anyway. I was a right clever wee chap in those days. I could fill an exam paper with information of which much was new to everybody, including myself. True information? Some or all of it might have been, for all I knew.

I would probably never have given it another thought, unless for my own purposes as eventually happened, but that one day in the Glasgow Veterinary College in Buccleuch St., at some time between sitting the written professional exam and finally passing in Surgery I happened to notice a group of students gathered round a table in a part of the big, central covered area at street level. Someone was demonstrating to the students a hysterectomy on a bitch. The demonstrator was not our professor of surgery but someone closely connected with him. Here, if this story is to have any point, I must explain that the professor of each subject, so far as I ever understood, had the duty of reading and marking the professional examination papers of each of his students before the papers were passed to the external examiners. What was my surprise then to see there in front of me my very own method, now apparently no longer mine, for dealing with the uterine stump. If I had been the most talkative chap in the college I could not have said a word just then. I dare say, looking back now, a large part of my astonishment would be due to the amazing coincidence of my arrival at the demonstration, about which I had heard nothing beforehand, precisely at the moment when the demonstrator (who had probably also seen the Surgery papers) was dealing with that difficulty in that particular way. A very few minutes later in arriving and I would have missed it.

Now it may be that that identical technique for dealing with the stump was devised and in use in veterinary or human surgery or both, long before I as just another examination candidate, set it out. Indeed the wonder would be if it had never been devised and set out. But in that case an even bigger wonder would be that it got no mention in any of the veterinary textbooks which were standard works on surgery at that time and of which one had appeared in its second edition only a bare two years before then. Neither was that method (which I still regard as being originally mine) ever mentioned to us in any class I attended in college. And if it had already been known and used in human surgery it would almost certainly have been passed on to veterinary surgeons somewhere, at some time. It is probably of little or no consequence and has very likely been long ago superseded. I claim only that I described it originally some time in 1936 and successfully used it some years later.

All the foregoing is good and true. We had dealt with the stump and more closing the abdominal wound when the Tilley lamp went out. The words then uttered by me cannot possibly be repeated here. My colleague was not a swearing man, but I was. I had shaken it beforehand to estimate the amount of oil in it and judged that we had enough when, sadly, we had not. It was soon replenished and, hot as it was, easily re-lit. As our suturing progressed so did our patient, a rather adipose Scottish collie, and she began to wake up. My colleague continued to suture while I dashed for the chloroform and a pad of cotton wood. Soon after that we had got her fully stitched, dry-dressed, bandaged and lying fairly warm and comfortable. She looked as if she might be giving us some room for hope. In fact she made a leisurely, steady recovery without interruption.

My second case of surgery for the relief of dystokia did not require quite such heroic measures. It was a straightforward caesarean in a Scots collie and, for that operation, I had the help of a friend, a doctor, back at his old home in Arran for a holiday.

Presentation of the patient, preparation, anaesthesia, surgery, recovery etc., were all according to the book. Everything went according to the best textbook lines and recovery was rapid and uncomplicated. That was number two. Dash it all, this sort of thing was threatening to become a bore.

For my third such case, this time in a Border terrier, I had the help of her owner, who was a good help but who knew about the job in hand what I told him and nothing more. The bitch, by her history, seemed to have started three or four days earlier and stopped. I first attended her in her own home where it soon became clear to me on examination of her that she was not going to have her pups in the normal way. Once again I got a two-hour start in my surgery-dispensary before the owner arrived with the patient, this time from a considerable distance.

In the course of a plain of long delayed caesarean we removed four or five somewhat decomposed pups in about a quart of black liquid and complete the op. as before. The patient being quite hardy and in good vigour despite some auto-intoxication, slept through the night as the others had done, all three operations being done in the late evening. I do not remember for sure now, but I think each one got a large saline injection before being left for the night. Of course they were seen very early the following morning in each case. This one was taken home again the day after the operation and, the owners told me later, escaped from the house on the third day, went off somewhere and was found conducting her own private rabbit hunt.

I was becoming quite vain, inwardly, about my successes. Three in a row, a hundred per cent success rate and all in the short space of about two years. Quite, quite hectic. There ought to be a check somewhere – if only to see that the equipment was still in working order, and I must have other interests.

Still, with that last caesarean, performed virtually singlehanded apart from the help which one completely untrained helper could give, I had come a long way from the first piece of surgery I was ever called upon to perform in that district. So far as I remember, my first surgical case while I was at home immediately after qualifying was a haematoma in a dog's ear.

My approach was fairly casual. I was at home, not long qualified, waiting for a job and my total surgical gear was made up of the scalpel and forceps I had in Anatomy, some cottonwool, lint and tincture of iodine. The scalpel was the kind one sharpened on an oil stone, the forceps were not required. I proceeded to the house where my patient lived, got acquainted with him, a placid natured retriever or some such breed, and taped his muzzle, just as a precaution. After a generous swabbing with iodine on the hot, shiny skin, one slash with the scalpel, towards the tip of the ear, did the trick. With a piece of lint or cottonwool damped with Tinct. Iodine over one finger I scooped out any fibrin between skin and cartilage, lay a piece of clean boric lint over the incision, a pad of wool over the lint and had the whole ear held against the head with a simple but efficient retaining device.

The 'simple but efficient retaining device' was the heel of an old, hand-knitted, woollen sock, cut just in front of the heel and again just above it, and a hole cut in it for the other ear. It fitted admirably; the dog seemed to like it and left it in position long enough for the skin flaps to make perfect re-attachment to the cartilage. Seen two or three weeks later, healing was complete and perfect. There were: nothing to it. With the dog, the owner and the vet all in blissful ignorance of possible complications 'twere surely folly to be wise'. Mind you I had seen elaborate and troublesome techniques which got results no better than mine, if as good, but for my case I had decided beforehand that the treatment to be used would be the simplest imaginable or nothing.

I was told, some weeks after attending the case, that the slightly elderly and talkative lady in charge of it had stated firmly, as her opinion of me:

'He knows his job.'

What greater praise could any young, new graduate reasonably expect?

CHAPTER 10

The name Shiskine is a corruption of a Gaelic word meaning 'the marshy place' and having that meaning some folk would say it was well named. Geologists have said that the valley was at one time a lake – no doubt here in Scotland I should say 'loch' – until the natural barrier between valley and sea at Blackwaterfoot eroded sufficiently to allow drainage of the basin. Today, especially after prolonged rain, some of us might be inclined to ask why should we use the phrase 'at one time' a lake? At the present day, though, it is not one bigger lake; it is in part a number of smaller ones – that is to say it will show several big shallow pools of flood water.

According to the Ordnance Survey map on the scale one inch to one mile one must go inland from Blackwaterfoot about three quarters of a mile to gain the first fifty feet of altitude. After that one can go another two miles and still not have gained the next fifty feet. Less than a hundred feet of fall for drainage in two and a half miles is not a lot of fall – something like 1/160 or 180 and those farmers involved can be left to express their own views on the cultivation problems arising from that. The veterinary surgeon, especially if born and brought up in the district, tends to see the situation through different eyes.

Fields which cannot be used for root crops without a big risk of part or all of the crop drowning and which are used only exceptionally for a corn crop because of the hazards of harvesting it, tend to become permanent pastures. Such pastures are looked on by the dyed-in-the-wool rural veterinary surgeon with a cold and sour regard. He does not readily forget one old and well known dictum in parasitology: 'permanent parasites perpetuate parasites', an aphorism attributed to one man, Noel Pillers of Liverpool, in his time a well known member of the profession. Permanently wet pastures also favour the survival of the white snail essential in the life circle of the liver fluke.

The farmer may see certain fields as being and having been for a long time past the best grazing he can get anywhere. His vet at the same time most likely sees the same pastures as hotbeds of worm eggs and larvae, white snails and other pests which in certain permanent pastures could be ticks and the protozoan parasites they may carry and which is the causal agent of the redwater in cattle. Not that all ticks are carriers of the redwater parasite. Though much, possibly all, of the Arran hill ground is tick infested redwater is or was found only in two or three small areas.

In my own case in those days my sour regard of such parasites, no sourer than the pastures themselves, usually carried with it the feeling that my farmer clients should be one and all more parasite-conscious. Any feeling I might have had of some moral obligation to tell them more about the parasite burden possibly being carried by their livestock was countered by the thought that I might be seen as simply trying to create more business for myself. So on the whole, no doubt like many another practitioner in the same position, I tended to stay quiet on it all.

How much was lost to the stockowners in Arran, and indeed is still being lost not only in Arran but whenever stock is grazed in any appreciable concentration through lack of countermeasures against contamination of pastures, is always a matter for speculation. In Arran, so far as I can see on looking back, there seems to have been little if any veterinary advisory services before the mid 1930s and probably not a lot even then. Consequently any early talk, for example by anyone building up a practice, on subjects such as parasites, while it was not refuted since refutation was not an option nor yet rejected, it was heard with what I suspect were a good many inward reservations and no noticeable accompanying action. Farmers are cautious souls. They found out long ago they had better be.

Shiskine however is not all dead level bottom. As with some other parts of Arran which also have dead levels it has hillsides, more or less steep as the case may be. These are cut up by gullies of which the sides may be quite high, rugged and steep or changing in places to sheer drops to be regarded as cliffs. These are very far from being the most important or the most dangerous cliffs in the island but they have been the scenes of occasional fatal falls for cattle. Far more dangerous are the sea cliffs which skirt most of the island and there are a great many other much higher precipices in the hills too.

Where one of the bigger cliffs was the scene of a fall there was usually no need for a vet. Such animals died on the spot, how quickly we do not know but in those few other cases which had fallen shorter distances where they seemed to have some chance of recovery I was called to such of them as were within my practice.

On examination the patient might seem to all outward appearances not too bad. The pulse would be as good as could be expected, temperature not too low, conjunctiva probably pale but not excessively so. The patient would be willing but unable to rise.

Looking back on such cases now it seems to me that what I did not realise sufficiently was the full extent of internal injury which was found to have been present in such cases: the probable rupture of ligaments holding abdominal organs in their places, displacement or possible rupture of some of these organs themselves plus other injuries unseen and undiagnosed all in total too much to permit recovery. But 'hope springs eternal'…, etc. In such few cases as I had, I generally optimistically aimed at a recovery and invariably lost.

There have been occasions when a big group of cattle on high ground driven by continuous heavy rain and strong wind have simply kept their rumps to it as is their instinct and travelled with it. At those times, more so when the movement was during a pitch black night with the whole group gradually approaching the top of a cliff, the animals at the rear pushing forward or perhaps only trying to huddle among those in front, the latter on finding an ever increasing downward gradient under their feet could do nothing other than go over the cliff to which the gradient had changed.

There were other causes of such falls over cliffs. Sometimes where the group was of mixed ages and sexes containing an assortment varying perhaps from aged dry cows to six- or nine-month-old bull calves (many bull calves especially if they were good looking and well bred stuck for long periods at nine months because after ten months they had to be licensed for breeding and licences were not always granted) one or more of the older stronger cattle would take a spite at another which was younger, weaker or both. A common example of that was the dry in-calf cow versus the bull calf which was probably undersized in any case. If that little bull calf old enough to serve should be unlucky enough or careless enough to find himself between one or more of those cows and the gradually increasing downward gradient he was on very dangerous ground. But he generally had the sense to stay well behind his elders.

Hostile members of a group were not necessarily the only agents of disaster for that group. There were sometimes low flying aircraft either coming in off the sea at hedge height or appearing suddenly from behind a hill and while it was difficult to prove that they directly or indirectly caused the death of animals at grazing there was strong evidence to that effect in places other than Arran.

I do know that a calf on hearing what we human beings regard as the simple sound of a motor bike at close range, if it does not understand that the noise is harmless it may start bawling in sheer blind panic and if it is free, stampede in any direction regardless of its own safety. Obstacles in its path mean nothing to it and its heartbeats when it is caught are almost painful to hear. That much I have seen for myself. But there did not seem to be any direct evidence of that kind in respect of aircraft about the Isle of Arran yet Arran seemed to get at least its fair share of low flying aircraft.

I might observe here in passing that there were during the war years a total of at least thirteen aircraft crashes or forced landings on or very close to the shore off Arran, an area of 164 square miles. Of the thirteen, three were in the Shiskine and Machrie districts within four miles of each other. I remember being a little astonished one morning in Shiskine going south on one of my rounds to see a Anson of Coastal Command parked neatly on top of a hedge, nose on one side and tail on the other, a few yards from the road. The same ratio for Scotland, England and Wales, an area of some 88,000 square miles, would have represented nearly seven thousand crashes or forced landings of aircraft not engaged in battle. If there ever was any such statistic for aircraft it was never commonly mentioned. They would seem on available evidence to be only very doubtfully guilty if at all of being a cause, direct or indirect, whole or part of deaths among cattle in Arran.

The hills and low moss ground too held another menace: bog or boggy ground. An animal of any age might be found stuck fast in a morass of peat and water not merely up to its flanks but right up over its back. The cause in this case might again be the pushing of it by others in the group or simply an error of judgement such as can be made by even the most experienced animal in the herd.

Where the victim was found after only a short time of being bogged and the process of extrication with ropes and spades and so on had not been too damaging, prognosis might be moderately hopeful. There were, as one might expect, better prospects for a young vigorous animal than for an old one. Where on the other hand the victim had been held many hours before being found and the rescue operation carried out with perhaps more haste and strength than skill, prognosis was not good. For the poor prognosis the reason which applied in some degree to all such boggings was not too hard to see.

As the animal was almost totally immobilised it could not maintain body heat by muscle movement and bogged as it was, most of its skin area was in contact with cold water. It could not reach anything to eat to help itself instinctively to maintain its body heat by chewing which according to the Physiology textbook can produce as much as one third of the heat production of a ruminant animal at rest. Thus placed it could no other than get colder and colder, very often, though we did not know it at those times, cold to 'the point of no return'.

As the length of time for which an animal had been bogged was usually unknown to anybody we usually somehow acted on the assumption that it had not been so for very long but too often we lost the patient.

From what I have said here it may be seen that hill grounds with unfenced cliffs and level moors with bogs, though less insidious in effects than heavily contaminated pastures as in a valley bottom, can also be sources of livestock loss. I have not said anything about sheep because we were never called to sheep which had got into similar 'sticky' situations in bogs or others as on a cliff face though there was always the odd one which did just that.

In addition to the sources of loss above mentioned I here claim to have discovered a new disease of sheep. Perhaps it can hardly be regarded as being new now. It appeared only for a few years, first seen at the start of the war when meat was tightly rationed. It was quite a seasonal incidence and invariably fatal. For lack of any better name I called it 'potato digging disease'.

Sheep affected by it (like braxy it seemed to affect mainly well nourished specimens) invariably died without premonitory symptoms. Almost the only noteworthy pre mortem symptom was profuse haemorrhage from the anterior cervical i.e. laryngeal area, post-mortem findings being severance of major blood vessels, the carotid arteries and jugular veins, no doubt at all but sudden bacterial action quite unforeseeable by anyone. 'Some bacteerie can be very vishuss.'

I was never asked to post-mortem any such carcase. I never even saw one but relied on reliable hearsay but I know the mortality rate was 100 per cent. No sheep affected by 'potato digging' (also called 'potato lifting' or 'tattie howkin') ever got over it.

There were heavy losses in the pig population too. At one period between the end of the war in 1945 and 1957 there was something almost like a craze for pig keeping. Pigs for slaughter were the thing to have for a time and nearly everybody who had a pig-habitable corner of any kind was installing a pig or pigs in it.

But besides all such proliferation of porcine representation as by that sudden boom in pig-ery there was here and there always the odd quietly placed old campaigner who kept the odd pig or two or four. These pigs never evoked a single query from the Ministry of Agriculture, Fisheries and Food. Many of them died very suddenly and the local butchers on their rounds – for there were no butcher shops on the west side of the island – found from time to time that some people were not using their bacon coupons. The cause of death in all those cases was undoubted concussion following percussion with coincident haemorrhage.

There was however one pig I remember well which did not die suddenly, at least not very suddenly. The subject was a young gilt bought as a piglet and reared by the owner. She was near breeding age when she developed an illness with no clear symptoms which would allow a diagnosis to be made. When I was called to her I found only vague symptoms, could not do much and left the case on a nursing and observation basis. That was all right and probably justifiable, or least excusable in the circumstances, but there was a sequel. Alas, alas and much woe; on which brought me no joy.

Young miss piggy-wiggy, then aged between a year and eighteen months, became more obviously unwell again with no definite symptoms only a very few weeks after I first saw her. At my second visit she had not shown any recent bowel movement. In fact she had not shown anything except that she was not well. Not knowing what she might have eaten which might be delaying her bowel movements I decided to administer to her a purgative. So using the traditional method I cut the toe out of an old shoe, stuck it into her mouth and poured my fiendish mixture into the shoe. She seemed to object very little if at all. My labours were a classic demonstration of the art craft of dosing a pig. The only trouble was that she very inconsiderately died in the middle of it all. Not choked, just stopped breathing and quietly sustained.

There were a few muttered words of a deep purple colour and the atmosphere immediately around us suggested sulphur. Some of my earlier laboriously gained learning came to my aid. I remembered that in cases of chronic swine erysipelas as distinguishable from the acute form which is easily diagnosed, the classical post-mortem finding is 'cauliflower-like growths on the valves of the heart'.

About the case I had been treating I began to suspect something. Definitely. I got suspicious, did a post- mortem there and then, and cut open the heart. Often it is only at a post-mortem on a pig found dead that chronic swine erysipelas is diagnosed. In this instance, to my great satisfaction, I was able to demonstrate absolutely classical cauliflower type growths on the heart valves.

I do not know if I sent the specimen to Glasgow Veterinary College or not. I think I did for GVC always welcomed classic specimens illustrating conditions well known but less frequently seen and it seemed to get at least a fair share of contributions from me.

Death from disease there was, and deaths in the hills and the bogs. These did no good to anybody. But casualties in those other categories like 'potato digging' or concussion with sudden haemorrhage: that was, eh well, that was different again.

CHAPTER 11

Sometimes in my leisured moments I have wondered, and who has not, about the way other people saw me. Did they, having seen that I did not speak in quite the usual way, have more interest in my mode of speaking than in what I was saying or more interest in either of those things than in the speaker? I seldom knew.

How many times I do not know but anyway too often have I had to take a seemingly eccentric line of action or on the contrary take no action at all, displaying behaviour which at times was probably very puzzling to the other party or parties observing it. Many such occasions there were, now largely forgotten, and all for lack of a few phrases as being some explanation from me and said to the right party at the right time. The phrases were not forthcoming not because I had not got them to say but because they did not get spoken simply because I could not utter them.

But there was one time when whatever might be my way of speaking it was no disadvantage.

I was sitting in my dispensary one afternoon looking out of a window and thinking about nothing in particular. I did rather a lot of sitting in my dispensary looking out of the window and thinking about nothing in particular and found I had considerable talent for that sort of thing. Who did I see striding up the yard but the Duke himself. Yes it was the Duke, all the erect six feet and more of him in the kilt he so often wore and bringing with him a spaniel on a lead. The dispensary was in one corner of a building and had windows in both walls looking out on to the yard. But before I could gather my scattered wits he had reached the door and rapped on it with the gold-topped cane he carried.

Now I had always thought until that moment that only in novelettes of a certain calibre did dukes carry gold-topped canes and use them to rap on doors. Not so. And when I saw my distinguished visitor stand there and rap on the door in the most matter of fact way I did not swoon nor vanish through the ceiling or the floor, nor adopt any other unusual course. For one thing the paint flakes on the door didn't fall off – there wasn't time. Though I daresay had there been any old paint flakes on me some desquamation might then have occurred with great suddenness. Instead I simply dashed to the door and admitted him.

Although I had never spoken to his grace I knew he heard hardly anything if he heard at all. As for me I was not exactly the world's best speaker. How was this situation going to pan out?

We got on famously. He made no bones about his advantage and probably knew all about mine. He explained about the dog and asked questions in the usual way about what he wanted to know. I in reply simply wrote everything I had to say or wished to say, a procedure which was to me all too familiar from the past. There was no communication problem whatsoever.

I do not now remember what was the trouble with the dog except that while it was nothing serious it required further attention. This we arranged would be done at the castle at which I duly arrived a day or two later. The duke again chose to have charge of the dog in the time required for doing what little had to be done. Whatever that was is forgotten now but was probably a brief examination or an injection or both. Another small matter about the dog affecting his rear end and fairly trivial but causing him much discomfort had appeared in the intervening time, and it too was put right.

To me the most remarkable feature about it all was that I really could not remember having worked with anyone who held a dog quite as efficiently as my present client who might have been the least expected to do so. What happened was that when I drove up to the castle I went to the first door I saw, the one at the south-west end. After admission and while I waited a few moments for someone to bring the dog I had time to consider my situation and after that to admire the stags' heads and other trophies on the walls. After a few moments the Duke himself appeared with the dog; we took it outside on to some higher ground a little bit away from the gravelled area and gave it the necessary attention. Unthinkingly I uttered a hearty compliment to my handler but of course he could not hear me and there was no one else present. I suppose I had become so used and resigned to inefficient handling that to find a patient being well held without hurting it was refreshing enough to evoke my spontaneous comment.

That case occurred probably in the early autumn and helped together with the usual thin sprinkling of other small animal jobs and the routine chores of dairy practice to fill the hiatus between the turning out of stock to the spring grass and bringing them in at the back end of the year. At one time or another I had some canine cases of greater or lesser interest which could have turned up at any time in the year yet it seemed to be mostly in the summer months that veterinary attention was required for them.

There was for one example the case of the terrier Jimmy. Jimmy was not his real name but it will do. He had got hold of a bone, probably a mutton bone, and whatever was the animal from which it came it was light enough to be fragmented and splintered easily by his strong jaws.

One of his owners, the lady, saw him in the act of crushing and gulping down the fragments of the bone. Panic stations. Those jagged fragments were by some folk's ideas surely going to tear gaping rents in the alimentary tract beyond his stomach. That was for sure. That the client held but little idea of what lay beyond a dog's stomach was a circumstance in which some calming talk would quite likely do some good. I happened to have that kind of talk just then and it helped.

We sat down or maybe we stayed standing. I explained to the lady my idea that dogs with voracious appetites such as her terrier had would readily consume porridge and that into that porridge we could introduce flakes something like snowflakes but thicker, of cotton wool.

She made the porridge according to my directions; I added the cotton wool.

Jimmy gulped the lot without question and then after all that there was nothing to do but wait, wait and see. I had to go home but the next day I heard on the phone the triumphant news: Jimmy had passed the bone splinters with edges neatly protected in cotton wool. Later in the week I saw two or three of the pieces, probably fragments of sheep scapula, carefully kept for me to see and in truth the width and the jagged edges of them would have made a frightful mess of the dog's intestines, more than just possibly fatal to him.

It happened maybe thirty odd years ago. There was nothing I could find in the textbooks of that time to cover or resemble the case in hand. Whatever may have been printed since then, of that I candidly admit a large ignorance. Consolation is surely to be found in the other Great Thoughts.

Once again the British Genius for Magnificent Improvisation was made evident. And somewhere or other I acquired a magnificent dram of whisky. Leaving aside those Great Thoughts I had to give other thoughts to other things.

How I knew about hungry dogs going for porridge was because at the end of my first year at college and faced like most other Scottish students of those days with a long empty summer, idle, hard up and hungry for work if not for food, I fell in with a job as a gillie. 'Gille' or 'gillie' by its English rendering is a purely Gaelic word meaning simply 'boy' or 'lad'. I was a 'gillie'. I carried a game bag kindly given to me for transport of the dead grouse when they had cooled sufficiently in the 'game stick', a contrivance by which dead birds are carried suspended by their necks until they are cool enough for transfer to the game bag. I also had charge of a number of that fine breed of dog, the pointer. As a 'gillie' complete with game bag and pointers I did my tramping of the hills behind three or four 'guns' and carrying a gradually increasing load of dead grouse arrived back with the others towards evening at the kennels.

At the kennels here was the remarkable thing – to me at any rate remarkable. There was a massive dish of porridge, not of the kind which might as well have been made in a teapot but the kind in which a spoon could be stood up: the kind of porridge for heroes. The pointers invariably fell upon it and swallowed it in chunks with or without milk though they usually got some with it.

Thus I had gained that not very common knowledge and I had from my previous year my summer's joy of a severely sexually disturbed mare working beside a monorchid horse. That much and more I had acquired when I started my second year at Glasgow Veterinary College and the going that far had not been too light.

'No animal is wholly carnivorous.' Thus saith the textbook. My goodness. didn't I know that of old. I had known for a long time that while 'lions and tigers', etc. ate mainly meat they had to have vegetable material too.

Meat, I understood, was broadly speaking acid producing, vegetable matter alkaline in its chemistry, the body chemistry of the higher mammals essentially alkaline. My pointers were direct descendants of the meat-eating wolf – how did they make out on a diet of porridge? Of course it was not entirely a diet of porridge.

They got milk with it sometimes if not always which would have kept up their vitamin supply and they occasionally evidently got access to a carcase where the animal had died from natural causes. But broadly speaking their diet was vegetable and alkaline and the dog as a species although a carnivorous animal, could get by quite well on a wholly vegetable diet if need be at least for a long time.

There was another reason why porridge was especially suitable. Oatmeal has a high carbohydrate content, too high for some diets, and is often said to be too heating but pointers with their very shorts coats have a high rate of heat loss and are constantly generating more body heat by shivering. They have always seemed to me to shiver more than any other breed I know.

I was able to put that little bit of veterinary lore to good use one time in Devon when we had to nurse one kennel of pointers through a sharp outbreak of distemper. They had had their serum etc. In therapeutic doses they had been fed meat raw and cooked and had gone off it. What could they be persuaded to eat?

I prescribed porridge made according to my instructions, salted to taste and offered in quantity with milk. To the astonishment of those concerned, myself excepted, the dogs took to it right away and never looked back.

Another canine case, rather sad one, which came my way was a big golden retriever Labrador. This poor chap had not just one but latterly two complaints. He could have lived with the first one indefinitely but the latter one was a killer. He was just a big lump of good nature and had an unfortunate tendency to go with any party, usually children who would entice him from his home down to the beach about a quarter of a mile away. That might have been all right in the end but they persisted despite all requests and warnings in throwing stones for the dog to retrieve. That again might have been all right in the end but for the fact that the dog regularly swallowed some or all of the stones thrown for him.

When I examined him and palpated his abdomen it was possible to hear the stones 'chinking' against each other in his stomach: The treatment I devised was to fill the stomach with butchers offal by letting the dog eat his fill of it, waiting a few minutes then giving him a shot of apomorphine for a prompt emetic effect which I got. Along with the rejected offal he brought up two rounded stones, a rather disappointing result for I knew he had more than that many. His owner had at some time much earlier taken him to other vets in Glasgow who had told him that on opening the dog's abdomen and seeing his stomach they decided against any surgical interference with it.

Maybe I should have waited longer before making him vomit but in any case I never got another chance because by that time his other trouble had begun to show too plainly.

Just about one year earlier while examining him for something else I found one or two of his lymph glands abnormally large and told the owner what I had found: that it might be nothing serious or it might be incurable, we should know better about one year on from then and just about one year on from then we did. All

somehow got her left patellar ligament (*ligamentum patellae*) completely ruptured so that the joint could be flexed backwards much further than normal.

The owner had phoned me beforehand, made an appointment and duly arrived with the dog. My prognosis, I must admit, was a sort of double-barrelled or maybe backfiring type; I hardly knew which. Before I cut down on the patellar ligament, the one so easily felt at the front of a dog's stifle or 'knee' joint of the hind leg, I had blandly assured the owner that provided the ligament had not detached from the bone itself or too close to the bone at one or other end, stitching the two ends together should be no great difficulty. I duly exposed the torn ends only to find that instead of the firm white cords I had expected was more like two strands of pink darning wool but stronger than that.

On seeing what I had got, my hopes of brilliant surgery went way, way down and I told the owner as much. However having gone that far with much trouble directed towards asepsis etc. I did make an attempt and managed one suture of fairly light catgut and with a good hold of each of the torn ends of the ligament cautiously drew them together and tied the gut not too tightly. I was fairly liberal with penicillin or another antibiotic, closed the wound and in time got the whole leg encased in plaster leaving a window.

I then told the owner I had some slight hopes of recovery for the case but did not rate my chances of success as very high. I never saw her again for the owner was a busy farmer a good few miles away and he likely grudged the time though not the cost for bringing her back to me but he told me a long time afterwards that she made a good, I think virtually complete, recovery.

I was rather pleased to have won that one.

CHAPTER 12

As the years went past the number of draught horses in the island seemed to diminish. The foals arriving were fewer, the number of colts for attention, never very many, dropped to zero. The Scottish Milk Marketing Board and the various tractor manufacturers between them gently if not unwittingly ushered the farm horse from the scene. Farmers who supplied milk to the Board realised early that in place of two horses they could keep three cows. Some of the smallholders who were closer to the ground said the proportion was more like one horse to two cows. The horses showed no direct financial return such as could be seen in a pleasing hypertrophy of the milk cheque. Everybody concerned knew all the pros and cons on the matter.

Moreover the tractors were not subject to ailments such as lymphangitis, better know as 'weed' or 'Monday morning leg' which usually went away but never very quickly, nor were they subject to colic which could find a horse apparently quite all right in the morning and left dead that same day. They did not have to be bred, reared, steered past joint-ill, have bowel troubles, pick up nails and so on and on. Anyone who has tried opening the hind foot of a two-year-old or three-year-old Clydesdale horse, high spirited but unbroken and quite unaccustomed to having his hind legs handled under any circumstances, never mind unpleasant ones, or even a well broken, much handled farm horse which is nevertheless leaning on the hapless farrier like a dead elephant, needs no further comment about that. Not that such things happen very often but when they did they greatly strengthened the case for selling the horses and buying a tractor.

As I said earlier in this story regarding trouble in cattle so it was with horses. Trouble could begin at or even before birth though I was only once ever called to a foaling case.

That one and only foaling to which I was called in Arran happened on a fine typically summery morning in June. The owner had guessed right when he decided that the mare was in trouble; I knew it as soon as I saw her in a little field down below the road and that was before I had even completed the journey. I knew because the location being about nine miles from my base I took twenty to thirty minutes between receiving the call and getting there and when I did arrive I could see plenty of effort but still no foal. The owner had the usual pail of warm water, soap and towel all at hand or he very soon brought them. Quickly stripped to the waist and wearing black oilskin or plastic trousers, my usual rig-out for large animal obstetrics, I explored and found some simple position which was easily corrected and I got well smeared in the process.

We were all in a very small field, hardly more than a slight extension of the beach head which formed one boundary of it with the sea itself about sixty yards away. Near another edge of this tiny field stood the mare held by her owner on nothing more than a head collar. Along this edge of the field ran a tiny brook on its way to the sea and to this brook I went to wash off a bit before helping the foal out. While I was bent over the wee burn washing the worst of the muck off my arse I looked up at my patient. To my absolute horror I saw that she had certainly made progress, yes, but she was now held up because one forefoot of the foal showing a marked over-extension had caught the roof of the passage, made a pouch of it and was pushing that pouch out through the anus. I say 'pushing' but she had in fact already pushed it through the anus to a distance of what looked like six or eight inches.

We all got a fright. I shouted something, something unusual but not commonly heard at garden parties and dashed towards the mare. She on her part being understandably quite unaccustomed to seeing any kind of figure rush up to her from behind, least of all one with its lower half black, upper half white, and shouting at her, let fly with both heels. Fortunately I was still out of range though only just.

That one fling however threw the foal forward within her and thus immediately corrected the presentation before I could get to her. Next moment I had got a hand inside her and guided the aberrant foot. Delivery followed immediately. The owner being at the head of course had no idea what the devil was going on at the other end end except that it was something alarming until I explained the whole thing to him later.

Now come the questions. If I had not shouted and run at the mare from behind as I did, would the next few uterine contractions accompanied by the terrific abdominal pressure a working mare can exert have damaged the foal's leg with its over-examined fetlock joint or damaged her own passage or, as seemed quite possible, damaged both vagina and rectum? On the other hand if I had not shouted and run at her would she in any case have flung up her heels as an instinctive reaction to the severe additional pain caused by the deviation of the foot?

I dinna ken. (I don't know.) I'll never ken but it's interesting and astonishing. The number and simplicity of questions I cannot answer with the desired information is astonishing.

Looking back over the relatively few cases I have had all told, I find myself a little surprised by the percentages of some of the commonest categories of cases which were made up of the less common types in that category. What I mean is that taking for example the question of lameness in horses, we are told that ninety per cent of all such lamenesses are in the foot (which is probably true for all I know) and that of these foot lamenesses more than half are due to picked up nails (which may very well be the case). Yet out of the few cases I had of lameness in horses, probably little more than a score in all were definitely of the stifle joint (which is what the layman first suspects and which is seldom the cause) and one was a hock wound. There were possibly half a dozen lymphangitis cases and four or five of laminitis. Add a strained tendon or two and the foot is left well short of being ninety per cent of the seats of equine lamenesses in my tiny practice.

In colic, another common category of equine ailment, impaction of one part or another of the small or large intestine is thought to be the commonest form of that complaint. Yet of the few colic cases I had all, two were acute volvulus of the small bowel and died within a day; one was a peracute case of the same with rupture and lasted about two hours from first to last. In that case no treatment could be given because of the violence of the symptoms. Another was due to peritonitis of unknown cause.

These which had ordinary forms of their troubles, lameness or colic or whatever, are not worth any description here but I had a few others which might be worth some brief mention.

I was called once to a place in the south end of the island to some case or some routine job, probably in a bovine though I have forgotten and it does not matter anyway. Just as I was leaving the owners asked me if I would look at a young mare they had which had a peculiarity in her walk yet was not lame all the time. As their best descriptions conveyed absolutely nothing to me I got them to take her out and walk her down the yard. As she walked past by me she had her bad leg next to me and thereby I got my clue (which I hoped must have made me seem frightfully clever). In fact I had never seen a case of the kind before and cannot recall seeing once since.

I saw something resembling spasm yet not exactly spasm: a sort of momentary bunching and quick release of the quadriceps group of muscles mainly, it seemed to me on further examination, the rectus femoris. All four muscles, or four heads if they are regarded as one muscle, attach themselves to the patella and their job is to help to operate the stifle joint.

It is known now and was better known then when draught horses were more common, that in certain loosely built individuals of that sort with muscles probably excellent in quantity but showing hypertonus perhaps from over strenuous exercise the powerful quadriceps femoris can pull the patella a little too high on the gliding surface of the femur so that the lower part of the patella catches momentarily in a little depression or what is potentially a depression at the upper end of that gliding surface. That movement causes discomfort and quite probably pain to the individual concerned. It certainly caused a check in the stride which once seen is easily identified. The next time she passed me I walked, or I should say nearly ran, beside her and at the precise split second jabbed with my fingertips at the impeded patella. For that action I was rewarded with a half hearted kick in my direction though the apparent kick was involuntary but the release of the anatomical parts involved was quite obvious.

While the owners appreciated this demonstration I could not unfortunately keep up the good work by telling them of any cure for the condition because so far as I knew at that time there was none. All I could advise was that the trouble had been given a splendid name (subluxation of the patella), that it would probably disappear as she got older, and that meantime she should have more than the usual amount of rest. What was wanted was a combination of conditions which would tighten the ligaments holding the patella and at the same time relax the muscles which moved it. Such a combination would be difficult to obtain and really a 'do nothing' policy had much to be said for it. There the matter rested.

As for typical colic if there is such a thing I had the treating of one which was distinctly atypical. Treatment had been started by my colleague who having to go out of the island for a few days, left the case with me but without telling me anything about it because I think he thought the case cleared. This was all in accordance with the standing arrangement we had that each took the other's calls and cases in his absence and it worked well.

This patient, a very nice clean legged medium weight draught mare, had failed to respond to treatment. Not only that: her condition had worsened. When I examined her I reluctantly had to abandon the theory that she was looking worse only to spite everybody and might be quite ready to die purely in pursuit of that objective. She had a temperature of 104 degrees Fahrenheit or thereabouts, seemingly total immobilisation of the stomach and bowels, and other symptoms which taken all together gave a very convincing picture of peritonitis.

I knew she had already had a dose of purgative which had not had the desired effect.

To give more of the same would be worse than futile. I gave her two gallons of normal saline by stomach tube. The idea was to promote irrigation of the alimentary tract and to counter probable dehydration. That treatment by itself might, I hoped, be just sufficient to gain the desired result. It was not. At next visit she was no better though no worse except that the good people in charge of her had in my absence and with the very best of intentions not matched by the effect produced dosed her with one and a half pints of raw linseed oil. I would still like to know what the mare thought about having that lot in her stomach.

Fortunately I had to stomach tube her again to give her something else and before beginning the dosage disconnect the tube from the pump. The oil began to reappear. The entire dose must have lain immobile in her stomach overnight. The nauseating effect of that can be imagined but the withdrawal of it was not due to any special skill on my part as the owners seemed to think it was. It was in fact just a bit of good luck for all of us. Not disclaiming the skill wrongly attributed to me I tacitly accepted it on basis that a little credit which I was not due might stand against some of the times when I deserved some credit and got none.

I gave her another two or three gallons of normal saline by tube and more of the sulfa compound she had already been given intravenously. Further sulfa dosage was continued by mouth.

On my next visit I found a marked improvement all round. Her pulse, formally very bad, was now much better, her temperature had dropped and she had eaten a tiny amount and was in general much brighter. She had 'turned the corner' as the owner put it. We had won.

There was no doubt at all that had the treatment of that case consisted of no more than the usual measures to evacuate the bowel the patient would have died as much

CHAPTER 13

Nearly all practitioners soon recognise various types of clients among all those encountered and island practices are no different in that respect. There is the attentive and cooperative, the garrulous, the loud, the querulous, the argumentative know it all, the largely useless and sundry others.

For one example of one type, there was the man who sent for me to go to his place and see one of his horses which was not doing too well at work. Nothing in particular wrong but just not as able as he used to be. So I went to the man's place and saw the horse in the stable and a pretty well worn old chap he was. I saw him in the yard where he immediately wanted a drink of water from the cold water trough. He got his drink then backed a step or two over some not very rough cobbles. Tail and hindquarters immediately proclaimed at least one of his troubles, probably the main one if not the only one.

'He's a shiverer,' I said.

'Naw he's no'.'

'Yes he is.'

'How d'ye know he's a shiverer?'

That point in the conversation should really have been my moment for exploding, verbally of course, in my client's face with a brief but impassioned address in words which came immediately to mind but were not spoken.

'Look here; if you have got to ask me how do I know he is a shiverer how the *** can you say he is not one? What the hell do you mean by contradicting me you argumentative old thing? Why don't you find out something of what you are talking about before you start blurting out your contradictions? Awfully good, you know, you should try it sometime.'

Of course at that moment I said nothing of the sort but instead mildly explained to Mr Clever what were the symptoms of the disease we call 'shivering'. At the same time I got some inward satisfaction from being able to emphasize the facts of the case: that the trouble was progressive and that there was no treatment, let alone cure, for it.

There was the other client who took me to see his horse because it was shivering in the stable.

'Robert, I want you to come and have a look at this horse of mine. He's standing shivering and I don't like the look of him at all ...'

True enough, but this was a very different kind of shivering. Examination showed the horse to be normal in all discernible respects except that his temperature was slightly subnormal. He also displayed a vigorous appetite the moment he got a morsel to eat. A diagnosis was formed and given that he was shivering because he was cold from having stood for too long in a draughty stable and in fact might safely be given a bit more to eat because the muscular movements required for the chewing and digestion of fodder would generate considerably more heat in him. Shivering, I explained, was simply nature's way of generating more body heat.

Not at all. My client would have none of it. If a horse standing in his own stall was shivering he was sickening for something if he had not already got it. That was for sure. Anybody knew that and it was what the old folk for generations back always said. And they were pretty wise the old folk; they knew a lot of things. We had forgotten a lot of what they knew. ('Not before time' was my own thought about that.)

I managed to escape somehow before I could be told of any good books I could get which might help me and managed to creep quietly to my car and slip quickly out of the yard. All the same I never heard of the horse either needing or receiving any further attention.

There was another sort of client who might not call me once in six months which is not to say that that he had no need of any veterinary service within that time. The trouble might be chronic, the owner slow to seek help, but when he did seek it whoever was called was plainly expected to drop all else and come a-running. And if as sometimes happened there was unavoidable delay it was sometimes necessary to explain to that type of client that we did in fact occasionally have cases from other people and that sometimes one or more of these had to get priority even over his one. I sometimes longed to add that incomprehensible as that might seem to him, it was none the less so.

It gradually became noticeable as long term tendencies showed themselves that a big proportion of these clients were by no means the most prompt in paying their accounts however low priced those might be. On the contrary, I was on one or two occasions driven to point out to them when I took more than minimal time to reach them and they remarked on that fact.

'Yes, well, I have been longer than usual in getting here this time. But if I took as long in proportion to get here as some folk take to pay my accounts to them I would not need to bother attending because the case would be either dead or better before I got to it.'

To that expostulation a typical reply would be in a tone half fun, half in earnest: 'In that case I would just get somebody else ha ha ha.' They knew that everybody knew that criticism between clients and vet was mostly a one way traffic and that neither of the vets in the island could afford to reverse that flow to any extent or else …

Another interesting variant was the client here and there, fortunately for the vet an exceptional one, who would certainly produce the case he had explained in his call then after that produce another and another and even more. It might be that he had genuinely forgotten about his 'chronics' when he phoned me but just as likely he decided that mention of them would be in time enough when he had me on his place. The case first mentioned might have been something like a retained afterbirth or a mastitis, very common but still requiring prompt attention and have been treated before there was word of any other case.

'Before you go I wonder, would you look at a calf I have here. It hasn't been doing too well these last few weeks. We were aye thinking it would come on itself but it hasn't. Don't know what's wrong with it; takes its food all right but someway it just….och, you'll see for yourself.'

So I go and find out as much as I can about the calf, form some probably tentative opinion on it, prescribe something and begin to edge towards the car.

'Oh and I have a cat here. She was near hand so I just took her in. She's never been right since she had her kittens. We're very fond of her; a rare wee hunter she is. Would you take a look at her if you have time?'

There is the apologetic smile. 'You'll be thinking it's a hospital we have here. I'm sorry to be keeping you back. If you havena' time never mind the cat just now. You could see it some other time.'

All this commentary is spoken quickly. What can the vet do? He cannot simply hurry away without at least seeing the cat which for all he knows may not survive without prompt attention. The trouble could be a hung up kitten. Could be anything. All right, let's see what we can make of Mrs Pussums.

This place with its plurality of cases might be some distance off either the main road or the direction in which my next call lay. Sometimes only one of these considerations would apply, sometimes both. Meantime I had looked at my match and learned from it that the person next expecting to see me would be by that time probably at the stage of pacing his yard and scanning the road as far as he could see it for any sign of me.

But I do eventually arrive at my next visiting place on that round and explain as far as I have to, or as far as professional etiquette permits the disclosure of any client's business to any outside party. While I am this being scrupulously correct I am knowing full well as I scruple that I need not bother my nut about such things because hardly any of my outside work remains confidential for any length of time. Almost any of my regular clients needed only to hear where my immediately preceding call had been to have at his or her disposal a ready line of comment and query.

'Well you've got here.' (A just perceptible emphasis on the word 'got'). 'And how many extra patients had big Jock got for you this time? That mare of his, d'you think that leg will ever come right again?', etc., etc. 'Big Jock' in this context is of course no one in particular but could well be any one of many. Since then I have known other users of my time who were a lot more culpable than him.

Such unforeseen delays caused by 'extra' patients were not always necessarily represented by a name in the book before I left home. There was the time for instance when I was sailing along to see a case, luckily nothing at all urgent, when who should stop me at the roadside but the tinkers. Could I tell them what was the best thing to do for their horse that was 'a wee bit lame like'?

Inwardly I felt rather pleased that these folk, 'the travelling people' as they are sometimes called, had heard report of me sufficiently good that they bothered to keep a sharp lookout for me and stop me at the roadside. Why they chose that way of calling me I did not know and did not ask. Perhaps they were hesitant about using a phone.

Anyway I walked across the few yards of grass to their camp and saw their horse. The precise cause of his lameness was a punctured sole caused by a nail or something similar trodden on but not retained by the foot. It was easily diagnosed with a few cautious taps with a light hammer and easily relieved, the patient showing an immediate and pleasing response to treatment. The owners undertook to complete the treatment according to my advice to them. They would soon be moving off and would be needing the use of the horse. Their gratitude was almost embarrassing.

'And how much will that be?'

I really did not wish to take any fee at all. The time and effort required had been negligible and it had been a pleasure to be of some help to them. Ah, but that was not the tinkers' way. Naw naw. I had helped them and it seemed I must take something. So I made no further demure and when they pressed four shillings on me I accepted it. No doubt it maintained their pride. They had engaged professional services and paid for them. As for me, well, dash it all, four bob was the price of about thirty cigarettes at that time and not to be sneezed at. Coughed at perhaps but not sneezed.

I did not mind giving advice freely and liberally to friendly people who seemed to welcome it. What did generally dry me up or at least reduce my comment to a minimum was to have someone appear by deliberate use of wrong statements to refute my main contentions yet later act on them, thus making use of free advice without appearing to have done so. There is after all many an individual who simply cannot whatever may be the depth of his ignorance bear to be seen to have anything to learn from any fellow mortal around him, nor will he seem to be accepting something for nothing even when that something is nothing more tangible than advice.

In that connection I once got a very sharp lesson in clinical deportment and, unknown to the donor, in clinical psychology as well. While I was in my final year in Glasgow I saw a very restricted amount of practice with a practitioner in one of the suburbs. He was a man of very much the same eminence on the profession as Henry Caulton Reeks. Both were or had been external examiners of the Royal College of Veterinary Surgeons and both as the students might have put it 'knew their stuff'.

One day while I was accompanying this man when he was treating a case of milk fever in his own particular way I thinking I could make a small simple alteration to the patient's bedding to give her slightly more comfort and moved a little of the straw at the cow's head. Boy oh boy; did I get it for that; hot and strong from the great master himself. I do not mean that I got the cow's head but that must have been about the only thing I did not get thrown at me, figuratively of course. 'Impudent young bugger...etc. was the mildest of the invective bawled at me.

Later in the car it all started again. Out of it all the salient remark, the only one I can remember, was, 'I wouldn't take your advice even if it was good.' The fact that I had never at any point offered advice, I would not have offered advice even if I could have, seemed not to have been noticed. He was having a bawl.

But one eminent vet was by no means the only person who would not take advice even if it was good and free at that. And others like him on the other hand have accepted bad advice provided they had asked for it and been charged plenty for it.

Just as there are some individuals, fortunately few in number, who liked to dispute or query good information so that they might learn by the patient correction of their brash statements so there were others who made misstatements not to elicit correct information but to impart what were downright lies about the case in hand.

With the first type I soon learned to leave them with their assertions and bid others who might be present to hear what was being said, to take note that it was not being said by me. With the other type a vet might know from available evidence or from his own knowledge or both that a client was dishing out one full blown easily demonstrating lie, yet not bother to show he knew it. Every vet in practice gets them. The one I remember best is the one about a certain lame horse.

His was stifle joint lameness. Conitis (inflammation of the stifle joint) of long standing had flared up again, probably under pressure of work, and the horse had in consequence gone lame. I was called to it and found diagnosis easy. In fact there were at that stifle joint streaks of white hair in a coat that was otherwise bay or brown. Any old vet who is at all acquainted with horse practice knows that gonitis, is or was then quite intractable to treat and becomes chronic. A common procedure is to induce some improvement of the condition by use of a blistering ointment followed by a long rest then getting rid of the patient. There is no cure.

The explanation I got for the white hairs round that stifle joint was of all things that the horse had been working in a lime quarry and had got burnt with lime. Whether the teller of that beautiful story really thought that lime was quarried at quicklime or that limestone was burnt to make it into quicklime where it was quarried or thought I would believe that contact with quicklime would affect only the stifle joint of the lame leg I never did find out. I knew only that his statement did not bear a moment's examination.

Soon after that encounter I was faced with a problem about that horse though not about finding a cure for there was none. Another client was thinking of buying it and asked me unofficially about it without employing me to examine it for soundness, in other words to 'vet' it for him. The consequence was that I, like any other vet in the same position forbidden by the rules of professional etiquette to discuss another client's affairs, had to stand by and see client number two, who was only a smallholder, buy in a load of trouble.

It seemed to me a dearly saved guinea or at most two guineas which would have been my fee for examination at that time. Such saving caused him a loss he could ill afford and which need not have happened. That was about thirty years ago and still today when one looks around the same mistake is so often seen. One can see laymen who may be good amateurs or not even that trying to be their own car mechanics in buying used cars or their own house surveyor for a house purchase armed with an unwarranted faith in their own astuteness while blissfully unaware of most of the pitfalls in the path they set out to follow to its conclusion.

CHAPTER 14

Though my practice was so small it produced besides the routine cases like mastitis and retained afterbirth infertility and so on a surprising number which because they were so unusual were more than ordinarily interesting.

One such case which went suddenly completely and mysteriously off its food I clearly remember. On being called to it, an in-calf Ayrshire heifer in the Shiskine district and easily reached, I examined it as best I could. Mouth, conjunctive, pulse, temperature, lungs, stomach, bowels, everything seemed completely normal.

'Is she drinking?'

'Aye well, I expect she is. She's got the water bowl there in front of her like the rest of them.'

The bowls were the type which had the tongue not on the bottom but placed vertically at the back part of the bowl. Now, I don't know whether I have inborn a nasty horrid suspicious nature or whether I really have a beautiful trusting nature which has been soured by repeated deceit such as that practised by old cars. Old cars, one or two of them that I drove anyway if not many of them, could have one believe that because they displayed a lovely lively spark at the top end of a plug they showed the same spark of enthusiasm at the points of that plug when all the time, the dirty cheats that they were, they did nothing of the kind and had no intention of doing so.

Almost as a last resort I tried the tongue of the water bowl. Not a movement. Not a drop going into the bowl. The heifer had not eaten for a couple of days beforehand, her consumption of food being no doubt gradually reduced to nil as she dried up. They were being fed sliced turnips as part of their ration, the turnips being sliced one by one beforehand in an implement for that purpose. The machine was of a type commonly used in south-west Scotland and probably elsewhere which resembled some exotic unclassified animal in having four legs, a round head on a long thin neck, a tail, and in between them a belly which was an arrangement of parallel cutting blades. The turnip was placed on top of these; the operator then pressed down on the 'tail' which he had previously lifted to push the turnip down between the blades. It was pushed right clear of them by the next turnip on top of it. This procedure resulted in slices of a uniform thickness of about one inch.

One such slice of exactly the right size had got lodged neatly between the tongue and the wall of the bowl. Nothing that the heifer could have done could have dislodged it.

I let her have a little drink to start with and told the owner to give her two two-gallon pailfuls of water with a kettleful of boiling water in them. He was then to wait for two or three hours after which she could have whatever quantity she wanted. I did not know how much she would have drunk given an unrestricted intake but I remembered reading while at college that in hot climates horses too long deprived of water had when they reached it sometimes drunk until they died, presumably from rupture of the small intestine. In this case, not knowing how my patient would react to unrestricted access I was not taking any chances.

A human being in the same situation would probably also drink to excess and then probably reject what the stomach and bowel could not retain. A horse cannot so reject. I remember seeing a bovine animal do it though I know that since then I have seen a cow somewhere or other lying and copiously throwing up the contents of her stomach. I saw her only momentarily and never knew what became of her.

I believe I have read or heard of similar cases where more than one animal in a given situation was presumed to have a constant supply of water when in fact the water supply was either not enough or none at all and they in consequence died of thirst. Such an error of omission based on unwarranted assumption is all too easy to make and surely underlines the need for frequent checking that things are as they are supposed to be.

Many a time since then I have wondered: suppose there had been not vet nor anyone else to play the part not so much of physician as of detective – in that case what would have become of the beast? Would she have had to remain in the stall enduring increasing thirst until she died? It seemed highly unlikely that that would have happened. Yet on the other hand why should the man in charge of them or anyone else connected with them suppose that the heifer's trouble was caused by nothing other than a total lack of water when she had a perfectly good water bowl in front of her, the same as all the others and all of them quite normal? I suggest that a likely answer to that question is that depending on the person in charge of such cattle in some cases the trouble would have been discovered in time and in other cases it would not.

On the subject of unusual cases I remember another one, a cow I treated over a period of a few days. This six year old Ayrshire cow in milk was about three months calved when she began to show symptoms of incoordination and amaurosis (blindness without apparent cause) and general decline of all her activities. Temperature, pulse, conjunctiva, respiration, etc. all non-committal giving absolutely nothing away; appetite capricious.

It might just possibly be milk fever which is simply one lay term for hypocalcaemia, an insufficiency of calcium in the blood. I hoped it was. How atypical can a milk fever be and still respond to calcium? I did not know so I might as well try some calcium boro-gluconate the usual medicament. No response or if any nothing like enough. I waited a day or so and tried calcium again. I most likely tried a few other things I cannot remember now. No luck with any of them. One thing I had learned about her in the interval was that she had been trying to walk 'through' a wheelbarrow which she had not seen standing in her path some days before I was called to her.

She conveniently, as it turned out, died a few days after treatment was begun and with the carcase I did one thing. More with the idea of eliminating the presence of any brain lesion than of finding any I removed her brain virtually intact, steeped it in formalin for a day or two and sent it off to Glasgow Veterinary College.

I still think that to have used only four tools on that job of removing the brain, a knife, an ordinary saw, a two handed axe and a heavy hammer, I made a remarkably neat job of exposing the entire brain intact apart from a slight damage to the cerebellum. What, as the French might say, was my astonishment and gratification too to receive a report from the College saying that cross-section of the brain had revealed a tumour, a neuro-glioma I think they called it and a haemorrhage as well.

I showed the report to the owners of the animal thereby giving all of us the comfortable feeling that we could never have got a recovery no matter what we did or might have done.

At quite another time I had another cow on my hands: this time much more like a milk fever and she may have had that to some degree too but that was not her main trouble. She was an average sized well nourished Ayrshire of good type calved and gone down in the byre. With that syndrome and an age somewhere between six and eight years old I did not fuss too much about diagnosis but simply warmed the calcium and injected it intravenously.

The patient rallied to some extent and may even have got up but if she did she soon went down again. More calcium produced almost no effect but this time I had noticed that the skin around her rear parts instead of being the usual colour for a white haired cow was unusually pale. Her pulse was very poor. Her conjunctiva, hastily examined, was white to diagnosis; internal haemorrhage probably from some undetected injury at calving and therefore if there was not excessive blood loss externally at the calving, which there was not, it should still be lying in the peritoneal cavity.

The patient saved us all further efforts in thought and treatment by dying soon afterwards. The owner wanted a post mortem and once he had got the carcase to the spot selected for the burial got me to open the abdomen. Either by chance or design he was absent for a few minutes while I did this. Almost the first thing I found lying at the lowest part of the abdomen in that position and quite unattached to anything was a massive blood clot much the shape of the bovine spleen but several times larger. I lifted it out as one might lift a liver off a butcher's counter and laid it on the grass where it was the first thing that caught the owner's eye when he returned to the scene. He said nothing.

'There is your haemorrhage,' said I jabbing my finger dramatically in that direction. Inwardly I felt no small satisfaction at having been able to produce incontrovertible evidence of what I had diagnosed for I had a strong suspicion, the sort of feeling one gets at such times, that he had been quite sceptical of my diagnosis and was ready with a small fund of jocular comment on my clinical abilities, comment which bad luck for him had to be put into cold storage for some other day.

Speaking about haemorrhage I had at different times not one but two cases of it, both acute and needing no skill to diagnose.

'Barbed wire. Dammitall haven't I told you all till I'm tired of telling that all its good for is tearing cows' teats and udders and now we've got a milk vein to contend with.'

Oh well, better try something.

'I can't stitch the skin to close the wound but I don't know if that will stop the bleeding or not.'

A little later came what was practically a soliloquy in the form of some sour mutterings from me.

''s lucky for us there's not much pressure in the big veins, in fact pressure's something like negative and we might get enough clotting to seal it completely. I'll have to cast her to get a fair chance at it. Don't want a dirty big hind foot coming up at me just when I'm making my first stitch, likely sending the needle anywhere at all.'

That was how my thoughts ran. I had never before seen a milk vein ripped open by barbed wire. Maybe stock keepers in other parts managed things a bit better or the grasses on the other sides of fences in other parts did not look all that much greener, not enough to tempt the hungry cow to try and clear the barbed wire.

Anyway we got her down and I got I my two or three sutures. The bleeding stopped: a fact which left me probably the only surprised person in the place. She made a gradual steady recovery.

The other case occurred in a really good Ayrshire cow, in her day the champion Ayrshire at the Arran agricultural show. If ever Providence was tempted, and disaster, it was in her case.

There was between her and where she grazed and some tempting two foot high green corn a single strand of barbed wire about the same height from the ground. I do not know whether the owner had been warned of the potential danger or not but even if he had not been he might have seen it for himself.

She eyed the corn, jumped the wire and got over it but at the cost of tearing her milk vein (also known as subcutaneous abdominal or anterior mammary vein). She was taken in and I was summoned. Again I did not have far to go but even so she had lost a great deal of blood. I got the wound sutured and the bleeding stopped but she was very weak.

At that point the owner asked me whether he should milk her or leave her udder untouched. It was a question I had never considered but a moment's thought about it was enough. If the udder could fill itself or even part fill only at the expense of the total blood volume, as was thought to be what normally occurred, surely it was folly with that volume gravely reduced to induce further reduction in its volume and quantity for whether such reduction actually happened or not the tendency would be to secrete more milk and therefore the risk would be created or at least increased. I explained my ideas to him as best as I could and firmly advised against milking.

The sequel was indeed grave. He decided after I had gone that as she had a big udder (and on what other grounds I never did find out) that he had better take away the milk she had already secreted. Perhaps she seemed sufficiently better that he thought he could risk it; I do not know but I have little doubt that on that stimulus she produced more milk with the last of her vitality. I knew about it only when the bitterly regretful owner called on me to tell me what he had by then learned. His cow, his beautiful champion cow, was dead. Thirty years on I still clearly remember the occasion but not my comment on it. Perhaps I had none.

I had in the past tried various agents for making up volumes of blood lost and had come to the conclusion that the safest course was to do nothing in the way of injection but to give plenty to drink, slightly salinated, if so desired. Left to herself and not too warm she stood a good chance of recovery. To take her milk, milk being akin to blood in composition when every fluid ounce of blood might be quite literally of vital importance to her was – well, I like most folk would have my own comment on that.

Now thinking more about horses and their troubles, although obstetric work among mares could hardly be described as uncommon, yet in my little practice horse breeding was itself becoming so rare that anything out of the usual about it or connected with it became a matter of note.

A certain mare again not far away from my base foaled and cleansed or all but cleansed of her afterbirth. The owner however was surely sharp eyed and knew a little about horse breeding. He called me in to check that everything was as it should be. In due course an examination by me of the membranes when they were spread out on the stable floor showed that their conformity to the well known description 'a pair of trousers' was incomplete. One part, the closed end of one cornua, was missing. Where was it? Oh well, let's get the pailful of warm antiseptic, the soap, towel, etc. and in we go again. Yes, it was there and from there duly removed and replaced by a suitable pessary.

Again I was left wondering about a case. As the placental fragment had been quite firmly attached would it eventually have separated and been expelled spontaneously without undesirable sequelae or did it stand every chance of being retained as the uterus contracted? Suppose for example the os contracted and closed before the cornua and the corpus uteri had contracted sufficiently to achieve expulsion of the fragment which would be by that time putrefying and could the equine uterus behave in that way and if it did would I then have got a classical textbook case of laminitis following one of the classical causes of that trouble metritis consequent on retained afterbirth? Not to any of those questioned did I have the answers. I still do not have them.

Speaking of laminitis it occurred a surprising number of times considering the sparseness of the horse population. Now on a backward view of those cases, another surprising feature of them was the variety in breed, age and other conditions in which the complaint occurred. There was the pony with a heavy body, tiny feet and little work to do, a combination about which the intending purchaser was warned beforehand and advised on the style of husbandry most likely to avoid laminitis but in the course of time laminitis arrived just the same. As a beast which supposedly ran on rough grazing all the time without any other food it got steadily and remarkably fatter as time went on. Its only work was on the public road in a buggy and not very often at that. With a relatively big body, overweight, its small feet probably overgrown after a time, the trouble when it came was no great surprise.

Laminitis or 'founder' was a complaint of which I had seen almost nothing during all my time as a student and then assistant. Consequently when I was confronted with it on my own with no principal of a practice to whom I could turn for advice, not that any employer I had ever had ('employer' here not including those men with whom I saw practice) would have known much useful stuff about laminitis; anyway I simply had to try to evolve something useful of my own. Goodness knows, I had plenty of time to think of something.

A third and possibly older name for the complaint is 'fever of the feet'. All right. As might be guessed without that third name any blood drawn off from the sensitive laminae themselves of tissue near enough to them should give some relief to the pain which came from the pressure of fluid from engorged capillaries and the exudates from them all pressing on nerve endings far worse than in other parts because the horn of the hoof could not swell at all to give relief from that pressure. As I saw it, it was really the near equivalent of an imaginary human being who somehow took all weight on one main nail of each hand and foot, the horse's hooves being in terms of evolution his sole remaining nails; then something happens inside those nails. I had always found my own nails very sensitive, like most folk, and I regarded the horse's feet as being no less so internally, of course.

With that aim in view we could generally get some blood drawn off from the sole of each foot near the toe. I well remembered reading in an ancient textbook, good in its day, that in the Army of that day, two or three wars back, horses that dropped out of the column with laminitis were often simply shod with rocker-bar shoes and then brought slowly along behind the column and that such horses often made a full recovery or at any rate became workably sound.

Our local blacksmith had done many a thing for me but to ask him or anyone else to make a set of rocker bar shoes to fit any given horse for them and nail them on to feet already very tender seemed to me not much of an idea. I daresay the old time army farriers did not think it much of an idea either. But then they were not issuing the orders nor writing the textbooks. They simply got the inexpressible pleasure of applying their superior's orders not at his pay but at an army farrier's pay and at the kicking end of a restive horse.

What we could do and what we did do was to take off whatever shoes might be on, if any, and lower the wall of the hoof round the toe of each foot making the greatest reduction at the foremost part and tapering off from there to the quarters. This procedure, although it put more weight on the quarters, gave the same effect as a rocking shoe and quite possibly better because by bringing the wall closer to the ground it restored to the frog more of its natural function, something which a shoe would largely have prevented.

At any rate the patients given that treatment seemed to like it and to walk better after it provided the walk was on smooth ground with no small stone to land exactly in the opening in the sole. They probably liked walking better than standing on account of the easy pumping action which they would have got from the intermittent frog pressure alternating with moments of ease.

I suppose I would also go through the time honoured procedure of unloading their alimentary tracts; I do not remember but I know they would not have waxed fat on the diet I prescribed for them; bran and straw and water, something like that, and nothing more. At any rate they all seemed to recover: I think really and truly because of the treatment and not in spite of it.

CHAPTER 15

Any time from August onwards one could expect the first of that season's crop of husk or hoose to attract attention because by that time the animals had been at pasture long enough to show symptoms. The young calves would usually be the first to show it followed in the later autumn by the yearlings, the six quarter year olds and a few two year olds but not very many all told. I do not seem to recall any serious outbreak of it in cows though there may have been an isolated case or two in them.

I had much earlier learned a little at first hand about husk through a somewhat abrupt and roughish introduction to it during the whole of September of 1936 shortly before I qualified. The scene was North Wales where I had obtained a very brief locum-ship and after it ended stayed on for the rest of that month as assistant to the principal on his return. I saw many cases of husk in its more advanced stages including one post mortem examination. One long look at these lungs was worth days of purely textbook study of that distressing complaint.

Treatment as I first saw it was of the crudest. It consisted of the intratracheal injection of a fairly hellish mixture of oleum terebinthinae (turpentine) phenol creosote, probably chloroform and more such stuff all in a bland base. Dosage was 10cc for the little ones, more for the big ones. The unlucky animals that got this were always in advanced stages of the trouble before treatment was sought and in some cases it was sought only because the animals were due to be sold at the autumn sales. The owners would call the vet a few days before the sales, apparently hoping that somehow the over-prominent bones, the long staring coats, the shortness of breath, the coughing and so on could all somehow be put right enough in time to present the animals for sale. I knew little enough about such sales at home and less about those in North Wales but was at one point a little bit shocked to hear my driver, who seemed to know everybody, tell me that so and so there was taking his beasts home from the sale because he did not or could not get a bid for them.

At that time I simply could not understand the sort of mentality of the owner who could see his beasts steadily deteriorate in physical condition for weeks or months before being put to a sale and then seek treatment for them at the last gasp, as it were. 'Last gasp' in this context has a certain macabre and unintended aptness about it. Forty-odd years later the mentality is quite easily understood.

Remember the year was 1936. The whole country was just beginning to climb out of a historic depression. Farmers were as usual left at the cow's tail in the recovery process and those men in some of the smaller hill farms in North Wales or if not exactly hill farms, marginal land, land which was chronically parasite-infested and under-manured at that were probably more bothered at times to know from where was coming their next week's keep than with the immediate welfare of their cattle. For them the money just was not there. So they were not going to employ a vet for treatment which might in any event be of only doubtful benefit when in the first place they could not pay for it and in the second place the cattle might somehow get better themselves – their owners hoped; and even if there was no improvement the owners would still try to sell them for what they would fetch.

I was supposed to tell them that the most effective part of the treatment lay in feeding liberal rations of good quality cake to affected cattle and so I usually did or got someone else to tell them in the Welsh they understood so much better. What their comments in reply would have been I neither knew nor wished to know. I had complied with my instructions.

All this seems a long story just to explain how it came about that when husk came up for treatment at my hands on my home territory, I had a clear enough picture of it and was well aware of the difficulties. The explanation may make the picture or bits of it a little clearer to others. Looking back now at this distance in time I have the impression that although quite a large proportion of the cattle in my little practice (which after all was representative of the island and thereby of sundry other islands) had outrun on to the hill than which there is no pasture more permanent husk did not seem to be a very noticeable clinical entity among them. The husky cough seemed to be heard less often among them than, for instance, a bunch of calves even when the calves were running on good well drained pastures which should have been less contaminated. The explanation lay no doubt in the vastly different concentrations of animal per acre. We are told by the parasitologists that the larvae of the husk worms from being lodged in the soil climb up to the tips of the grass blades in damp conditions such as those occurring after rain, descending again to the grass roots when drying conditions set in thus avoiding death by desiccation on the grass tips.

As one man was heard to observe on being given that information: 'Hooch, it's likely a' a pack o' dampt lies and yit man there might be something in it tae.'

When I started treating husk in Arran I used the same crude mixture, similar if not identical to what I had seen used. The old style materia medica books recommend prescriptions all very similar to what we used. Use of it had two results: one, the beast which was intended to get the injections slowly coughed the bulk of it straight out, and two, the man holding its head said, 'By gosh, that's strong stuff.'

Luckily for me I soon found a more modern more refined product and began using it in my own way. I did not inject slowly; instead I 'fired' it down the trachea and because I could usually feel the breathing on my cheek, could often time my shot to go with the ingoing breath. It did not require a lot of skill which was lucky. I did not have much.

The patient hardly seemed to know it had got anything and did not cough it up. I could only suppose that with the force I used the jet formed a spray of some kind which got carried down to the parts where it would do some good. I probably hit the wall of the trachea or a mass of catarrh or something similar. Tracheal damage seemed less likely than damage to the parasites. Anyway, I generally seemed to get good reports. All that was long before the arrival of 'Dictol' or any other product giving similar effect. I do not suppose there is a single intra-tracheal injection anywhere nowadays but I do not know.

About the same time of year or earlier as the new season's husk appeared another and far more quickly lethal complaint would appear; more in some years than in other. And it never in my limited experience allowed even one recovery. That complaint was bracken poisoning and some summers produced more of it than others. It seemed to happen more during a long warm dry spell when the reduced growth of grass seemed to induce some cattle to eat bracken. But really nobody seemed to have any sound theory as to why bracken should apparently suddenly become for some cattle not merely toxic but fatal. No doubt if all the cattle exposed to it had eaten enough of it all would have died. But the question remained: why did some eat sufficient of it that they died while others did not?

I was never at all keen to see what I diagnosed as a case of bracken poisoning and such a case was really not too difficult to diagnose. Given the main symptoms: a raging temperature, evidence of subcutaneous or submucous haemorrhages or usually both, signs of blood in the dung, a recent history of access to bracken, one could hardly go wrong. I soon found I suppose like many another vet before me that about all one could do was to try something or other and tell the owner not to expect a recovery.

CHAPTER 16

Things at home and outside having gradually moved away from a scratch start were becoming more comfortable. There was progress from the state of affairs as they were in 1940 to being near enough fully equipped for all the practice I could tackle, not that I seemed likely ever to have that much. I had a good dispenser surgery, a new car, an adequate stock of medicines and instruments for large and small animals, the main accessories such as casting tackle for horses, anaesthetics, muzzle for horses, rope hobbles, lengths of rope, etc. There was also an awful lot of spare time, time which added up to years and the years were slipping past. I was making a living for myself but very little more. With these considerations in mind and the additional one that the accounts I issued were taking longer to come in making me a creditor to others who were mostly much better off than I for much longer periods than the medical supplies firms would allow to me as their debtor, it was all a little dispiriting. Not that the problem of going longer and longer without payment was mine alone. My colleague suffered in exactly the same way only more so because he had more work. I know because we had more than once discussed it and what we could do about it, which seemed to be very little.

Not only were a certain few notably slow to pay but of those few laggards who were at fault in that respect some of them, when they did get around to making a payment, had a large pale yellow moan to go along with it. One saw them as writing their cheques by the light of the silvery moon. Short of working to them for expenses only, and some of them would not have thought of that as being a bit too much, I do not know how they could have had more reasonable charges.

One interesting long term observation was that whereas when I started practice from nearly nothing my accounts, all of them quite tiny, were nearly all paid promptly, as the years passed and I became less visibly an impeciounious party the average delay in paying got longer and longer. Latterly it became a very real consideration. One point odd to consider now was that as the 1940s passed and farmers' incomes got bigger, on paper anyway, my charges would have rated proportionately less and less to them. Although some livestock prices were multiplied by five in a decade as e.g. the £40 heifer in 1940 which became the £200 heifer in 1950 or '51, did veterinary fees increase in proportion? Perhaps in some regions of the country they did. In my home island the fees for clinical work seemed to be increased only with the greatest difficulty where they increased at all. As an instance of things said about fees here is a story of one case in particular.

I was called to calve a heifer which certainly needed help. On examination I found a grossly hydrocephalous calf. The cranium instead of being the usual size for an Ayrshire calf was at the very least the diameter of a full size football. If she was going to be calved it would be either by embryotomy or by caesarean section. I had a good embryotme and with it I got busy.

The thin bony shell of the cranium was soon sawn through and a large slice removed. I did not get the whole head in one cut but I did get it in bits and pieces. After that with calving lines on the forelegs and a long hard pull the rest of the calving was straightforward.

The heifer had had a hard time. No doubt internally bruised and sore she would be but she was not torn nor cut so far as I could detect. Externally she had some of the stretch fissures which unhappily so often occur at a first birth but with a good deal of after care she made a full recovery. She escaped the obturator paralysis she would have suffered had the intra-pelvic pressure been as much as would have been caused by passage of an unsectioned calf.

For anybody who may be wondering what the devil is obturator paralysis I shall try to explain here (after sneaking a look at the textbook) that the obturator nerves on both sides enter the pelvis from the front and pass out of it again through two oval openings (each one called the obturator foramen plural foramina) one on each side of the floor of it to supply those muscles that are attached between the pelvis and each hind leg inwards and backwards. Excessive pressure within the pelvis, as for example by passage of a calf too big for it, crushes or may crush those nerves between the bones of the calf and the bony floor of the pelvis. The most obvious result seen externally is that the hind legs of the dam project forwards and outwards in the 'ten to two' position. What is less obvious and that serious is that she cannot get up and usually cannot turn herself. I had had one or two such cases before then and had had only partial luck with them. That was before I got an embryotome and learned how to use it.

I reckoned I had displayed a little skill and a lot of hard work from first to last. My bill, or rather that part of it which related to the heifer, came to something like one third of her market value, not very much in those days, a result which I thought was a lot better for the owner than to get nothing for the job of digging a hole for her. There was no knackery on Arran.

Did I get any thanks or any word of appreciation from him when he sent his bill? I did not. The main and lasting impression I got from him was that he thought the whole thing should have cost him less. Maybe I was different from other practitioners but I admit here that comment of that kind made me wish that somehow as soon as possible I could be in a position in which I would not be costing him and a precious few others anything at all.

But it would really not have mattered much whether all my clients were fully appreciative of my efforts or not. I simply did not have enough work to justify the time I spent in that situation especially at the fees then charged. So when one day early in August 1951 a senior officer of the Ministry of Agriculture Animal Health Branch suggested to me that I might become a Temporary Veterinary Inspector (TVI) for work solely on tuberculin testing and outlined the terms of employment I made notes and gave the idea a lot of thought.

After thinking over every aspect of the proposed new move as far as I could see into the existing situation and future situations as I imagined they might be I began the process of application completed and returned the usual forms and was in due course accepted for work as a TVI.

In the conditions of employment as I was told of them by word of mouth and nothing in writing, on some of the most important points in my favour there was existing a 'gentleman's agreement' by which the TVI, not being eligible for pension at any stage nor holiday pay nor sick pay nor anything much else at all by way of additional benefits, would be given a regular change of stations about every four weeks or so. That as it was explained to me in my innocence kept the TVI on night subsistence which lasted for the first twenty-eight after each change of station and was at a much higher rate than any day subsistence. Neither rate was taxable because subsistence came under the heading of expenses. We would be paid two guineas per day for every day on which we were necessarily absent from home on Ministry business plus night rate plus mileage plus garaging allowance etc.

Fine. Having thought about the new proposition and decided in favour of it I sold my little practice, put all my stuff into storage and then on the chosen day stowed my luggage in the car and took the road early that morning in late September 1951. I was to report to Divisional Office Carlisle. I soon learned that the work rate expected was about 200 head per day whether made up of one herd or several herds; about 200 of them were ordinary beasts to handle.

Wednesday's output was not expected to be quite so much because Wednesday late afternoon injections would have involved readings which would have encroached some way into Saturday afternoon a time when even the most zealous worker might be expected to stop, come up for air, step out, go downtown or whatever. Monday morning of the second week was started with the beginning of the test of something like 120 Galloways right up in the northern end of Cumberland. The total was not more than 120 I know because for one reason we could not have done any more. The first forty-odd of them had come straight off the fells to which they returned one by one as they were tested. None of them was acquainted with anyone other than their usual attendant.

We started sharp at 8.30 a.m. which meant that I had been up bright and early and on the road well before eight o'clock. We finished neatly at 7.00 p.m. having had between times a one hour break for lunch and two ten minute breaks forenoon and afternoon for cups. I know I was extremely tired at the finish and by what I heard at my next visit the hardy lad who had done most of the handling was even more tired and he was hardy, no mistake about that.

At least when I did get finished I could count on what remained of the day as being my own; something I had never been free to do in practice I liked the country I liked the folk the weather was good. I was all right.

So the work went on for the next three, nearly four, weeks without a thought from me about where the next station would be. The matter had hardly crossed my mind at all and entered it only when I got back to base one afternoon during my fourth week in Cumberland and found in my desk a crisp typewritten note. Simply it instructed me to report to Divisional Office Welshpool on Monday 29 October at 9.00 a.m.

Only a few months earlier sitting one day in my old home in Arran looking for some name on the map and finding it I lingered over the map. Here must be a confession to being fond of lingering over maps, good, bad or no use at all. I do it given the slightest excuse at any time and that time my eye caught the name Welshpool. If I had ever come across the name before then it did not stay with me but from that time somehow it did.

I remember quite well my idle thoughts on seeing that name on the map. 'Welshpool' – that's an unusual sort of name. Seems to be on the Severn. Wonder if there is in fact any particular pool there which as at one time call the Welsh pool? And if a Welshpool why not a Scotspool (no allusion to hobbies or cameras) or Scotchpool (no allusion to whisky) on the river Tweed? And for that matter why not Englishpool on both rivers. Fair shares for all and all that sort of thing. It never occurred to me then, as it did later and probably erroneously, that the 'pool' may have been originally '*pwll*' which has a quite different meaning.

Among those dazzlingly brilliant inanities which I kindly called 'my thoughts' there was never the one that I would ever at any time, never mind so shortly ahead from them, be living in the place. Anyway the point was that when I got that note on my desk about Welshpool I knew where to look for it on the map.

The weather had been consistently good all through that October in Cumberland and was still good on the morning of Sunday 28th of that month when I set off in my Ford Prefect. I had only shortly before then got it back on the road because on my second Monday in the job and after my tiring day among the Galloways I had put the car and nearly put myself as well off the road.

When after the day's work I finished up at the main farmhouse and set off for base again, before I could get on to a thoroughfare I had some very twisted dipping and sharply turning track to drive. I soon found too that I was right at the corners and the dips before I began to do anything about them. In other words I was taking them late, a discovery which was slightly worrying. As I had almost wholly avoided alcohol, having in fact declined a kind offer of a whisky just before leaving the farmhouse, I could think only that my late reactions were due to the fact that for all the morning or whatever two or three hours it took to test the forty-odd cattle I had reached their necks only by standing on the second top bar of a high railing and bending over the top bar until my head was about the level of my knees. I reckoned my intra-cranial pressure had somehow changed and had not had time enough to readjust. That one I leave to the doctors.

If that had been all the trouble it would have been nothing.

I could simply have taken more time; but I was hurrying. I was hurrying because on the Tuesday afternoon of the preceding week I had injected for the test of a herd of nearly 140 head on a place about nine miles south of Carlisle when, unknown to everyone concerned, one animal had been left out of the test. This was explained to me and she was presented for injection when the test of the others was read on the Friday which meant that she had to have her test read on the following Monday. And on that Monday I was twenty miles by road north of Carlisle, the time was eight o clock at night and the daylight had gone. So there we were.

There was more dips, short and deep, to negotiate. Coming up out of it the headlight beams were pointing to the sky and I was doing something I had never done in my life before. I was depending on the road being where I expected it to be, straight ahead of me when the headlights came down on it again. What the headlights showed in fact was a strong hedge at which the road turned without warning at a sharp right angle to my right and uphill. The hedge when the headlights got on it was seen to be not more than twenty yards ahead. I found out slightly later that it was of the kind which is planted on top of a bank of turf and stones, especially stones.

Having put on a fair bit of throttle to get up out of the dip the case was that however fast my reaction time which was normally fairly fast I had not the slightest chance of avoiding that bank. I went straight into it. The briefest look showed that I had rammed the radiator back against the fan, bent the steering wheel, fractured it at the eleven o clock position and cut my nose on the sharp edge of the fracture. But before I discovered all that, believe or believe not, acting I suppose on something like Pavlov's conditioned reflex well known, I pulled the starter to see if I could get out again. Of course one pull was enough: no response at all. Clearly Mrs Ford Prefect was not going to convey me home that night nor for some few nights to come. I really felt I deserved better than that. Dammitall I had been doing my best, hadn't I, and this was what I got. Ah well; anyway I had at least shown that I could fill in the first week's work without incident. I left the scene of the crash and wandered up the road in the deepening dusk, turned left at the next right-angled junction and arrived at some cottages where I got a response at one door. The dear old gentleman who opened the door as soon as he understood that I had crashed my car and that he was being asked for a little help simply kept saying that he did not understand. Just what was so incomprehensible about the statement: 'I have crashed my car back there,' or some similar brief statement I never did know. He ventured as far as to ask me had I been drinking. By that time I had remembered that I had accepted one small glass of Port wine at one place at four o clock that afternoon and in my simple innocence I told him so. 'Well, there you are,' said he with the triumphant air of one who had for long sought to prove something and had at last found a proof. Alas, any information additional to my first answer was again not understood. There seemed little doubt that if the one small glass of Port four hours earlier had not enabled him to wash his hands of my plight something else would have been found to allow him to do so.

So it was back to the road again where I was soon overtaken by a car driven by a lady with passengers. She very kindly gave me a lift to the nearest police station which was not very far ahead. A colleague collected me and took me back to base.

Someone next morning read the test on the animal we had missed. But all that time, looking back on my efforts and my progress since I set about the job, I felt that if ever there was a case for not shooting the pianist as he was doing his best I had that very case.

The month in Carlisle was nearly completed before I got my car back on the road again; in fact latterly there seemed to be some doubt as to whether I was going to have it in time to leave with it or not. There was at that time everywhere a chronic meaning of longstanding severe delay in obtaining spare parts for cars. However all essential parts did come through in time and Mrs Prefect was ready for the road again in time enough. I like Cumberland or 'Coomberland' as some of the good folk in it called it. I liked the folk themselves of whom as I recall about every other one to whom I spoke claimed either to be Scottish or of Scottish descent. I like the good sized herds of really beautiful beef Shorthorns, the fields the fells and other natural features. I was sorry to be leaving them all. But with the Black Galloways on these same fells however I did not find the same reluctance to part. No.

CHAPTER 17

Sunday morning, 28th October found me heading south at a pace varied enough to suggest a sharp conflict between prudence and rapid progress. There was anxiety to get to journey's end before too much of the day had passed versus a strong desire to avoid any mishap which might delay me. I had previously been on that road as far as Penrith. Beyond that point it was new to me. I had heard tales about Shap Summit seething with buses in high summer and Shap Summit swathed in swirling snow in mid winter burying heavy goods vehicles, never mind anything smaller. At the end of October however there was simply nothing remarkable about it. There were a good few heavies moving and parked gradients to be respected but otherwise nothing to cause my any delay.

I was all against delay anywhere and in due course wended my way through Kendal, Lancaster, Preston, and the middle of Liverpool. I was by no means well practised in driving through a big city, not even Glasgow which I knew fairly well in those days let alone Liverpool where I had never before been by any means of travel. When by following the numerous large signs I arrived at the tunnel, or rather somewhere near the entrance, there seemed to my apprehensive eye to be an area extending to about two acres wherein vehicles of all sizes might dart about at will or possibly for all I know play games of tig with each other. However the whole area seemed quiet, almost deserted. By golly, was I glad I had chosen Sunday to make that journey. Perhaps if I picked a quiet moment and scuttled across the open space I would be allowed to bolt down the hole after I paid the man in the box at the entrance.

That in fact was more or less what happened. I soon found myself in Birkenhead and making for open country to the south. Chester, Wrexham and Oswestry were all duly reeled off and I arrived where I had to be. Most likely I stopped somewhere for a cup of tea and a sandwich but goodness knows where or when. But I was quite used to going for long spells without food or drink and I quite possibly did Carlisle to Welshpool in a 'oner' apart from occasional stops for a walk about.

Monday morning 29th saw all the introductions over and me back on the road again. Whether by chance or design I do not know but my work for that first day lay about eight miles back up the road I had so recently travelled – eight miles then turn left and ask. I was well and truly in Welsh Wales again and I managed that day's work and succeeding ones without snags. It seems odd that after more than a quarter of a century I can remember without records where my rounds lay on each day of that first week which is more than could be said about my first week in Carlisle.

The weather stayed good. Just as the whole of that October in Cumberland had been sunny and mild so was the next month in Montgomeryshire nearly if not quite as good. Such good weather for starting off was a very big benefit to me or to any other stranger who had to be in different parts of the surrounding countryside every working day. Besides allowing better visibility, which allowed me at all times to get my bearings and with the aid of the map to navigate about the countryside, it was immeasurably more cheerful for the stranger than if he had had to crawl about the byways and in and out of farm tracks in fog, mist of haze low visibility from whatever cause.

Having thus once penetrated into Montgomeryshire I had left the Shorthorns and Galloways of more northern parts in exchange for Herefords and Welsh Blacks. Many of the cattle were Herefords crossed with either the Black or the Shorthorn but on most farms the white face was predominant no matter how crossed the breeding might appear to be. So mixed did the breeding appear to be in some cases that I sometimes felt tempted to enter the 'Breed' column of the tuberculin test notebook not the usual for Hereford cross or Shx for Shorthorn cross but something new and bold like IGE. This would have been annotated in the 'Explanations of Abbreviations Used' space on the test chart as 'Indeterminable Genetic Entanglement'. Alas, such liberty in description however tempting for used by the veterinary inspector in the field tended to be coldly regarded by clerical staffs at all levels. Besides it would have taken longer to write; we already had far too much to write and who was going to be all that much interested anyway?

It was easy to see why the owners would not be interested in the breeding of the animals as the vast majority of them would be going to make beef just as soon as they could be brought to whatever stage was wanted, unless it could be shown clearly that a purebred or a first cross animal was more economical to feed or gave a better carcase for the same feeding or something like that there was really no advantage in having a purebred beast since it would not fulfil its purpose one with better than the most outlandish mongrel.

I am not suggesting that their breeding was any more complicated than can be found in other parts of the country but I saw there a feature I had never seen before. There was a young bovine, maybe six maybe twelve months old, with the usual common red and white markings distributed in no particular pattern with in addition on its off side a patch or two of black hair, so a proper description of its colouring would have been 'white, red and black'. On my later travels I saw a few other cattle with that combination of colouring but very few indeed. The sources were easy to see; white and red from either the Hereford or the Shorthorn, black from the Welsh Black but as indicated the combination is uncommon.

In due course at the expiry of one month I was moved on again; that is to say I was given a change of station and posted this time to Newtown. Having arrived in the hotel I was not long seated in the lounge when I found myself heavily engaged in conversation with the rest of the company, some four or five people. The main part of the talk went something like this:

'Where do you come from?'

'I come from Scotland.'

'Oh we knew that as soon as we heard you speak, but what part of Scotland?'

'Ah well, I come from a place you've probably never heard of; I come from the Isle or Arran.'

'Well now,' said one gentleman in the company 'will you believe me when I tell you there's hardly a corner of the Isle of Arran that I don't know? My wife and I spent a holiday there a few years ago. We were into nearly every part of the island.'

When I heard the name of the village Blackwaterfoot, the name of the house and the name of the owner I found that my new acquaintance and his good wife had spent at least one holiday not more than two miles from my old home. There was I sitting in a hotel at a distance by road of something like 300 miles from my home ground, confidently assuming and I think quite reasonably that as I was a total stranger neither I nor my background were known to anyone there nor was my background ever likely to be. Later by some years on looking back I saw that that little occasion was only the first of numerous similar ones on which I in some place or other, fondly believing I was totally unknown, was approached and usually named as well by someone who was at first sight a complete stranger.

I may get around to mention of some of them if this story goes on long enough but that first experience of that kind made me resolve to be from then on very correct and careful. I must not tell lies nor thinking of doing so. I had always heard on all sides from Sunday school onwards that that was a very bad thing to do. But if I was going to tell lies make sure they were good ones, nice big round ones which when led out would glide effortlessly off the tongue and could be trotted out around the company without anyone prodding them in tender areas and declaring them to be unsound statements fit only to be put to the knackery or else turned out to grass. And my brand of lies should have no teeth to reveal their uncertain age and other things about them.

By the time I had done a few days rounds based on Newtown the days were becoming very short, not that they were ever less than 24 hours. It was just that as folk in Scotland might say, 'the nights were creeping in'. And just in case this to anyone hearing it read aloud might evoke a vision of plumed armoured warriors leaving their lances and charges and stealthily effecting entrance somewhere on their hands and knees, all that is meant here is that the hours of daylight were becoming fewer.

The places to be visited to the north-east of Newtown would not any of them be located more than halfway back to Welshpool, perhaps not even that far but to the south and west and north-west I no doubt had some long fairly slow journeys back home in the dark from the more distant points. But what a nice feeling it was to turn the car for home, possibly about four o'clock in the afternoon with the thought that the rest of the day was my own. And if it was my own what of that? I probably had not eaten not from choice but from lack of opportunity since breakfast time, would be a bit tired and taking my time with nothing much to occupy my thoughts.

These as often as not would turn to the Welsh place names of which I sometimes asked people the meanings. There was one time anywhere trundling along gently homewards in the dark from a tiny place called Llanbrymair (pronounced I think like 'Hlanbryn-mire') when possibly because of its very smallness and quietness I began to invent some action for it. Suppose there was a public meeting with people seated in the local meeting place.

'There was a wee man of Llanbrynmair'

Yes, well, that was all right as far as it went which was not far but what did the wee man do or have happen to him? Let's see:

'There was a wee man Llanbrynmair
Who started jumping higher and higher.
His quick jumps from his chair
Made the folk near him stare
But the seat o his breeks wiz on fire.'

Splendid. Hardly suitable for *The Oxford Book of English Verse* or anything like that and I don't mean that it was splendid about the wee man's trousers. Pity about that; perhaps someone had dropped a burning match or a burning cigarette end. One couldn't be too careful. But what a splendid if brief moment of action that would have been if only my wee man had ever existed. Anyway while following that brief if somewhat inane fantasy I had progressed several miles nearer to Newtown the hotel and an armchair.

There were plenty of other journeys home in the dark with or without verse but soon my time in Newtown had elapsed and I transferred again to Welshpool. The expiry of the next four weeks would take me up to 24th December and I was looking forward to getting home for a fortnight as any shorter time had to be a week which hardly justified the length of the journey. I might not make if for Christmas but I would be in good time for Hogmanay, bringing in the New Year and a few visits.

Before that happened however there were marked changes made in the terms of our employment. Broadly they were that we were all, i.e. all temporary Inspectors, being dismissed and at the same time offered re-appointment on revised terms. Of these the main provisions were that we would be paid three and a half guineas instead of two guineas as previously per day but payable only for those days on which we worked. A half day's work brought a half day's pay. Saturday afternoon work was firmly discouraged so we received pay for five and a half days per week. Also we could be and frequently were required to stay on in one station for long periods after the expiry of twenty-eight days in them and therefore after expiry of our night subsistence which was all that made the work worth while. During those periods we had less money after tax than we had had when we first took up appointments as TVIs.

All this we were apparently expected to accept philosophically and without demur. I had often before noticed how very philosophical many people could be about other people's injustices or poor fortune. How clearly and easily they could see in such things a 'challenge', to other people of course.

Cost of living was rising all the time. The value of our work surely increased with increasing experience but of those things never a word.

CHAPTER 18

I think it was probably in the spring of 1952 that I was first stationed in Llanidloes. Llanidloes is said to be very near the geographic centre of Wales and is situated firmly astride the Severn as is Newtown further down that river. From Llanidloes one had a wide choice of directions in which to travel. Roads of one sorts or another seemed to lead off to all the main compass points, not that any of the roads held their direction for long. I know; I tried them all many of them much oftener than once though I remember little about them now. One minor road I do remember however is one which heads north over the hills and debouches at, yes, again Llanbrynmair. Between those two points it passes through a hamlet known alternatively as Staylittle or Stay-a-little. I have seen both versions. The place so far as can be seen from the map is almost exactly on thousand feet above sea level.

Getting out of the car there on a February or March morning with an east wind that seemed to be whining only because it had not managed to bring along more snow, one tended not to forget the place however much one might try. There was not a scrap of shelter to be had anywhere and there was already snow on the ground. Fortunately there was little occasion to get out of the car: one gate to open or something like that. Some weeks, indeed months, before I ever saw the place itself I had seen the name on the map and wondered had some joker given it that name to leave the uninformed to wonder whether it was intended as an instruction or as a suggestion. ('Stay little' (the shorter the better?) or 'Stay-a-little' (you'll like it here). And though on a February or March morning with a heavily overcast sky it might have little appeal, yet at other times, as for example during most of the summer of 1976 when the valleys were sweltering, it would have had its points. A thousand feet is a tidy height anywhere in Britain and there is no doubt at all that farming on an unsheltered plateau at that altitude would call for a few special tricks besides all the usual ones a farmer knows and has to use on occasion.

For a variety of scenery Llanidloes probably had a narrow points lead over any other station I ever had. It seemed to be the starting or finishing point for numerous small deep valleys which themselves often branched into smaller ones and everywhere there were roads of various grades which left the main roads and ran along the valleys or climbed the hillsides and traversed the uplands. All of them I travelled in turn to reach my jobs every day. There were interesting little interludes too. There was the time when I had taken the car along a high fairly lengthy stretch of empty track to the small place at the end of it where there was a small herd, very easy to do. It was a warm sunny spring morning and my programme was not too full to let me stand and talk for a minute or two.

The man of the place kept sheep, as one might expect in such a situation, and he had been losing lambs. More than that, he placed the blame, or a good part of it, on the ravens in the vicinity. After all, he was on high ground, most of it round about a thousand feet, and lonely at that. Rightly or wrongly he had shot at least the one raven that I saw and hung it on the yard fence. Possibly fearing that I would leave without remarking on it he drew my attention to it and made some mention of his problem. I on my part could do no more than sympathise with him. The pro's and con's of the ecology of the raven/lamb question I had to leave entirely for those people who know about such things to settle, if settled it can be.

One thing about the scene did impress me then as it has done since then. I still reckon I had never seen black until I saw that raven's wing. With the sun glinting on the feathers it was black, black going into something like an impossibly deep blue. There and then I learned the full meaning of 'black as a raven's wing'.

Of course at times like that with the odd few minutes in hand here and there we got talking, the farming folk and I, about lots of things though seldom for long enough to get anything sorted out and firmly wrapped up in an opinion which the people whom we deemed to be at fault ought to have been told. Besides the peoples to be blamed were all far away in Westminster or Whitehall or they were dead or something like that so there was not much we could do about it.

One topic which did pop up sometimes was the matter of placenames and accents. I knew a few words of Gaelic because I had heard it spoken a lot in my childhood and youth and on that account was able to cope pretty well with the Welsh placenames; in fact I was once complimented by a Welsh speaker on my pronunciation of them. On one occasion while speaking to an old lady maybe six maybe nine miles out from Llanidloes when we were comparing Welsh and Gaelic so far as we could which was not very far, I told her that in the Highlands of Scotland the Gaelic accent could vary within quite short distances. I then said something like:

'I expect it's something the same with her in Wales. While all Welsh sound the same to me you can probably detect differences in accent with the different districts.'

'O yes,' she said, 'I could tell or I think I could tell someone from Llanidloes down there someone coming from [I have forgotten now the name she gave]… by the way they speak.'

I thought to myself at the time that that was pretty good going and needed a nicely discerning ear because the distance between the two places as I understood at that time was less than ten miles, probably a good deal less.

Whatever the volume of the work, very full day or not so full day, to have attempted to reach it all from any station nearer Divisional Office than where I was would have been a very lengthy business each morning. But in due course all the jobs outstanding in that area were mopped up then it was back to Welshpool for me as per instruction received.

Some time before or after that spell in Llanidloes I had a succession of rounds right up or near the northern boundary of the county which was also the Division. 'Division' here is or was an area quite often a county administered as such under the Animal Health Branch of the Ministry of Agriculture and Fisheries. Montgomeryshire for example was one such Division; so was Cumberland.

I think it was very shortly after my arrival in Wales that I became acquainted with places such as Penybontfawr, Llangynog, Llanrhaiadr and a few others n that area. '*Pen*', I learned early meant 'end' '*bont*' was fern and '*fawr*' was 'big' fem. gender. Together I took them to mean 'the end of the (area of) the big ferns'. I clearly remember reflecting idly that fern as part of the name was not too inappropriate suggesting primordial moisture and while there was nothing noticeably primordial about that place there was certainly plenty of moisture. As I drove down the long slope approaching the place in the morning there was rain and passing through it on my way home in the evening there was still rain falling as heavily as before.

By that time I had been in Llanrhaiadr or if not actually in the village had found the name in the list of addresses given to me. This place was of course Llanrhaiadr ym Nochnant, not the other Llanrhaiadr. Having found the place I had to find and done my work at each I then had a longish drive back home to the hotel, tedious because of the deepening dark and a twisty unfamiliar road back to town. As my speed had to remain low my mind wandered back over the day and the places where I had been. There was Llanrhaiadr (pron. – approninmately *Hlan ry'adr*) tucked right in at the foot of the hills with an almost claustrophobic closeness. Couldn't it have even one just one highly unusual character, maybe a queer old man or a queer old wife or something like that?

A certain old wife of Llanrhaiadr
Accidentally swallowed a Spaiadr.
That spinner within 'er
Got thinner and thinner
Because there was nothing insaiadr.

Aye. Ah well, she's likely had this modern age craze for slimming and carried things a bit too far. Kind of tough on the spaiadr though with not even a solitary fly to put him by unless she had accidentally swallowed a fly as well and most probably not a drop of drop of cider insaiadr either. Wonder if he (or maybe it was a lady spider) ever got out again. Would he or she have got out if the old wife had coughed or sneezed? Of course maybe he or she didn't really want to get out. Interesting line for speculation here.

Ah, now we're coming on. I like that slight glow I see in the sky and over there the first of the lights of the town coming into view now.

The day's work was often long and tedious not because of large numbers of cattle to be done but because of various circumstances which made rapid progress impossible. It was very seldom that the cattle were not at hand housed or otherwise enclosed if not all of them at least enough for a start. But very often labour was scarce and what there was of it not very able on the smaller places, perhaps one man at most two, probably no longer young whose method of handling was to rope each animal in turn and pull it up to a post or a rail or some such thing. In such cases the inspector could only hope that the cattle were going to be quiet and they generally were. It was quite common also on arriving at some of the smaller more outlying places to be told by the goodwife or a housekeeper or whoever was asked for the man in charge something like:

'He's not in. He's just gone up the high field a moment ago. He won't be a few minutes.'

Ah how many times have I heard that earnest affirmation: 'He won't be a few minutes' and resisted in impulse to reply, 'Well I hope he'll make them as few as possible,' when I knew perfectly well that the speaker was much more at home in her native Welsh. What she really meant of course was that the man we wanted would not be more than a few minutes.

Whether he was or was not a few minutes in appearing we always got started in due course and generally made a good enough time to the end of the job but never at a pace anyone could call fast. In fact just to be on the place was often half the battle. One might be able to drive into the yard or one might not. All too often the car had to be left at the last place on the track where there was a reasonable chance of turning and where some other vehicle could pass if necessary. The distances to be walked varied from a few hundred yards for one place to several miles, perhaps again for only one place but more likely for several places to be taken in a circuit over ground where no car could go. I remember one round on which between forenoon and afternoon walking I clocked up something between four and six miles in locating and testing everything I was intended to do. I remember it very clearly because the landlady I had at that time, not long after I had arrived in Wales, kept asking me why didn't I go out for walks in the evenings like some other inspector who had stayed with her. When I told her I had already walked up to six miles that day she replied, 'I thought you might be going to lose the power of your legs for want of using them.'

I with what I considered was a display of masterly restraint refrained from telling her that the cleverest things I did each day was to avoid using my legs whenever opportunity allowed and that her inspector friend, whatever he told her, probably walked no further each evening than his favourite pub and back again.

Gradually I began more often to try to work out beforehand with the aid of the map and the place names on my list roughly how much walking I was going to have to do on the first three days of that week. The next three days would of course be repetitions of the first three. I learned to watch out for any name beginning with 'Blaen' which I was told meant 'end' or something like that. So by that meaning 'Blaen y Owm' is the end of the valley or hollow and there are quite a few places of that name up and down Wales. I suppose the nearest equivalent in Scottish nomenclature would be 'Glenhead' or something like that. Surprisingly enough the few 'Blaens' which I had to visit were by no means the least accessible places; in fact the roads into them were usually very well kept. This was the more surprising because as far as I could see the County Council or other public body seemed to have a policy by which it laid down tarmac as far as the second last house along a track whether along the bottom of a cwm or up a hillside but beyond that point the last tenant whatever his status was very much on his own in both senses. That may not really have been the case but very often that was what it looked like yet as I have said, that part of the road to the last house was usually good. But however might be the surfaces of the road as I am calling them when what I mean is single track lanes branching off the major ones, the length of the road visible ahead was often very limited. Because of an endless succession of blind corners a driver simply dared not crowd on full sail but could stand on with caution always ready to go hard aport or drop anchor.

CHAPTER 19

I believe though I am not sure it was the early summer of 1952 when I had my first out stationing of one month in Machynlleth. Pronunciation of that name is something of which my one attempt will be given a little later.

There was one time when my station was Llanidloes at an Easter or Whitsun weekend, some public holiday anyway, when I was proceeding towards Aberystwyth and parts beyond on pleasure bent. As a matter of fact I believe I was going first to the Devil's Bridge to see it for the first time when a short distance past Llangurig I picked up two hitchhikers, a husband and wife from Lancashire. Of course we soon got talking about our intended destinations and from that to our respective occupations and so on. I learned that they were telephone exchange operators, a fact which immediately led on to a mention of some of the Welsh place names. As might be expected they as experienced telephonists had heard most of the place names in the country incuding Machynlleth, about which they admitted quite frankly they just called it Machine-leth. My own best attempt at it was something like 'Mach-un-hleth' with 'eh' guttural and the accent on 'un'.

One might suppose looking at the map that there could not be much agriculture around that area and perhaps all there was could be regarded as a great lot yet to anyone engaged in testing or re-testing the cattle in small lots they seemed to be unexpectedly numerous. Apart from the obvious places for finding bigger farms namely distributed along the valley of the river Dovey there were still the smaller ones along the cwms round the backs of the hills on top of the hills and no doubt in other places too. I think it was in that area I had to do a small retest at the far end of what I should think was the narrowest twistiest lane in the narrowest cwm ever I was in and in it for about four miles each way twice. My guess is that even to the most unhurried operator there comes a time when, constantly watching the next bend only a few yards ahead and constantly anticipating the obstacles he cannot see, of wondering will he make good time on the job he is trying to reach and wondering what is the time anyway; he has had enough.

Summer holidays were drawing near and I reckoned that though Machynlleth might be only five miles from salt water and about ten from the open sea in Cardigan Bay I knew places much closer to the sea than that quite a bit to the north of where I was and in due course I reached them. I got back to the Isle of Arran of course with the car.

Starting again after that holiday I suppose I would have resumed in Welshpool and stayed somewhere in Montgomeryshire until October 1952 when I was a little astonished to receive an instruction to proceed again to Carlisle, Oh well, it's always another two hundred miles or thereabouts nearer home. Whether it was during that spell that I had my first spell in Cockermouth or not I cannot remember now. One thing I do remember very clearly because I could not forget it is that I spent half of one January and half of the following February in Alston, the highest market town in England, probably the highest in Britain. According to the map I had, the OS 1in/1mile, the upper end of Alston was about 1,200 feet above sea level. I think I was there in 1953 but if anyone happens to remember which of those winters was the very hard one he or she will know which one I mean.

Snow. There was already too much on the roads for driving to be easy when I struggled into Alston from Carlisle. We soon got more after that. I got most of my listed work completed but not all of it. The snowfall reached a stage where RAF planes were dropping fodder to outlying cattle which could not be brought in nor have their usual fodder taken to them.

My two main recollections of that place were firstly standing under a tree just across the road from a house not far outside the town and waiting while the owner of the cattle decided whether he was able and willing to start the test or not. After waiting perhaps ten minutes without sign of him I decided he was not willing so I moved on but while I stood under that tree I saw something which was new to me. It was only a small tree; fresh ice was constantly forming on its branches and when sufficiently thick was being broken off like broken moulds from the smaller branches by the action of the wind. There was quite a quantity of such ice on the ground beside me while more seemed to form and fall as I stood and watched. I had never seen freezing fog if that is what it was. I still do not know exactly what I was seeing.

My other vivid recollection of Alston is of that day when having taken my car as far on the main road as far as was going to be any help, I saw from the higher ground on which I was that the whole of the side road which I should soon be using to take me to the farm I had to reach was blocked. Where I stopped I was in fact nearer the farm than I would have been if I had gone to the end of the side road.

I have said there was snow. There was much snow and it was frozen hard. I took my callipers, notebook and some disinfectant, all I needed, and set off on foot. There was a beck and a fence or two between car and farm between them but not in the way for I found that I could walk straight over everything, which I did.

The farm stood well up on a hillside on a steep slope with a high retaining wall going across the slope below the house to allow some levelling of the ground of it. This transverse wall was most likely not less than nine feet high but could as easily have been twelve or more for all I could see of it. In normal times it would have caused me quite a detour but not that day. I simply walked straight up over the wall, placing my Wellingtons carefully, and arrived at the farmyard without mishap. Mind you, if that frozen crust had broken I would have disappeared and the farmer who had been quietly watching it all would have had a hearty laugh. I went back to the car by the same route but that time not caring whether I went through the crust or not. Gravity would have been working in my favour.

Somehow or other I managed to get something to fill the diary for every working day I spent in that elevated situation until just before I was due to leave again I saw the interesting spectacle of one of the biggest snowploughs in the county stuck near Alston on the road I would be taking to get back to Carlisle. But I took it and got back to Carlisle without incident. Thus ended my one and only spell in Alston. I wonder what does it look like without snow?

That spring was probably spent between Carlisle and Cockermouth but by summertime I was back in Montgomeryshire again starting with Welshpool. By then I was gaining a fairly useful knowledge of the entire county. The trusty Ordnance Survey maps were not nearly as often in my hands as they had been not merely during my first working in the county but for pretty well a year after that. They were still brought out for some of the smaller details like the names of some of the farms and to find some of the less well known lanes. I often used some of my spare time in the evening to see the routes I had taken and compare them with those I might have taken whether for better or worse.

I think it was on my first summer holiday when I was home from Wales that I was able to claim, though I suspect my claim was heard with some reservations, that there was not a square mile of Montgomeryshire within which I had not been. Looking at the same maps now the claim seems incredible. Here are long stretches of main road and umpteen lanes I cannot remember at all, whereas for a long time in the past I reckoned I could remember every place where I had ever been and go back to it without using a map or directions. When I say any place I do not mean every street and house but every locality of any size where I had stopped for any time. Such a claim would probably have been true for a long time but there must come a time when even the best of memories, let alone mine, given sufficient overloading must fail. And that goes for more than memories;

The job was not entirely humdrum. It did have its moments of high risk and in contrast moments in which to pause and enjoy a beauty spot. As an example of the former, one of my first jobs on arrival in Montgomeryshire was to test a large herd of Friesians and in doing so I spent a large part of two days. Last items of all in the herd were the two bulls, one six years old and sire of the other, a three year old. They lived out of doors in a field throughout the year with a shed for shelter if necessary and kept themselves fit by sparring with each other, so I was told. They were of course well fed.

The farmer and the farm hands all made out a very good case for not testing the bulls and I was inclined to accept their point of view and leave it at that. Not so the bosses in the office when I got back there and explained the situation. Oh no, that plan was not going to do at all (possibly none the less emphatically disallowable as they themselves would not be going anywhere near the bulls). So the phone was used and I went back to the farm at the time the bulls were being brought in. Each stood about fifteen hands, i.e. about five feet at the shoulders, and must have weighed anything between 15 cwt. and one ton. Each was well fed, fit as a flea and quick. Fortunately for all concerned they were both good natured. With the sort of neck skin measurements they had I do not think they knew I had stuck anything into their necks, nor did they feel the injections which although only one tenth of one c.c. each often caused quite a fuss in other cattle.

Both bulls were indoors. Each in turn was haltered with a proper halter with a cotton rope shank and hauled, or rather coaxed, close up to a post of some sort. Had either beast chosen to show any marked disapproval of the proceedings I could not have seen the halter lasting more than about five seconds even if the man in charge of it could have stayed that long to hold it. For my own part if either bull had chosen to hasten my departure I could not, being lumbered with rubber coat and boots as I was, have got myself removed in the time allowed, say about two seconds. I do not know if there is a record for a standing up macintosh and Wellingtons but if there was one at that time only that if one existed I was ready to attempt a new one. On my second time around I was better placed because of not carrying syringes and my hands were empty. As before nothing happened.

But life as a Temporary Veterinary Inspector did not really have many such scalp-tingling situations. There were other less strenuous, more soothing, activities in connection with the work. I do not recall and cannot say which time of year nor hardly even in which year I was first up around Lake Vyrnwy but that I was there several times I do know.

Lake Vyrnwy as it is called is a man made reservoir about four and a half miles long and a third to a half of a mile in width. To go up there at any time was never an unpleasing prospect even when the sky was grey, rain was falling and the wind whipping up little white-tipped waves on the water. To go there in sunshine as in early summer with all the trees newly in leaf and little if any wind blowing and drive round the lake as was necessary to accomplish what little work there was to be done, made up for some of those other times like sharing a loosebox with about two tons of lively Friesian bull of temperament still unknown to me and about to have injections.

There was one such time about the lake, not the bulls, I remember well. It was either early summer or well into September. I had been round the lake on my errands which may have been retests or more likely merely queries to be answered. It was late afternoon; I was tired, probably showed it and had a strong notion of a cup of tea. I had most likely had nothing to eat or drink since morning, a state of affairs not all uncommon with me in that job. There in front of me was the Lake Vyrnwy Hotel ,at least I think that that was what it was called, one nice fair-sized hotel anyway.

So I thought to myself 'Why not? At worst the staff can only decline in whatever words to serve me. At best I shall get my cuppa and feel a lot fresher afterward.' So I got out of the car, mounted some steps, found my way into the lounge and presently had my order taken for afternoon tea.

Whatever time of year it was I had the entire lounge to myself, large and comfortable. In fact I seemed to have the entire hotel to myself, a really noble view from the windows and a very nice afternoon tea in comfort at a moderate price. It was, all said and done, a most refreshing half hour. Unfortunately a chance to repeat the experience never occurred though I was about the Lake at the other times after that.

CHAPTER 20

Autumn 1953 saw my arrival in another county, another Animal Health Division, but not involving a very long journey this time for my transfer to it. From Montgomeryshire in fact I went south one cool autumn afternoon and took up my abode in Llandrindrod Wells. It got the 'Wells' part added, I suppose, because it was at one time a famous spa and a very expensive one too but perhaps no more so than some of the others.

There was not a great deal to do in spare time in Llandrindod Wells: televiewing, talking, reading, pubbing on a Saturday night pretty well exhausted the list. The professional staff permanent and temporary included Irish Scots and one naturalised Briton. Oddly enough there was not a Welshman among us. Usually on a Saturday night some of us went out for two or three whiskies or beers or both as the case might be in one of the local hotels. Quite often there followed after the visit to the hotel an invitation to one or other of the homes of the kind couples whom we got to know. They provided the armchairs, the coffee and the sandwiches while we were always happy to provide the other items. All these plus lights and bright conversation were a combination to which we looked forward each week.

There was the occasional dance at which I might contrive to be present, not so much with the idea of dancing but usually successful in loosening the flow of conversation with the usual aids to conviviality. The dances announced were seldom any that I knew. I was anyway generally too tired and all the girls were already attached. There was one dance in particular being held on a Friday night. I received an invitation which I gladly fulfilled and after an appropriate length of time at it tottered home weary but mellow. The following night there was another dance at which I was expected and was present but it was not quite so near at hand.

Llandrindod to Welshpool by the shortest main road route is about 41 miles. This route should be taken if one has any choice only for fun and never in a hurry. Some of the residents in those parts said that between the Newtown and Llandrindod Wells there was a bend for every day of the year. A few miles along it after starting with the first of January at one end of the road I took their word for it. I reckon I gave up some where about the middle of March. It might have been into April or only the end of February; I did not know and I did not care. Half the time I within my mind was driving round the south end of Arran. The combination of hairpin bends and blind bends going round abutments was much the same for both.

To get from Llandrindod to Welshpool via Rhayared is 54 miles but the difference in time required must be small and which of the two routes would take lesser time is something I never found out.

While I was in Montgomeryshire I had enjoyed the privilege of membership of the Caledonian Society of Montgomery and Oswestry. The Society was having its Halloween party on the Saturday night after the dance in Llandrindod; I had some short sleep on the Saturday afternoon, changed clothes and eventually got my car as far a Welshpool.

It was a good party and it finished late. More than that, there was the party after the party and from that later party my genial host would hardly let me leave. A very nice chap but he had not got fifty-odd miles to drive. Leave however, I eventually did, having stood talking outside on the pavement until I was thoroughly cold. But no problem there: the car was new and had an efficient heater which heated things. Too efficient.

All went well as far as Newtown yes; Llandiloes yes; now we reached Llangurig, the car and I. Ah, wouldn't I love to stop somewhere just for twenty minutes maybe half an hour in any place where I would not be noticed. Can douse everything and save the battery, think I passed one suitable spot there. Never mind soon come to another one. Terribly sleepy, must open the window. Oh, rain on this side is it, it would be, of course, dammit. Just my kind of luck to be on the west side of the car this time. Heavens I was nodding there, nearly slept, mustn't do that whatever happens. A little further on there it is again. I must perk up, sit hunched up over the wheel. A little further on... on... BANG: Then I was really wide awake, very much so, and for the rest of that morning. I had bashed the near side parapet of a stone built bridge with the near side wing of my nice new car. My rage knew on bounds. What filthy luck especially as just a few yards from the bridge there was a place where I could have parked and remained undisturbed if only I had reached it. Why hadn't I left the window partly open and endured some rain on me? Might have helped to keep me awake. Sad words those two, 'if only'. It was in fact the place I had been thinking of using but Dame Nature stepped in and administered to me a sharp lesson.

That is how I see the incident at this distance in time and though it ruined the new car in that despite protracted and costly repairs she was never the same again I reckon it was cheap at the price. It taught me that in future when or if I should be in such an attenuated state of fatigue and sleepiness made more so with sundry whiskies, even though these were some hours earlier, by any considerations of the simplest most common sense kind for any sake to stop in the first available safe parking place. In short get off the road. I must not merely think about stopping and keep crawling on intending to stop but STOP: passengers or no passengers, protests or no protests. Park if possible where not even another driver in the same egregious state as mine could bash my car.

It taught me if there should ever be a next time not to expect to be as lucky as to get off with nothing worse than repairable damage to a new car. I knew places where I could have gone through a fence and landed goodness knew where or into what. I could have been in any one of dozens of places where there was no obstacle between the side of the road and deep water or a long drop or both. Worse of all, I might have hopelessly maimed, almost worse, to have killed some third party of any description. I might have killed myself. In that case so far as I had seen up till then such an outcome would not have made much difference to anyone anyway. But I would not have liked to have been permanently disabled such as to become a burden to other people and myself. All in all, though I did not claim under the comprehensive policy I had but kept my no claim bonus by paying for everything myself, I reckoned I had got off lightly. A lot of drivers in the same case did not. I found a piece of wood and managed to prise the wing off the wheel enough that I could drive with only a little difficulty but making a lot of noise. In that manner I got through Rhayader early that Sunday morning earnestly hoping nobody would be wakened by the sound or if wakened would not bother to look for the cause of it. The whole story was bound to have been known to nearly everybody very shortly afterwards but fair dues to all, not one person ever said so much as 'accident' nor 'bridge' to me afterwards. They possible took the view that someone working among their herds as I was might well be the object of complete discretion on their part.

I had progressed the twelve miles form Rhayadar to Llandrindod when just within that town Fate struck again. Not a stunning blow this time, just a good cuff on the car. I ran out of petrol. If strong language concentrated and suppressed because the air was deathly still had been of any use as a type of fuel for the motor then I had no problem. As things were however I had to walk between half a mile and a mile to the hotel, and let myself in waken a friend quietly and explain my trouble to him. That, I told myself at the car, was what I would have to do and it wouldn't take long.

'Won't take long won't it? Are you quite sure, you silly little man?'

I did not actually hear any voice saying that but I might as well have heard one as some early counterpoise to my thoughts. About forty or fifty yards from the car the entire heel came off my left shoe leaving a lot of short nails and stuff in its place so that I could not put much weight on that heel but had to hobble along using mainly the toe.

'Here, Mrs Fate. This is bloody well carrying things a bit too far, dammitall: to hell with this. I know I dropped off to sleep for a moment in the car while driving. All right. I took the rap for that. Yes, I said rap. Can't we leave it at that? Perhaps you'd care to break the lace in my other shoe now just to even things up or should I say down a bit? After all why have this 'up today down tomorrow' mode of progression? Maybe you think I just love hirpling along 'one shoe off and the other shoe on deedle-deedle dumpling my son John' on unfamiliar pavements at six 'o clock on a Sunday morning first of November?

'Well I don't and I'll tell you something else, Mrs Fate, if you think you'll teach me to stop drinking whisky you bloody well won't.' And whereas I might have gone straight to bed if I had got the car straight off the road, now I won't. Soon as I get it into a safe place I am having not one but two big ones. Lucky it just so happens I have a bottle of my own. Shan't have my own car now for weeks so am having party number three. Friend won't take much if any; will probably decline cordial invitation. In that case number of people at party one, myself. 'There you are now old Mrs Fate, see what you've done. I don't like you very much this morning.'

The residue of my thoughts were of the kind which on paper are usually indicated by rows of asterisks mingled with dashes. With such thoughts I arrived at the hotel, let myself in and woke my friend. He immediately grasped the situation and began the first steps of the rescue operation like the hero and gentleman he was. He rose quietly, dressed, slipped out of the house with me, rescued my car with some petrol and got back to the hotel and bed all between 6.10 and 6.40 a.m. on a Sunday morning and he did not even have a drink despite my cordial invitation to have a good one. But I did.

If I chose on that occasion at any rate to avoid the shorter route between Newtown and Llandrindod Wells there were many much better known drivers who did not avoid it on another much better known occasion. It was in November of that year, I think, that the RAC Rally had that stretch of road as part of the route for one of the sections with one of the Llandrindod hotels as a stopping place. Whether it was a check or had some other designation I do not know but certainly it was a stopping place.

Here were real drivers, men and women who 'stayed not for brake and stopped not for stone' though perhaps hesitating to swim the Esk River where ford there was none if any such need had ever arisen. And the cars they had: how they came roaring into the town square and were so to speak reined back on their haunches opposite the hotel of choice. All this was late at night with headlights blazing and heaven knows how many other lights blazing as well. It went on for quite a time with the cars arriving as near as could be managed at regular intervals. Yet we noticed that the drivers so far as we could observe them did not all seem to be noticeably above average. While some of them, apparently the older hands, wandered calmly in and stood talking eating and drinking a few of the younger ones seemed to head straight for the nearest armchair or settee and just flop. No doubt they too would eat and drink in due course. But all too soon each crew's time was up; they got aboard their cars again and roared off into the dark of the night leaving the little town as quiet as before.

Radnoe had its fair share of places in unusual situations and of those places a fair proportion had unusual approaches to them. Two at least I can remember, both of them in the Rhayadar area. One was on the far or west side of the river Wye which thereabouts is not very big. It could be reached by starting from the main road on that side of the river and following a rough track either on foot or by vehicle to the house. An alternative and in some ways shorter route to this place was by a wire suspension bridge over the river. The wire so far as one could see was simply over heavy gauge fencing wire, the rest of the material apparently home produced, and the entire structure looked as if it was home made. To use it, had the visiting Veterinary Inspector have wished to do, so he had better have been wearing all his protective clothing and carrying all his tuberculin testing kit in his pockets because he was going to need both hands to hold on to whatever might help him to stay on the bridge.

One colleague who had also used the bridge in discussing it with me one day reckoned we should have got danger money for using it. I heartily agreed but we did not get any. The track on the west side seen from a distance looked rough for cars so the bridge saved us a much longer walk and long walks on wintry ground in Wellington boots, rubber coats and high winds are not at all popular with HM veterinary inspectors, no doubt among many other people. Rather a few moments suspense on a suspension bridge.

The other unusual situation was reached by driving about two miles along the track beside the Elan Valley Reservoir. If Montgomeryshire had its Lake Vyrnwy no less had Radnor got its Elan Valley Dams as they were called. Like Lake Vyrnwy they were created by damming a big stream at a chosen point in its course. Choice of site for the dam would be, I suppose, as one speaking under the slight disadvantage of not knowing the first thing about it, based on the idea of having it far enough downstream to obtain the maximum catchment area yet high enough to have the necessary fall of head of water and still have at whatever point compatible with the foregoing desiderata the two opposing hillsides closely as possible in opposition.

On reading over that last sentence I realise that I am most likely potentially a great civil engineer of inestimable genius now forever lost to the nation with the nation never suspecting what might have happened had that become my profession. But don't we all have narrow escapes of which we remain blissfully unaware?

Reluctantly to return to tuberculin testing, the everyday business of that time, I remember I was at least once but I think twice up at the first reservoir and along one shore for what seemed to be a couple of miles. If I was there but once that would have been either on a query or for a retest of an animal or group of animals no longer there but I rather think I did a retest which means that I was there twice. I think it was so and that each time was with the last of the daylight of a winter afternoon with the sky overcast and the water dark. I did not see any trees. The contrast with Lake Vyrnwy as I mostly saw it could not have been more marked. To me the Elan looked quite peaty, very much like a Scottish loch seen in the same light. It also looked very deep so far as I could judge from a moving car when the road on which I was driving seemed uncomfortably close to the water's edge.

I should have felt at home beside such a stretch of water and to a certain extent I did. At the same time I had the feeling on the return journey along that shore that the place I had just left seemed to be as lonely and isolated as any I could ever remember visiting, perhaps the loneliest of all. Fond as I might be of a quiet spot above a stretch of water I reckon that that one would not be my first choice.

I was never out right around all the dams there unless on some Sunday afternoon run not remembered now but I reckon there is plenty of time yet to do that. The whole area should go on to my list of 'Places I Must See Again' though how many if any of them I shall see again who knows?

But if those dams in the Welsh hills were not very well know to me they were well enough know to certain units of the Royal Air Force for it above them among other locations that the bomber crews who were involved did much of their rehearsal for the immortal Dambusters' raid.

CHAPTER 21

Whether it was before or after Christmas of that year when I finished in Llandridod I am not sure but it seems likely that I went from there to Welshpool and possibly other stations after that before being posted again to Cumberland first to Carlisle then to Cockermouth some time later.

I was certainly comfortably parked in Cockermouth in October of that year which seems to have been that one and thinking I was probably settled there for the winter. Christmas and New Year were not too far ahead and there was I nicely placed for a light scamper round the end of the Solway Firth then heigh ho for the Arran boat on some date near Christmas or sometime between that and New Year.

Not so. Some time near the end of October I received by the mail one day a brief note in which the main information was in some such words as 'You are instructed to report to Divisional Office Welshpool on …'.

I did not hear any kind of voice speaking to me at that time either though it was the perfect occasion for me to hear one say in tones part reproving part mocking: 'There you are you silly little man. You see? Will you ever learn? Come and sit with me and I will tell you a little story.

'There was once a clucking hen and it liked to sit on a nest of eggs as much as it could. It could count up to seven which was very good for a hen because very few hens can do that and it counted up to seven eggs under it. Well anyway, it thought it said to itself because it was a very foolish creature just like you: "soon shall have seven chicks to parade about for people to see and admire." But it had damn all of the kind because four of the eggs were china eggs ad the other three were golf balls.'

That was the end of the story I did not hear and no doubt it showed clearly there are right and wrong times for counting chickens. The only voice I did hear was my own and it was saying things I could not possibly set down on paper.

There was nothing for it but to pack the travelling trunk and the suitcases once again pay for my lodgings, pile into the car and head for the deep south once more. I must have been getting to be a kenspeckle traveller on that route, that was what I felt however absurdly but traversing it a mere twice a year or so each way and meeting innumerable vehicles at speed there was likely to be very little ken and a great deal of speckle.

So to Welshpool I returned to sojourn a while and weary not in well doing. Perhaps I did not quite measure up to that high precept because I did weary for a change. There I was when some time either just before or just after Christmas 1954 it was decided by others that my services were more required in Ruthin, Denbighshire, or if not actually required could be usefully employed there so to Ruthin I would go.

Some time previously I had already been from Welshpool as far as Llangollen to see at least one long evening in an International Eisteddfod. One result of that journey of 28 miles each way was to that it enabled me to have a pleasant stroll round the scene of all the various activities and see many of the groups of artists from many countries practising their various arts. They sang or played or danced with only the grass underfoot in the open air on that beautiful evening. The next thing to do then was to try for a seat in the great marquee for the concert which seemed to produce the elite of the elite in the various performances.

I reckoned even in those days that I was possibly just a tiny bit too difficult to please and impress but by golly, those concert artists I am perfectly certain had everybody in their audience (including one crabbity old Scotsman) completely under their sway. The marquee had a seating capacity of thousands. It was packed.

The audience responded right from the start. The artists seemed to sense quickly that they had got their audience; everyone gave and received of the best. I did not notice within myself either hunger or thirst though I had not eaten or drunk for several hours before then and smoking was forbidden. But if I went for a few hours without those things I probably made up for that when I got back to Welshpool.

That was how it came about that when I was due to take the road from Welshpool to Ruthin I already knew it as far as Llangollen. But I had never been over the Horseshoe Pass for which the road rises to 1,367 feet. However I had been many times over the Ross Road in Arran for which the road planners surely made some of the best ever attempts to tie knots in the line of a road without using complicated modern construction and though the Ross reaches only to a height of just under one thousand feet I was most interested to see how the two would compare. In the event I simply drove over the Horseshoe Pass and on to Ruthin in the most ordinary way.

That arrival, when I come to think of it, must have been on some date well into 1955. During my time in North Wales in 1936 I had been several times in the town square in Ruthin. I had now made a complete circuit and was back in some of my earlier tracks.

I found the hotel for which I had been booked or so I had been told before I left Welshpool. I found it because I could hardly have missed it despite my well known talent for missing places which cannot be missed. I knocked and rang or pushed a bell push anyway, called out walked round the place and repeated my procedure at any likely looking door I saw. No response. Ah well, perhaps this was how they did things in North Wales, surely a different type of approach to the catering business; still it made a change.

'Approach,' did I say? Somehow that did not seem quite the right word. Management here seemed to have taken a somewhat detached view of their undertakings and responsibilities. Yes, that was the word. They had detached themselves and buzzed off to some other place some time earlier. Presumably anyone expected or not arriving at their hotel in their absence was free to make instant alternative arrangements about accommodation if they could. That I believe is what I did for first I simply had to find somewhere to stay and there was a guest book not too far away. Fair play to the native Welsh who might conceivably have been concerned about the hospitality rating of their own town had they heard anything of my dilemma; the hotel manager was English or if not at least had the most English accent for miles around as I discovered later.

However I know I did stay in that hotel eventually for some time.

Ruthin is a small town with a slightly unusual layout. The town square is on the top of a small steep hill and although my directions for finding Divisional Office were clear enough yet I managed to go wrong and take the long way round. But I could not have failed to find it eventually so I found it and with it the Divisional Veterinary Officer and had the usual introductory chat with him. From there my next move was out into the Denbighshire countryside, Denbighshire, thought I, then at an age and stage better able to appraise it than my first view of it some eighteen years earlier, was more open country than Montgomeryshire and prettier than Radnor. Also it had what neither of them had, a fair length of attractive coast. On the other hand, though it had a big reservoir or two it had nothing of that sort to compare with the size and beauty of Lake Vyrnwy and likely not with the Elan Dams either if only I could have seen more of all those places and been better able to make comparisons.

The features of Denbighshire which I best remember are the two towns, Ruthin and Denbigh, the road between them and beyond Denbigh to the coast into Colwyn Bay and almost into Llandudno. I was never actually in that famous holiday resort. The county boundary between Denbighshire and Caernarvonshire was always an obstacle and so too was usually the information gained from various timepieces. No doubt if I had really been keen to see it I would have got there sometime on some pretext or none at all.

Though I was never in Llandudno I was often enough in Colwyn Bay and at a good few of the small places on the hill behind it. I was rather surprised one day to see when passing one place there, not a smallholding, on its front gate unmistakeably the name of a very well known mountain in Arran. Mentioning this to someone at my next place of call I nearly allowed myself to be introduced to the owner of that gate and house but time did not allow.

I was in Ruthin either over Easter or over the Whitsun weekend or more probably both. I know because I remember on Saturday forenoon unless it was a Friday afternoon coming back from Colwyn Bay. Coming along the coast road through Abergele to the junction at St. Asaph and again at Trefant the outward bound traffic from being the usual well spaced out few changed with seeming suddenness to a high speed nose to tail stream. All were heading for the coast and all were driving as if the coast might not be there if they did not hurry. So they hurried. Once I got past Trefnant I could forget it was a holiday weekend. Traffic south of that point was pretty much as usual. The heading rush further back was no doubt made up of people from nearer or maybe not so near towns and cities of England heading for a few breaths of salty air with at the same time their feet on the sand of the beaches. And a very good idea it seemed to be though maybe a wee bit on the cool side even in that bright sunshine that day.

Looking back it seems very likely that I was still at Ruthin well into that summer because I was there when another International Eisteddfod came along and one evening I wandered at leisure in the car over the Horseshoe Pass and joined the crowd as I had done before.

That pass; and those sheep forever on the road or roadside at the top of it. All right perhaps on a summer evening when one was in leisurely mood with time to spare but not always so acceptable at other times. There was the wet morning with low cloud when the first of the jobs lay over the hill in the Llangollen district. We start climbing, the car and I, up the first part of the hill on and up into the mountain mist or what the weather men might call hill fog. Speed was perforce reduced and we were late in starting. We did in due course reach the summit and dimly perceived some scattered grey shapes in the grey mist.

'Gerroff the road y'old bitches. GO ON. GERROFF.'

Blee-eep. Bee-be-be-be-be-be-be-beep. 'Hoppitchubitches.'

They hardly even look at me. They are clearly unaccustomed to being hustled off the road by anybody, anybody never mind an insignificant looking to turnout like mine. They have held up Rolls Royce's and Daimlers and Mercedes with no more effort than they are using now and I and my car matter less than nothing to them. One turns to the others. She does not speak. It's all done by thought transference.

'Tell you what, girls, you stay here, don't let him get past and I'll go round to his windows, look up at him with my most plaintive expression and see if he does not produce a few biscuits or at least one sandwich. If you see anything come out through the window you can let him past. And if he hasn't got anything for us this time we'll make sure he understands it'll pay him to have something for us next time. No reason why we should wear out our feet and our teeth on the hill when we've got a system here.'

'Hoppit. Gerroff.' Beep-beep-beep. BRRRRM. 'Hoppit. Dammit. Buzz off .'

'Listen to him. I say. Ovis, old girl, hold everything. What if he's one of those veterinary creatures and throws out something that looks nice but really has a big dose of …you know how some of their stuff tastes…Suppose we get that sort of stuff from him and it makes wish we ---'

'D'you think I care one hoot whether he's a veterinary creature or not; he's got to give us a – oh well perhaps you're right. We can always stop the next car. Let this one go.'

That very broadly speaking seemed to be something like the tactics displayed on a damp spring morning. The tactics on a fine summer evening were such the same but I did get past them to reach my destination in time enough.

It is of course my second time at an International Eisteddfod in Llangollen. At the concert I enjoy among other delectable items some great violin solos by a man considered by many people to be one of the greatest if not indeed the greatest violinist in the world at that time. It is wonderful, wonderful and I had never heard even a rumour (not having seen a programme) that there was to be any violinist there that evening. I forgive the sheep. I forgive everybody regardless. My only trouble now is that I shall not be able to endure the sound of my own fiddle playing for several weeks to come. After that perhaps if I start with a slow air on the back strings I can maybe work my way back slowly to the odd reel and strathspey again. Anything lacking in tone, likely to be rather a lot, I shall probably make up with volume, tempo, temper, and things like that.

The concert reaches its end as it must. I slowly make my way back over the Pass to Ruthin and prepare to face the old routine of the following day and many more days after that.

I think I must have been back in Welshpool before it came time for my summer holidays because somehow when holiday time came I seemed to leave oftener from there than from anywhere else. While I was still in Ruthin the Divisional Officer in Welshpool acquired the very commendable idea that a change of air for me might do me a lot of good and it did. Somehow or other I got a posting back to Welshpool, a change which was markedly conductive to my general well being.

The summer holidays came and passed. From Arran I returned to Welshpool and was still there late in November. The Caledonian Society was observing an occasion in the town hall and I was there. Normally no 'shop' is talked on such occasions except when two or more vets get together and then they talk nothing else or tend to do so. Thus when the SVO as that rank was then designated asked me how would I like a move to Scotland I said, 'Yes please.' Only after that did it occur to me to ask him which part of Scotland did he have in mind. I was told that part of the proposed move had not been quite decided just at that time. I gathered however that the particular part of Caledonia stern and wild most likely to enjoy or endure my services would be Orkney.

Before I could venture much surmise about that I was told that the Orcadians as a matter of fact do not regard themselves as being really Scottish at all. Much more do they regard themselves as being descendants of the Norsemen of old rather than as anything else. Such information did not trouble me at all as I reckoned I was by no means clear of Norse blood myself and could adduce some slender evidence in support of that theory.

Briefly the theory is that while the Norsemen for hundreds of years carried on sporadic raiding right round the coasts of the British Isles and other coasts too when King Haakon rather overdid things and came to grief by the ravages of the weather and the fury of the Scottish defence at the battle of Largs in 1263, many of his men, perhaps a majority of them, failed to re-embark. They were not all killed or drowned and so a proportion of them survived to be taken prisoners and eventually to marry or at least pair off with some of the lasses of south-west Scotland. The name Sillars seems to have appeared originally and solely in SW Scotland so far as the British Isles are concerned. Where it is found in other parts of the world it can usually be traced back to the south-west of Scotland.

I cannot think other than that from those wild Vikings of old there was handed down to me (and a lot of other folk too) through the many intervening generations those poaching, plundering, pillaging, piratical propensities which are so sternly suppressed for most of the time and at other times I hope never noticed. Anyway I was not at all averse to spending some time in Orkney; in fact I rather looked forward to it. But first there was to be Ruthin again up until some date about Christmas or New Year.

I was back in Ruthin and walking one evening along one of the narrow thoroughfares when I met a colleague. He had little time to spare but there was a little bar right beside us and in we went. The bar was small and we were almost the only customers. The barman who had been in either the Royal Navy or the Merchant Navy during the war, when he heard me tell my friend that I thought I would be going to Orkney, could not refrain from joining in the conversation. I think he was English and the gist of the conversation went something like this:

'Orkney? Excuse me, sir, but did I hear you say you were going to Orkney?' And then on my affirmation he went on:

'Cor, that's some place, that is. That's the only place and I've been all over when I was at sea, that's the only place where I've ever seen a waterfall flowing upwards. That's right. We were sailing up the west side of Hoy, I don't know if you know Orkney at all, up the west side of Hoy and there was this waterfall coming over a high cliff. But there wasn't a drop of it going down not a drop. The wind, cor they do have some wind up there, was carrying every drop of it right up into the air and away...' His voice trailed away as if still muted by recollection of the sight.

'No I don't know Orkney at all. But now that I've been warned I'll know what to expect. Eh... could we have the same again. Have one yourself.'

'Thank you, sir, of course it isn't like that all the time but it can blow very hard sometimes,' as he spoke he got the drinks. 'Your very good health, sir.'

My companion could not wait longer so we left and immediately parted, leaving me with this fresh piece of information, very fresh indeed by the sound of it, to digest.

As the days dropped off and Christmas drew nearer, the office staff spent more time deciding the details of the Christmas party. They no doubt had one every Christmas but for me it would be the first office party ever though I was by far the eldest member of the company. My colleague and fellow TVI decided that he and I would put on a short sketch or skit; we didn't know what it was about – well it seemed in the end to be about nothing in particular except that it was absurdly Wild West. Just pure distilled light hearted inanity.

He by some planning all his own decided that he was going to be Wild Bill Hiccups and I was to be Hopalong Catastrophe or else it was the other way about. Not only that but for the purposes of this remarkable production he, whether he was Hiccups or Catastrophe, was to be a superb step dancer and I was to be his musician and manager. We were touring the USA finishing in New York. We had been into Chester on the preceding Saturday afternoon when I had picked up a couple of cowboy hats for children. Those hats, something or other to represent sleeveless jerkins, and very little else were our only props.

There came the night of the party. We all having first assembled at the office adjourned in cars to the appointed place and the party began. In due course my colleague and I took the floor. Our dialogue we assured our vast audience (at least six and quite possibly seven) was entirely spontaneous, unscripted and unrehearsed. I had forgotten that news when on hearing him muffing his lines I poked him with my fiddle bow in his left rear ribs and told him he was at page three. His dancing was somewhat impaired by the size of the footwear on his feet and by his inability to maintain his gravity by the gravities of the sundry beverages he had absorbed up to that point by his marked preference for holding on to an armchair, and by the strongly pervading Christmas spirit: and though I played 'The Chicken Reel' with great vigour to make up for any missing notes he really did not dance at all well and clearly on that showing had no hope of touring the States and taking New York by storm. Sadly I realised that there was no fortune for us in his footwork and as I looked at it I turned away in pain, not wishing to see what he would do when he or if he quit partnership with the armchair. He had on his part evidently deemed it best that the audience should not see too much, in fact any at all, of his footwork.

The audience, except the VO who were rather younger than us, had probably never heard of Wild Bill Hicock who was a real person, nor Hopalong Cassidy who was not but it didn't matter. I reckon what happened without any intention on our part in fact further hammed up what already was meant to be pure ham. We as it were double hammed unintentionally.

When my colleague told us all as part of the 'unscripted' dialogue that Old Mother Riley who had the finest herd of Welsh Blacks in all Texas was deeply in debt from boozing, I had to pull out a wad of thousand-dollar bills and peel off a handful with a suitably casual comment. It was a very sad and serious thought and a more sympathetic audience would not have laughed as ours did. Mine was the only serious face in the room.

Just how the star of a one-man dance act and his manager could get themselves so abruptly involved in the financial rescue of a highly improbable Texas rancher left one of those large gaps in our 'unrehearsed' script for which there is no explanation except perhaps 'Christmas'. Such gaps are jumped only by the strong spark of the Christmas spirit. There may be scope here for comment on 'plugs' and sparks and points but it eludes me. Clearly we had no future as scriptwriters nor any better hopes as producers. The dancing was not the international success it was said to be, at least not without the aid of an armchair. But we enjoyed it all.

Throughout the week that followed between the party and the Christmas break we so far as our routine work was involved were less heavily engaged. Then came the final Saturday afternoon when there was nothing left to do but pack everything for what might be the very last time in Wales, load everything into the car and set off for Scotland.

CHAPTER 22

It was early in January 1956 when several of us veterinarians gathered in the chill of early morning at the Airways terminal in Aberdeen. From there we were conveyed out to the airport at Dyce and in due course after being hoisted up aloft and conveyed northwards I get my first aerial view of Orkney. It was not strictly speaking my first view because I had seen some parts of it in a blue haze across the Pentland Firth several years before that.

Looking down from the plane I was rather puzzled by what I saw. Until then I had been totally unaware of the existence of the Churchill Barriers as they are called, the name for the causeways linking the small islands on the east side of Scapa Flow. I remember my brief astonishment that so much work could have gone on during the war years and existed for so long afterwards without my ever hearing a thing about it, never a mention that I could recall anyway. There had been plenty of war rumours flying about all the time of happenings real and fictitious, yet somehow I had missed all mention of those massive works at one of the main anchorages of the fleet. Clearly my private espionage network had slipped badly and I was going to have to shoot several of my spies. For instance there was Lord Goan Finoot, that thrustful and enterprising peer and pillar of my private intelligence network. There was General Sir Isidore Kent Fyne who generally signed himself I. Kent Fyne and his beautiful accomplice Miss Anne Ethererd who was notably less successful in her inquiries. All had come suddenly into existence and all were to be as abruptly destroyed.

On landing at Grimsetter the first words I really heard were spoken not by an Orcadian voice but by an Ayrshire one belonging to the DVO who met us there. Not that the Orcadian accent would have fallen on unaccustomed ears in my case anyway for wasn't my first or almost first ever teacher when I started at Shiskine school in Arran a pleasant Orcadian lass from Stromness. And had she not told us about the quality of the 'cham' she had brought in the local shops (that would be about 1918 or 1919). Had she not read to us from little books how the Eskimos got their hair out with the 'chaw' bone of a shark (and other things like that which every child ought to know or so the educationists of that day seemed to think.

In May and June 1919 the 'cham' would no doubt still be showing the effects of the war and the young teacher's comments on the quality of the jam were probably thoroughly justified, whether they were or not the Orcadian accent forty years on was just the same.

After a cup of tea and a bun in the canteen at the airfield we all proceeded to Kirkwall for a briefing in Divisional Office then on to our hotel to rest, gird our loins, burnish our armour, etc. for a start the next morning at the unholy hour of 5.00 a.m.

We were all up at the appointed time, had a light wash, a drink of tea made the previous night and were all aboard the boat before 6.00 a.m. or possibly an earlier deadline depending on what her sailing time for that particular morning might be. This was normal procedure for anyone travelling to the North Isles and might have been new to some of our party but such an early start to catch a boat was nothing new to me. I had done it many a time not by any means from choice as a youngster in Arran leaving home to start another term at secondary school. All the youngsters from Arran who wanted further education under County Council auspices had to do the same or use alternatives which were no better.

The steamer was at the first pier of the journey before there was any sign of daylight and did not have a lot of it at the second pier either. Whether the second pier was Stronsay and the third one Sanday or whether it was the other way about I cannot tell but I do know that the fourth call was at the island of Papa Westray. At each preceding call point one veterinary officer, permanent or temporary, had disembarked to stay on that island for as long as might be necessary to test all the cattle then due for test.

Now it was my turn to get off. I disembarked all right and immediately re-embarked. This seemingly futile procedure consisted of my leaving the vessel via a square opening in her side and settling in some part of a small open motor boat by which we reached a jetty where we got safely ashore. Not for me apparently the dignity of stepping down a gangway on to a pier. But the small ferry boat was something again not new to me for when I was quite small as a child I had hopped on and off between ferry boats and the Campbeltown steamer which in those far off days sailed between there and Gourock or the opposite way every weekday and had contact with Arran both by Lochranza pier and by open ferry boat.

Papa Westray had between six and seven hundred head of cattle distributed in a good many small herds over quite a lot of ground of which much had to be covered by walking. This meant testing a good two hundred head made up of herds of various sizes each day. The six day cycle went on non stop which is to say we did not have a break on Sundays.

At this point some further recollection uncovers the fact that after our arrival in Kirkwall on Monday of that week we must have spent the whole of the following day in that town because we sailed on the Wednesday morning. I know because the time when I reached Papa Westray was mid afternoon, the ship had still to go to Westray and would not be returning to Kirkwall that night though at other times of the year she did make the round trip every Tuesday. So I arrived in Papa Westray on a Wednesday, started work that same evening, finished on the following Tuesday, crossed over to Westray by ship that Wednesday and as best I cuold got ready for the fray in Westray.

I am unlikely to forget that crossing. To join the ship we had to leave as we had arrived by small open motor boat, this time from a tiny sandy bay on what was that night the lee side of the island. Darkness was rapidly falling. There were short sharp flurries of hailstones carried on that offshore wind.

Almost the only other cargo besides myself and my luggage was a coffin containing the body of a man. From what I learned of his case during my week on the island he, poor soul, seemed to have died ultimately of cachexia, that is wasting away which in his case seemed to be a sequel of the condition know nowadays as anorexia nervosa.

So there I was standing on that beach and being thrashed every now and then with bursts of hailstones watching the men launch that little boat and load that particular cargo all in semi darkness. For my protection the rubber coat and boots I was wearing were only just enough. That particular point was further emphasised when about half way of the hundred yards to the ship the boat was found to be filling rapidly with water. The plug hole in the bottom of the boat no longer had a plug in it if it had had one at all for that journey. Someone said afterwards that the men had forgotten to put it into the plug hole. I do not know about that. I do know that on reaching the steamer I got aboard as if I was sixteen again and hurrying the remainder of the cargo was shipped safely and the boatmen made the beach again without being swamped.

Looking back on that scene which to me at the time was strongly suggestive of something from Edgar Allan Poe, I felt that all we needed to obtain a completely macabre effect was the presence of a tall dark gaunt man in a long black cloak with a raven perched on his shoulder and from time to time carried to our ears downwind from the raven a creaking voice saying 'Nevermore.'

My queries about the anorexia case when I was first told of it drew the information that the unfortunate subject of it had most probably suffered severe mental trauma associated with the taking of food. The story was that one day when he and his little sister were both young, she it seems being hardly more than a toddler, they were both playing on the kitchen floor when a meal was about to be served. There was a large pot of boiling hot soup standing uncovered on the kitchen floor and into it the little girl toppled backwards. We can guess the rest. I never heard what diagnosis if any was made in his case nor what treatment if any was attempted.

I joined my colleague in Westray. We had another week there, maybe two, then the order was 'back to Kirkwall' for me. The vets from the other islands arrived back there as they finished their stints. That stage of the 'blitz' as it was called of the North Isles was over. The permanent staff members who had come to Orkney from Aberdeen went 'sooth' (south) again. I was given various duties on the main island or Mainland as the Orcadians call it until the North Isles should again be due for their next round of tests.

That was exactly what happened and when the next round came due I was given the work in Stronsay to do. Once more I was to catch the very early boat this time by myself alone of all the vets. I did not catch it. I failed simply because the wonky little alarm clock in the hotel bedroom did not go off at the time for which it was set. In fact I do not think it could be induced to ring at all except in a very erratic and half hearted manner. My story was met with considerable scepticism until the same thing happened to one or two of the sceptics who would test the clock and see for themselves. So they tested and they saw.

The main consequence was that after much phoning around I reached Stronsay in an open motor boat from the intermediately situated island of Shapinsay at a cost of £5 and most of the day. As finance branch were unlikely to accept a story about a wonky alarm clock against a claim for £5 I paid it myself: keen type I was in those days.

I arrived on Stronsay in the evening at a beach in the south end of the island with still enough daylight left to test one of the biggest herds in the island. I wanted to bet a pay for that day and got it. I finished about nine o clock at night which in those days in those parts was closing time for the sort of catering establishment I wished to visit. I had had a long day. While in no way fussy about where I was going to sleep still I was not sleepy. Someone conveyed me from the farm to the village of Whitehall in Stronsay where I checked in at the house where I would be staying. The catering establishment was closed but I got my dram and the hour of relaxation I felt I had earned that day. Thus did I get my introduction to Stronsay, little foreseeing then how much more extensive and prolonged my acquaintance with it was going to be.

For a fortnight, three weeks or whatever it was I stayed on Stronsay then it was back to the Mainland for another spell there then another outstanding, this time on Sanday. It was my first visit to Sanday and once again there was a small feature, a little out of the usual thing, to mark my first visit to one of those islands. I could not, it seemed, just arrive, do my whole visit and depart without incident like anybody else. At Papa Westray it was an unusual departure at Stronsay and unusual arrival at Sanday; my feet had hardly touched the pier when one of the more prominent local citizens approached me with the information that they were having what he called 'a little concert sort of thing' (or some such description) that evening. He had heard that I played the fiddle and would I care to join in and play a little something or other, anything I liked to help out?

Having myself been born and brought up in a small rural community I thought I knew right away the sort of situation he was facing: the permanent dearth of talent, not merely of talent but of performance of any kind, good bad or middling. It would be the sort of situation where such brave souls as did volunteer faced a audience of ten maybe twenty folk, all utterly informal but no less critical on that account. I believe I quizzed him about the size of the audience and gathered that it might be more than just a few. Oh well, no good in being sticky about it. I had good hopes that it would be a small audience maybe about the size of the average political meeting in those parts and agreed to try and play something not too woefully badly.

That was in the forenoon and I still had a very respectable day's work to do. However, I thought as I went on I should enjoy the little light entertainment whatever form it took in the evening. That was what I thought. But as the day wore on casual mention by other people of the 'little concert' as I had first heard it described made more and more evident to me that it was going to be nothing like as little nor as simple as I had assumed it would be. In fact it turned out to be a full blown concert in the biggest hall the island had and with the hall packed at that.

I suspect my reputation as a fiddler mainly of Scottish country dance music had been inflated away out of all recognition by word of mouth beforehand and if not beforehand I certainly heard that happen to it at the hands of the compere just before I went on to that platform.

Why I went on at all was because by the time I learned more clearly the scale and nature of the social function in which I had become involved to have withdrawn would have left some sort of gap in the programme and possibly also have caused some annoyance. The atmosphere in the hall by the time I went on to the platform was very warm and humid, just the sort I had known so often before to muffle a solitary fiddle as effectively as if it was played under a blanket. As if that was not enough I was very tired, tense and not recently practised. Anyway I went ahead and did what I could. No doubt the audience had heard worse, probably never much worse but yes, worse. They were very kind and gave me an encore. Even the people at the back who could hardly have heard me at all applauded loudly. I am still convinced that those who heard at least applauded most.

Maybe the dram had been circulating briskly in certain quarters thereby greatly enhancing appreciation of anything resembling a strathspey or reel coming out of a fiddle. Orkney, by the way, is a real stronghold of the fiddle and contains many fiddle players who would hear another such player with very discerning hearing: fiddlers are generally very kind about another fiddler's playing.

In the day that followed the work went on as usual and I was glad to forget the concert so far as I could. But long as the work list might be inevitably after a time I had to make my way back to Kirkwall once more and carry on with the annual renewal tests.

The job of doing the renewal test dull and routine work as it mostly was still left some grounds for thankfulness that not all the herds were chronically undermanned for test purposes and quite exhausting to do. A striking example of the difference in speed of testing with the differing behaviour of herds or sections of the same herd came my way one afternoon. The total was 123 made up of 80 milk cows and 43 lively two-year-old heifers. The cows all stood in a large byre where people with implements and utensils were clattering in and out all day every day. In effect nothing that I did caused them any unease whatsoever. They were all constantly housed in a warm byre and consequently all as short haired as they could well be. With minimal control and minimal hair clipping required they paid not the slightest attention to me or my work and I tested the lot in forty minutes. The heifers were a different proposition. They were running loose in a big shed and they had lots of space. All were Ayrshire as were the cows. I had a good team of able hands catching yet as best speed we took about sixty minutes for the forty-three. Those heifers were pretty able too.

CHAPTER 23

About this time when I was coming up towards completion of my fifth year as a temporary Veterinary Inspector two considerations were more in my mind. The first one was that after all the time spent on the job and the solitary rise in the rate of pay coupled with new conditions of employment which left me worse off overall there was no sign of any improvement on the way. We were paid salary and expenses lumped together in one payable order each month and it seemed to me on comparison of figures I had noted and kept that I was receiving less per month in the spring of 1956 than I had been paid for each of the months November and December 1951, all these payments being amounts after tax. That was in the face of ever increasing cost of living.

Besides all that my much increased experience of the job was surely value, I thought, for some increase of pay for which there might have been some provision made in whatever regulations governed our activities. I knew and knew very well that some people were always ready to tell me I would get my reward in heaven etc. and other forms of heavy unoriginal humour were not lacking in the verbal replies I received to my written statements. Of those verbal replies of course I had no record and with no record no adequate retort. I would have preferred to receive instead of lumbering attempts at humour just some more plain ordinary British money at that time. It all amounted to giving at least the same if not better value of work done for reduced value of pay received. Repeated representations on my part over the years never produced more than verbal replies of which of course I had no record nor would record have been of use if I had had one. Anything than that I never got.

I really did begin to think somewhat unhappily that I had really been rather naïve in my belief in British fair play. I was almost tempted at times when being knocked about among a bunch of rough cattle to wish that some of the clever ones who made the precious regulations or those who neglected to amend them might have a week, just one week of constant work among a number of herds which I would select for them 'with the greatest of animosity' as the man said when he was being very polite. The other main thought in my mind was that many of the stock owners in the North Isles had told me when any discussions of veterinary matters had arisen between us that they had a great need of a vet of their own, a veterinary surgeon resident in those isles. It was quite an idea, a big one which others may have had before me but which no one had ever tried.

I still had all my veterinary equipment at my old home. I had a car. All I had still to get was a house of some sort a fresh stock of medicines and the goodwill of whatever area was judged to be right for me to take over. With these requisites I could be in business again as a practitioner.

During one small social evening I mentioned to some of my colleagues when we were as usual talking shop that the North Isles seemed to be 'crying out' as I put it for a vet of their own. I soon learned that if I pursued the matter seriously I would get support for it on all sides. I took a few days to consider the matter and came to the conclusion that I could not lose financially by any reckoning viewed from any angle. Perhaps I should have let my thoughts dwell longer on the full meaning and implications of that word 'financially'.

By simple arithmetic I could not but gain by starting practice there. The goodwill of that part of the Orkney practice which I proposed to take over could be bought and was bought for a sum trivial by comparison with the cost of an ordinary practice. I bought a house in Stronsay again for a price which would have been absurdly small in a less remote area but which in that part of the country was in keeping with other house prices. I also had a car still fairly new but acting on advice that I should get something older to run on some rough tracks and salt sands on the other islands I bought another one at a modest price, old and not too sweet to drive but sound.

Most important of all, or so it seemed at the time, I met and courted a young lady and after a proper length of time became engaged to her. Now I had a new practice, two cars, a good house and a lady to place in it. Apparently I had everything.

After a long holiday in Arran during which I got all my stuff started on its way to Orkney I got back up there and on Saturday 1 September 1956 stepped off the boat at Stronsay pier accompanying my car. The car was slung ashore in the usual way and I drove it up to my house. All I had to do now was 'get down on the mark and wait for the gun', the gun in this case being the first job that came in from the practice or the first batch of work to come from the Ministry. As I had been a TVI my appointment as a local Veterinary Inspector (LVI) was automatic, so I was told, and in any case was appointed.

There was no need for me to sit idle while waiting for work to come in; in fact I could not afford to do so. Having selected one apartment to be a dispensary etc. it then had to be freshened up and specially equipped for its various purposes. But soon there were to be far bigger changes had I but known.

I stayed as a boarder in the house I had bought and in that way was in the curious position of being both landlord and lodger. (I never seemed to manage to do things the same way as other folk did them.) Work began to come in. there was a little practice first of all then a lot of Ministry work necessitating my staying away from home for periods of a week or more at a time. In November and December of that year there was Eday and Papa Westray to do and a beginning to be made in Westray.

However well before Christmas had drawn near things seemed to move against me. The very weekend before I was due to leave and did leave for Eday by the Monday morning sailing from Westray the husband of the couple who were keeping house for me died very suddenly. His widow remarried a very few weeks later and went to live elsewhere.

My fiancée decided that she did not wish to continue our engagement and returned the ring. That particular moment was no doubt the best one for showing the sharp difference between us the incompatibilities etc., but her action was no help to me at that particular time. But these things, as I reflected, had happened before, they would happen again and one just had to accept them readjust to them and soldier on as best one could.

In Westray I was half way through one week's testing and was about to issue my postcards for the following week when I got urgent word to go south to Arran as my mother was nearing her end. So as I was able to break off the work between two six-day cycles I got away in plenty of time to be beside the old lady for the last of her days.

Return to Stronsay was in the latter part of December of that year. I was by then very much on my own and welcomed friendly help from wherever it might come. The whole scene had changed almost like a third rate play. I may have been suffering effect of which I was not aware at the time though that seems unlikely because as far as I could see there was nothing recently gone wrong which would not come right with the passage of time. Apart from a deep determination to stay on and make a success of this new thing I was trying in the North Isles of Orkney I had at that stage not a single idea of what the future held for me nor of what the next move was going to be.

Something I knew within myself though not the sort of thought which was often expressed was that one deep need within me was for companionship, somebody of my own kind with whom I could talk over my affairs and discuss what the past had held and what the future might hold for me. There was plenty of company of a kind: not unfriendly, not uncongenial, but none whose position was much like mine or who could be expected to discuss mine with me. The other three professional men in the island, if they had problems of their own would no doubt have found little in them in common with mine. We simply did not have many points of contact. My colleagues in Kirkwall, the Ministry men, the only colleagues I knew at all well, were far off, had very different relationships with livestock owners and different viewpoints regarding them and their livestock. Owners and stock taken together of course constituted the reason for the very existence of the veterinary profession.

I was in Papa Westray when I got back the engagement ring my mail having been re-directed to me from Stronsay. A tiny parcel the size of a cube on an edge of one and a half inches separately wrapped and sent to a man known to be engaged did not call for very astute guesswork as to its contents. I was asked point blank by the lady of the house if that was the ring sent back to me to which I could only reply to the dear lady that it was. I forget what comment if any she made but it did not matter anyway. Ah well, the rest of the folk in the North Isles had to know about it sometime in any case, so why not start the process right there and then. That break must have happened in late October or early November I think because I know the other two losses happened in that November and December.

On returning to Stronsay just before Christmas 1956 I found that if I had lost one housekeeping couple I was quickly fixed up with another, this time a young newly married couple. To all outward appearances I had in current slang 'got it made'. I had arrived. There was no denying I had arrived at something even though I was not too clear as to what that something was. Whatever it was or was not may emerge if I am permitted to tell the rest of this story.

CHAPTER 25

When I first arrived in Stronsay as the new vet in a new practice I also ran into another new experience which took me pretty much aware one to which I have already made reference a little further back. I was a new house owner. I do not mean that either the house or I were by any means new. We were not though both fairly durable. It was just that I was new to being the owner of a house. It was a funny feeling, 'funny' in both senses. I felt I must be rather like the young man in the old music hall song who had never been twenty-one before and whose papa had given him the key of the door. I found myself somehow chuckling quite absurdly at the novelty of it.

I had never owned a building nor part of one before. Now I owned a substantial house, two and a half storeys, thirty-inch walls, stone built, with outhouse, a large garden to the rear and full frontage in the public road. I walked some yards away from the house, turned round looked at it and told myself as if not quite grasping the fact: 'It's mine, yes, mine. Bought and paid for. Item one whole house perfectly sound, perfectly durable to do with largely as I please: improve it, neglect it, live in it, live out of it, etc., etc. Soon I found myself during this inspection viewing the house form another angle with further inward commentary.

'Yes pretty good. Not too beautiful in fact not beautiful at all unless with the kind of beauty a balsa wood raft might have for a tired swimmer in deep water. Maybe "she" was right in describing it as being like the county jail (presumably as seen in Westerns but not equipped with sheriff hosses, hitchin' rail nor nuthin' like that). It should keep out Jack Frost anyway whoever it may fail to keep in. but "she" will soon find herself jolly happy to be an inmate of said "county jail".'

That and more of it was the sort of line of thought I had. How wrong can one be on occasion in such a well recognised situation and with never a suspicion that one could be totally wrong as in fact I turned out to be. And who cares anyway? I did it for a time but not for long.

Getting further away from the house some other parts of Stronsay had various attractions for me and not necessarily of the two legged variety either. There was the long level stretch of good farmland down the middle of the island. as elsewhere in it. with rises in the level of the ground at most of its extremities and how many extremities it had. What an uncommon shape it had. Its outline on the map could with only a little imagination easily be a first year biology student's drawing of an amoeba, this one even extending a cautious pseudopodium represented here by the small peninsula called Housholm, properly Roithiesholm. It all made a very appropriate setting with just that mere suggestion of rudimentary biology to make a 1930s Glasgow graduated vet feel that tiny bit more at home. After all, my learning of biology began with the amoeba and never did progress any appreciable distance beyond it.

Something else which pleased me a lot now that I was working for myself was the size of the herds and the ease of access to them. With a few small possible exceptions every farmyard could be reached easily by car.

I remember on one occasion during the time when I was back in Arran in that first December someone who to my surprise seemed to know no more about Orkney than did I myself before I went there, asking me would I get enough work from the crofts in Stronsay. Taken completely aback, I had to have the question repeated to me. I then explained as gently as I could that I would have the work not only of Stronsay but of five neighbouring islands as well that at least three of the crofts in the islands which could and did top the 200 mark. There were, I added, between twenty and thirty herds of between 100 and 200 head each and a great many more between 60 and a 100 head. All told, as I explained to the questioner, I could have the veterinary work for a number between 1,300 and 1,400 head of cattle which made the proper question not would I have enough work but rather would I be able to do all the work which was likely to occur.

I had many a thought to myself and sometime expressed to others that the cattle population in my charge as a practitioner was about two and a half times what was in Arran and that if the distribution in Arran was bad enough to make the work sometimes too much for one person the distribution over six of the North Isles was incomparably worse. But I suppose I was an optimist not capable of being really and permanently cured of the idea that the best is yet to be as expressed among other things by the post. That pious thought, I must admit, is often followed by the less gentle one: 'By gum it had better be like that because if what I've had so far had included the best I ain't hanging around to find out what's the worst.'

It was early on one mild evening during that first September or October when I got an urgent call to go over to the neighbouring island of Eday where there was a cow to be calved. The attendants who were also the owners had investigated the situation, made a moderate attempt to correct it, then wisely decided that it was a job for the vet. When I got their message the first thing I had to do was to look for a boatman to take me across to Eday. In this quest I was fortunate and in due course we set off. The sea crossing including the time required for embarking from a beach and disembarking at a pier would probably have been well over half an hour. Total distance between my house and the scene of the case would be almost six miles as the crow flies. Of these about three were sea crossing. I reckon the time required from door to door would be about an hour.

Whatever the time it took I duly reached my patient, got stripped to the waist, got down behind and began. There was the usual and indispensable preliminary examination then began the pushing and grunting, the adjurations to the old blank of blank to stop her blank pressing, perhaps with some further sporadic commentary and I think I did make some progress towards correcting the position of the calf. But after most of an hour of that, clearly it could be seen that the advantages lay too much with the cow. Apart from the position of the calf it was a perfectly straightforward case but even with the cow's back raised no sooner had I repelled the calf and gained sufficient space to bring up the head or whatever other member was not then presenting than the patient gave another heave and we were back to where we had started: no worse off but certainly no better. This had gone on through repeated extensions of the process of 'building her up behind' which translated means raising that part of her standing which was under her hind end so that whether she stood or lay her hind end was higher than her fore end. For this purpose packed straw was usually the most popular material though various other materials might also be used.

I decided that whether the cow or the owners like it or not she would have to be slung up by the hind legs: not high and not for long. The owners were thoroughly cooperative and after a short time up went the hind legs. I tried again inside. Plenty of space this time and no interference, not that the old moo did not try with further expulsive efforts to interfere. She tried but she could not. Another very few minutes and the calf was straightened out, put under traction and landed on the byre floor. Once he was straightened out but before he arrived in this cold hard wicked world his mother got every chance to do her stuff and she did it.

There was nothing remarkable about the case itself unless perhaps that it was a very good example to show how a simple mal-presentation holding back a normal birth can persist despite vigorous corrective measures because the dam remains in a position adverse to the process of correction and therefore of delivery.

My whole time on the farm, including the washing off in the byre and the cup of tea afterwards in the farmhouse kitchen, probably took about two hours. The sail back to Stronsay was just as calm as the outward journey. During both of them I had the thought that this was but the first of many such journeys and that it showed things working out apparently pretty much as I had imagined before I started practice there. It certainly was the first such journey but not the first of many such.

The reasons for this paucity of small boat journeys was never very clear to me nor did any one reason by itself seem to provide much explanation. There may not have been the anticipated number of cases of sufficient urgency on the other islands or there may have been cases urgent enough but to which the owners chose not to call a vet, preferring instead to work at them without one. Some such cases may have cropped up during the many times when I was known to be away from home or at times when it was equally certain that no small boat could have made the crossing to another island. Those few times when more than my advice on the telephone was required and my presence at the case desired presented in themselves difficulties amounting almost to a miniature saga.

On receipt of a call of that kind, having hung up the phone, the first thing to do was to find a boatman. There were boatmen in the village and at some distance outside it. What were my chances? The short answer generally was 'not very good'. For one reason: if the weather was at all good the boatmen were likely to be away from their houses either out in their boats or doing something else which prevented their conveying me across the deep and dark blue to wherever I had to go. Conversely if boatmen and boats could be found at home the likeliest reason was that the weather was bad enough that they could not or at any rate would not consider a crossing. On an odd occasion the state of the tides might settle the matter.

But supposing the weather and the boatmen were favourable and a crossing was available, that was not the end of the matter. Even if the proposed destination was within safe boating distance from where we were, there remained the question: how long was I going to be ashore? A question to which I could only give an approximate time as an answer. If my time ashore was going to be too long the boatmen, who had their own commitments at home, would have to go home without me. I might be able to give them a reasonable estimate of the time required for all the work about which I knew but of course could not take account of time required for any other cases which might be shown to me. I could at a pinch have stayed a night or nights on whatever island it might be and get home with the ship sometime, yes, but when? And how much was I going to lose of time which might be badly needed at home to try and overtake the eternal clerical work? And who was going to pay for my bed and board for time necessarily spent away from home?

On me was placed the onus of showing that any expenses I claimed were unavoidable were justified were actually disbursed by me and I suppose of convincing those who had the duty of reimbursing me that I had not invented the entire claim anyway.

It was even suggested to me and from an official source at that but not in writing, that before I claimed for my sailing fares I should get receipts or duplicate tickets from the steward purser on the ship. I can imagine, but only imagine because I never asked that official what would have been his reaction and his reply to that idea. I noted well that any amount of effort and embarrassment on my part could be freely incurred so that officialdom might be satisfied that the signed claims I submitted for payment were genuine. At an off time or two I fell a wondering how honest were they themselves who required, at least desired, such proof of honesty in others.

It was difficult, you see, lacking the desirable documentation to substantiate claims for sailings fares, etc. and I sometimes did not or could not provide the necessary documentation. So once again I would most likely have paid that kind of expense out of my own resources rather than squabble about them with what I called the unreachable ones. Once claims for fees and expenses left my hands they were examined at various levels starting with Divisional Office. All who examined them knew that if any claim was queried or disallowed there was little the claimant could do about it without further correspondence which he would probably prefer to avoid because he anticipated failure of his claim in any case.

If ever I felt the need for a strong professional union of some kind to fight the cause of the solitary worker in an isolated situation, it was at times like these when as I observed sourly strong unions could get claims passed and fresh pay demands mostly granted without giving any improvement in production or service in whatever kind of job they did.

By considerations such as these it was perhaps more fortunate than otherwise that motor boat journeys were, as I said earlier, comparatively infrequent. Although practice was in theory my main reason for being in the North Isles and although officially I was under the auspices of the HIVSS, the subsidy paid to me in respect of it did not provide much income to supplement what little was derived from the total clinical work of the six islands.

Consequently I depended from the very beginning right through until I finished mainly on the income from the annual renewal test of the herds. Practice however could and did get in the way of those herd tests and the clerical work of them at the most awkward times. No man, we are told in the good book, can serve two masters and if in this context masters be taken as meaning those of whom one is responsible then I had at least three different sets of them. There was the Ministry of Agriculture. the HIVSS and of course the client who as things were then arranged seemed to come third or lower. This list of course takes no account of income tax which like the poor was always with us, in thought at least.

As for conflict of obligations, there was, for instance, that Monday morning I remember so clearly in the hotel in Sanday. I had got a good week's herd testing not for the preceding week but for the one before that. The notebooks had gone to that industrious one who did the 'writing up' of my test charts and had come back with the accompanying charts all properly written up. What I then had to do was to make out accurate accounts for all the lot showing proper scales of charges according to the rules, proper mileages charged and showing where these were already covered by another account, etc., not a terribly onerous job but vitally important requiring plenty of time and preferably to be approached with a fresh mind.

With a view to obtaining all these desiderata I rose at six o'clock on that particular Monday morning in the Sanday hotel and got busy in the lounge. I had it all to myself. The morning was a fine one in late spring just before the cattle would be turned out to fend for themselves on the grass. I reckoned that with any half decent kind of luck I was just going to manage to get that batch of charts all checked, signed and with their accompanying accounts into the large envelope down the pier and aboard the ship which I would see approaching when she came round the point. I knew that on having tied up she would not lie long but I thought I could fulfil my programme, just: that was what I thought I could do, that was. Eight o'clock it was by that time and at eight o'clock somebody opened the lounge door and spoke to me.

'Mr Sillars there's a message; Mr X----' who was the owner of a big herd fairly far along the island 'He has a heifer there newly calved with her calf bed out and can you go along there as soon as possible?'

I do not know whether or not there was a barely audible thud to be heard in that lounge just then. If there was it was the sound of my heart landing in my boots: Wellington boots of course. I was due to start wearing them at the first test beginning at 9.30 a.m. anyway. I thanked the message bearer and began to adjust to the new situation.

'All right, ship, you can come now or not come; you can lie long or not lie long as you please with no difference at all to me. As some worthy Orcadians might say in a case like this "Hid's makkin' nae differ".'

There was I thinking that just this once with a bit of extra effort which I would fain have spared myself and a little luck which I reckoned I needed, I would get a batch of test results and all papers connected therewith into Divisional Office in good time. What a very curious idea. However did I come to be so naïve? Now to relive the experience: I shall not merely not get away my test charts nor shall I get breakfast which seldom interests me anyway but I shall not even be on time for my first herd test. When I do get to it I shall probably feel like death only very slightly warmed up and not look much better than that.

I got to my heifer at a time around I should think half past eight. She was a big strong crossbred, probably half Shorthorn and half something else, and my goodness could she press: her back end was already slightly raised but such was her size that when she was lying which was most of the time the offending uterus was lying well below the level of the rest of her body. An unhelpful position but at least I had lashings of hot water and cold water, a strong white sheet and men to hold it, all of which I needed for the job. When I had finished with the warm antiseptic and got the uterus inside the sheet with the men twisting the ends in opposite directions I doused it liberally with cold water and the big push began. Sugar liberally sprinkled on a prolapsed uterus was something I had either used or seen used at some time in the distant past but had not noticed any specially beneficial effects from it and in this case worked without it.

I started the job cannily knowing it could be a long one. Every time she pushed me back which she could do quite easily I gained another half inch with my counterthrust when she relaxed again. There came that moment known to everyone who had done that job when after long and strenuous efforts neither he nor his assistants can see that he had gained much if anything at all. The next thing we know after that is that the mass is obviously reduced and the next thing after that again is that it is back inside her.

Right: and that was exactly how it worked with me that time despite all her vigorous straining. Then I pushed it as far forward as I could reach though I probably had not got it thoroughly and completely replaced. I asked my helpers to watch it as best they could and if she should strain again in the next few seconds to try to keep it inside her while I dived for my bag. I needed only a pessary, the iodoform tape and the big needle: a very few seconds to grab the lot.

I knew I was taking a risk which seemed to me reasonable and justifiable and I lost. Within those few seconds she simply gave one mighty heave got the whole lot past the men's restraining hands and had us all back where we started. I did not say very much but I formed a very low opinion of that beast just then.

Well, after that there was no messing about. Already a lot of time had been spent on her and the plan now was to sling her hindquarters. In what seemed no time at all the owner or his men had got a spar resting on the joist, the block and tackle in position and up she went. That uterus after that procedure practically flowed back into its place and stayed there with an iodoform pessary for company while I stitched her up good and proper. We then released her and allowed her to get to her feet again.

When we had everything shipshape again the time was coming up to ten o clock. The owner asked me would it be advisable to keep a beast like that to calve another time with him. I told him such was the impression she had made on me that while normally it is quite all right and safe to keep a beast that has put out her calf bed once and I had not heard of it happening twice to any beast, in her case and I emphasised the word 'her', I would get rid of her for fear she might do it again, perhaps at a time when there would not be anybody so near at hand to notice her and attend to her.

The time being then ten o clock it was time for the men's 'half yoke'. The owner and I made our way to the house where I found I was still not interested in breakfast. I was seldom hungry immediately after prolonged exertion but I did linger over and enjoy a large liquid refreshment which somehow arrived in my hand.

I think I was possibly about an hour late at the first place I had postcarded but for sure the owner would have been on the phone to the hotel and learned what had taken place if he had not learned by any other means. The test charts would have had to wait till Thursday of that week because the ship always came out from Kirkwall on the Wednesday of each week and lay at Westray overnight. But I know that they got Divisional Office eventually.

CHAPTER 26

I began to notice after I had been a while in Stronsay and from there sometime on to the other island not merely the scantiness of practice but the lack of variety in what little practice there was. There was hardly a case of that scourge of the dairy practice, mastitis, to which I was called. I certainly kept small stocks of the commoner antibiotics and sulfa drugs but they were usually wanted for use by the owners themselves without further attention from me.

There was very little digestive trouble: a very few case of traumatic gastritis leading to peritonitis and all manner of chest complications. With all such cases I was completely unsuccessful perhaps from not getting them soon enough or perhaps I was too hesitant about going for a rumenotomy as soon as I got them instead of pinning my hopes on the older treatment used in bygone days and which was quite often successful. It consisted of having the animal stand and lie on a platform which sloped from a height of eight or ten inches at the animal's fore end to floor level at the hind end. The only modern addition to that treatment was dosage of the patient with sulphonamides.

The idea of this treatment was that it tended strongly to move the entire mass of all four stomachs towards the rear of the abdomen taking with it, we hoped, the penetrating foreign body which seemed otherwise to be forced always in a forward direction by the stomach movements, penetrate the diaphragm, and set up pericarditis, pleurisy and goodness knows what else.

I myself at post mortems of two widely separated cases, both young, removed from the second stomach of the first one a thin blackened three-inch nail and saw an identical nail taken from the second stomach of the second case. The first one was in Arran and came from a carcase which was much altered internally. The next one came from an animal in Stronsay slaughtered as a butcher's animal, the carcase being detained only because it showed early localised peritonitis. Yet the nail I saw produced from the second stomach of the second case was indistinguishable from the one I had seen in Arran many years earlier. There seems to be a recognised critical length for nails or wires to do damage in that situation. The length most noted is two and a half to three inches. Shorter or longer they seem not to penetrate the stomach wall, or at least not nearly as often.

Although years earlier I had begun to assemble basic equipment to do a rumeotomy up to the time when I left Arran I had never done one. In fact I had never at any time seen one being done but it would not have been the first operation of which my first sight was at my own doing of it. After all, there must have been at least one occasion for each one of many operations which no one had ever seen done before because it never had been done before. I might have had a go at a rumenotomy, in some cases probably should have done so but never did. (Eventually I did manage to see one during my travels between leaving Arran and settling in Orkney.) The ticklish point is that if one tries non-surgical remedial measures which prove partly or wholly unsuccessful then by the time they are seen to have failed and because they have failed the operation may come too late because of the gross changes inside.

Another complaint, acetonaemia ketonaemai or whatever the newest name for it may be, did seem to occur fairly often but again seemed to be treated more often by the owner than by the vet and was of less importance in the beef herd than in the dairy herd.

There was, as I may have said earlier, no dairying in the North Isles apart from a little for internal consumption within the Isles. That is something which while it seems to the resident too obvious to be worth mention, may not be quite so apparent to the outsider who is not familiar with that region. It is a fact which I for one realised only slowly as nobody pointed it out to me. The reason for it I assumed to be that no one island produced enough milk to justify having a creamery of its own and the alternative of transporting the liquid milk into Kirkwall for processing was out of the question. Over and above that, the regime required for dairy farming is one which would probably not have fitted in at all well with the way of life of the North Isles folk.

Without a dairy industry or need of one the style of farming followed in those Isles was one which produced high grade beef on the hoof, good breeding heifers, and little or no egg production on a commercial scale although in past years it was large, and no doubt there were some lesser items unspecified.

Talking about breeding, many veterinarians and others believe there is some obscure but definite connection between iodine and fertility. In this context I refer in particular to the female bovine. I believe there may well be such a connection though I never found any evidence in direct support of that belief. As a barren beef heifer seemed to be about the same marked value as an in-calf heifer of the same size and quality I never seemed to be treating for infertility and was never able to judge for myself how much or how little it occurred but it did not seem to be a problem if it occurred at all. As to whether that was due in any measure to a possibly relatively high iodine content in the herbage of those islands, I had and have still no idea.

There was a noticeable absence of other diseases such as redwater, blackquarter or other colourful diseases all well recognised clinical conditions mentioned here partly for fear the reader should find any subsequent mention too ridiculous to consider. Any one of them might individually amount to very little but jointly they could do much to give the day book a full and prosperous look.

Any vet yearning for a bit of horse practice could have died of a broken heart in the North Isles for all he would have got of it there. There was a time, so I am told, when two of the biggest farms in Stronsay were run as one and with a common march they made a pretty impressive stretch of territory, all good arable land. Of those two places one itself could field eleven pairs of horse and still leave one horse in reserve. That number of head may have been between the two places but as the two between them made up more than a square mile of arable it looks rather as if the eleven pairs were the complement for one place only. That was in the days between the wars and most likely before the 1914 war too.

Whenever it was, to have seen all eleven pairs or even two thirds or half of them working in pairs or threes ploughing on a fine spring morning all within view of each other must have been a sight most people would not readily forget. There is one square field of forty acres which itself could have taken several of the teams; but that was all a long time ago. By the time I got there in 1956 I doubt very much if there were a dozen horses, probably not more than half a dozen to be found in the whole island. The cattle population on the other hand was something over 3,000 a figure reached most likely only after the clearing out or simply the running down of the horse population.

So far as I can remember now, and I do not think I am forgetting any – they were too few to forget – my equine cases in seven years totalled two picked-up nails which recovered and one gastric impaction in a two- or three year-old gelding which did not recover.

One of those cases of picked up nail I remember very well. A lively, very lively, mare about five or six years old she was. Her owner had tried with or without the blacksmith's aid to relieve the foot himself. After being briskly ejected from the stall two or three times, the foot being a hind one, he gave up and came to me for help: I heard his story, saw what we were facing, got him to assemble a few men at a set time and duly arrived at his place with my casting tackle and everything else required. We marched her well out from the farmyard and into a field to a clear dry spot. There I gave her a hearty dose of chloral per jugular vein to which process she did not raise any noticeable objection. While she was standing wondering if it was really the field which was heaving or herself who was swaying as she had never done since the first time she took her feet as a foal, we had the tackle on her; she was pulled down and well tied. In a way it seemed almost unfair to her because she never did have a chance to show what she could do like sending young men flying through the air with the greatest of ease.

The blacksmith had the shoe off in a very short time. I luckily found the spot easily, dug my wee hole in it against all the rules which say that the sole shall be levelled all around the puncture before opening the foot, and that was pretty much that. We got the discharge we expected, the foot got a dressing on it with a pad, the shoe back in place and two strips of hoop iron to hold the dressing in place. She got up and walked back to the farmyard a lot better than she had walked away from it. An eminently satisfactory case to all concerned: the owner, the smith, myself and presumably the mare. Afternoon tea among other things was served in the farmhouse kitchen.

The colic case, the impacted stomach in the young horse, was a very different story. The message was given to me by a neighbour of the owner. When I got to the patient and saw the external symptoms, got the recent history and noted the absence of any specific symptom on rectal examination, the diagnosis was not difficult to form; the prognosis not good to give.

All too clearly I remembered a case I had seen years before in Arran in the absence of my colleague. No doubt there had been others I had seen in other parts of the country but that was the only one on which I had a chance to do a post mortem. At the p.m., when I reached as far as the pylorus, i.e. the outlet of the stomach, I saw that that unfortunate horse must have ailed for some days before he was noticed and had anyone called to him.

For those folk not too well acquainted or not acquainted at all with the alimentary tract of the horse it should be explained here that the duodenum at that end of it which is next to the stomach has in it a sort of bend, something like the old fashioned s-bend below the kitchen sink. This is a feature which can be unfortunate for the horse because pressure on that bond, by gas or liquid or solid, has the effect of sealing the outlet of the stomach by a valve-like action, the same as that which a bag of sand left open at one end and stood on that end will not empty so long as that part of the wall of the bag is held pressed against the floor by the weight of the contents. At the other end of the stomach because the gullet joins it at a very oblique angle by going in a direction which is continued for some distance within the stomach wall, this same effect of closure by pressure from within is obtained at the entrance to the stomach. This feature also provides the reason why a horse cannot 'bring up' anything it has swallowed. It simply cannot vomit.

At that p.m. I found on reaching the parts involved that the food was in parts black, indicating that it had been there for a considerable time though there was no knowing how long. Such was the state of affairs, differing only in degree if at all which I suspected existed this time inside the young horse.

There seemed to be nothing to do save to see if anything could be gained by passing the stomach tube. I did that and got little in return. There might in some cases have been a small quantity of gas or something or other, not in this case. I pumped in a pint or so of the pailful of stuff I had prepared then I disconnected the tube from the pump. Some of the mixture shot back out of the tube thus showing pressure at the other end. The case looked now very unpromising, a very bad prognosis.

I had not got, in fact have never possessed, such a thing as a double stomach tube. To attempt to empty or even partially clear the stomach using the single tube was always in my experience quite futile. It always blocked shortly after return flow began no matter how many or how few inches of it had been introduced into the stomach i.e. beyond the oesophageal sphincter so a little more would then be pumped in; the return flow would back again and so on for as long as the process continued or until rupture of the stomach occurred.

Maybe I left too much fluid in that stomach. Maybe it was going to rupture anyway no matter what I did. That at any rate was what happened. I saw the horse and treated him in the late morning. By that evening he was dead. Lacking a double stomach tube which I suppose was not to be found anywhere north of the Pentland Firth and maybe not for a long way south of it either, I could not think of anything which was going to save that young horse. By that consideration then it could be argued that the sooner he finished with it the better.

These then were my main experiences with the surviving members of the horse race in Stronsay. With another representative of the same race and the same sort of trouble being again a colic but not a stomach case and on a different island I had a much happier outcome but I shall arrive at him later.

If twenty-three horses on one farm seem a lot of horses I have still a story to cap that one, a story related to me by the owner himself one day as we sat together in the saloon of the ship going between Westray and Stronsay. I am as sure as I can be that the good man who certainly had a very big farm would not have minded my retailing his delightful anecdote partly in my own words, partly in his.

Whether the story relates to the period of the war years or to some other period I am not sure; whatever period it was, my friend like all other farmers had to make extraordinarily detailed returns of all manner of information about his farm: number of cattle and numbers in each category of them; similar figures for sheep, pigs, horses etc. For horses in this case the number given was thirty-seven. The form all completed was then returned to the office of issue.

In due course back came a query. Would the owner please check the number of horses shown in the returns as thirty-seven to make sure a mistake had not been made?

'So I sat doon and I counted them all up wance again and sure enough I found I had made a mistake. Oh aye, they were right enough wi' their query, right enough to ask aboot that. It wisna' thirty-seven horses I had, it was thirty-eight.' And at that point the old man chuckled with just as much pleasure, I imagine, as if the story had newly come to light. When I asked him how in the world did he come to have so many horses about him he explained in whatever phrases he used that some of them would be mares in foal or that had foals with them, some would be young horses not broken in, and some would be on other places perhaps loaned to other people. And I would venture a guess that he got a lot of fun in replying in terms of his choice to the party who had innocently raised the query.

I mentioned another colic case on another island. It was on Sanday. Word came in to me one morning on Stronsay that a certain horse the only one his owner had and in almost daily use had colic. My chances of hiring a motor boat for my own use were not too good as the weather looked a trifle uncertain. But there was a party of some of the more prominent citizens of some of the other isles going to Westray for the day on public business and I could get with them as far as the south end of Sanday, get to my case, deal with it and be back at the same place on the shore to join the boat on its return trip to Stronsay. So equipped with 'the wee black bag', stomach tube and pump I duly join the boat at Stronsay pier, disembark on to a shingly beach at the south end of Sanday and start walking. I have about a mile of rough walking to get to the nearest farm but my case is at the other end of the island. I am perhaps halfway to the farm or rather a group of three separate holdings which were originally one farm when I see a tractor approaching. This is a man and a tractor out simply and solely to give me a lift as far as the road where there is a car and a driver waiting for me.

I do not know who arranged for the tractor to come out nor whose it was, but I do know I saw in that action an example of helpful cooperation if ever there was one. And the case was in no way connected with the tractor owner or the driver. I remembered at that time having some time earlier in that year or a previous one managed to do some good to a single rather severe case of husk on one of the three holdings and speculated that possibly the action with the tractor was that particular owner's way of saying 'thank you'. It might have been that or might not.

I made reasonably good speed to my case, diverging from the route only to replenish the body fluids against losses suffered much earlier in the journey and was comparatively happy to find that my patient, so far as I could discover about him, appeared to be suffering from nothing worse than impaction of the pelvis flexure of the great colon. I mixed my usual mysterious potion, about two to three gallons of it as much for irrigation as for purgation, and got the stomach tube into position without difficulty or objection from the horse. He was a useful fairly heavy vanner and was really his owner's motor car.

Neither the owner nor the driver had ever, I am fairly sure, seen a stomach tube being passed before; possibly had never known until then that there was such a thing for horses and I somehow did not offer any comment nor explanation of any kind. They never uttered a word from the time the tube was started on its progress into the horse until the last of the pailful of mixture was inside him. Neither did I catch a glimpse of their faces except once when I got a two second glimpse of the owner's which was frozen immobile but I could feel their eyes on me. I could almost feel their astonishment.

The horse in fact showed the least interest of any of us and stood apparently bored as if getting pumped into him two or three gallons of warm watery mixture was the most every day occurrence to be expected by any horse at any time. When he was led out on a halter, apart from a slight crouch or two indicating a twinge of abdominal pain, he seemed more interested in grass than in anything else. I told the owner to allow water, as much as the horse wanted, and that he probably would not look at any food other than grass for a day or two but should come all right without complications. And he did. I did not hear from the owner immediately afterwards but saw the horse at his old job again some time after that.

I made my way by car and on foot back to the point of embarkation, lay down on the stones on the beach head and had a slightly chilly nap while I waited for the motor boat and its passengers to reappear. Embarkation was, so far as I remember, probably between half past three and four o clock with arrival home possibly about half past four.

My journey had been necessary and useful but there was no escaping the fact that it had taken me from some time around half past eight a.m. until some time about half past four p.m. to do one case. Such a case might be, as on this occasion, a satisfying sort of job, one for which I could charge the man probably about £2 but clearly by that reckoning there was no fortune, nor even fair living, to be made that way.

Such was the outcome of one of those very rare cases in which I had cause to use the stomach tube. Seldom and all as that might be it was still required oftener than most of the other instruments and tackle of various sorts which I had brought from my former small practice down in south-west Scotland. There was, for instance, the cattle probing, a large and somewhat expensive instrument used for clearing the gullet of a beast which had choked on a potato or a piece of turnip or other object. In ten years in Arran it was used but seldom. In seven years in Orkney amid ten times the number of cattle I handled in Arran it was never required or if so certainly never within my knowledge.

I used to make the occasional casual survey of all the stuff I had accumulated in the rather large instrument cupboard I had had specially made for me. It stood in the middle of the one plain wall of the new dispensary I had had specially built in the garden of my house in Stronsay. There it stood with its contents which were made up of most of the heavier items such as sterilizers, trays, kidney dishes, equine chloroform muzzle, stomach pump and tubes, docking machine (docking was legal at that time though never popular with me), various other items such those for restraint of bulls, etc. There was heavy casting tackle for horses, plain rope and rope hobbles for casting cattle. There was other equipment like suture material, more highly refined medical preparations small in bulk such as almost inevitably accumulate over the years in the course of small animal work however little of it there might be.

That was what I saw in the first year when I was still of the opinion that once I was thoroughly settled into a routine if I could devise one and people became more aware of what could be done there would be more use for all my equipment. That was all during my first year and a half while my enthusiasm still burned brightly if with gradually dwindling flame. Gradually, either consciously or subconsciously, perhaps in both ways, I began to feel I suppose rather like a builder who had assembled his materials on a popularly approved site, built a general purpose building on it then found that very few people ever seemed to wish to use it.

Of those jobs for which people did call on my services two of the commonest, neither of them so very common at that, were the trimming of a bull's feet and right at the other end of the range between force and fineness of touch removing a chaff sometimes called an oat flyte from an eye. The first required prolonged vigorous yet fairly precise action, the second called more for the talents of a painter of miniatures or someone with a touch no less delicate.

Why the majority of patients coming up for hoof trimming should be bulls would be, I think, because most times when all other cattle would be outside walking as they grazed and causing normal wear on their hooves (for which the technical anatomical term is 'claws'), poor old bull, unlucky chap, who was in fact generally older when he required such treatment got kept in. So he did not get the horn of his claws worn down and gradually became not exactly lame, for he walked evenly, but short in his step walking in a way sometimes described as 'going short'. The next stage after that would be that he spent more and more time recumbent and eventually would hardly be willing to stand at all.

I occasionally had to attend a cow which for one reason or another had got one or more of its feet overgrown but the majority of my patients were bulls and really all of them so far as I remember were the most docile of creatures to handle. One reason for that was that the acute discomfort of their feet made them little inclined for movement. Anther reason was that in that practice anyway they were generally either Aberdeen Angus or Hereford, the two breeds which are, in my experience anyway, the most 'civilized' of any in this country. Had they been, for instance, Galloways I don't say I would not have been willing to trim them (assuming that we ever got the animal cast) but would have wanted a tree handy that I could climb at speed directly they were released or possibly some time before that.

For hoof trimming I needed a length of rope, rope hobbles and three instruments. Using the long rope to cast animal by Heuff's method so one simply attached one end to the top of the halter on a polled animal or if there were any horses tied the rope round them, took a loop round the base of the neck, another round the body just behind the elbows and a third loop just in front of the pelvis and the stifle joint. All loops were then tightened, a few pulls given here and there, tension maintained on the tail end of the long rope and the beast then quietly sank to the ground in most cases without any struggle. Any explanation of this minor phenomenon has thus far not come my way. Mention of 'pressure on nerve centres' such as was mentioned to us at college might be a lot more explanatory if it also mentioned the location of these centres and how in any case they could affect control of the standing posture in the bovine. Having thus got the animal cast, one then applied the rope hobbles and got on with the job.

Even the biggest bulls made practically no demur at this procedure and when I came to a bull I had to do for a second time I swear he took one look at the outfit, knew what was coming and practically lay down himself when the rope was put on him. I liked to think afterwards that he knew me and remembered me as an excellent chiropodist who should be given every encouragement. The actual cutting and rasping, first finding the best positions for the foot, for the operator could be warm work and did in fact cost me many a drop of sweat.

The other common complaint mentioned, an oat flyte in an eye, again arose from defective management but in a very different manner. Many of the farms had in their byres overhead racks for feeding straw or hay to their cattle and those racks were a prolific source of oat flytes which landed in the eyes of the cattle, most likely the only source or virtually so.

Once in the eye the curvature of the oat flyte exactly matched that of the eyeball and no amount of blinking or watering could dislodge it. It must in that situation have caused unremitting pain. Some of them as I knew by the changes they had caused must have been in the eye for days, quite possibly weeks, before any attention was drawn to them. There must have been many more of which I never heard nor saw.

Perhaps the hatching was all past and the youngsters were all very efficiently hiding themselves. Maybe the adults put on a show of indignation every time a stranger came near them just as a matter of principle not '*pour encourager les autres*' but quite the reverse. I found it all very interesting and was glad to escape without any wounding or depilation.

What sounds like a re-test in May, if in fact it happened then, could have been followed up by the annual herd tests for the island in March of the following year. I know beyond any doubt I did one annual renewal test in March because the test reached completion but the weather still did not improve, not enough to satisfy the ferry men. First one day which I thought was quite usable went past, then another. At last I could wait no longer and got on the radio telephone to the Divisional officer Kirkwall.

I had evolved a plan of my own in which by hiring a fishing boat which I knew was available I could get home to Stronsay on the Saturday of that week. To the plaintive query from that party as to what was all the hurry to get home, I explained, rather unnecessarily I thought, that I was due to get married in St. Magnus Cathedral, Kirkwall the following Tuesday.

I thought my correspondent was unnecessarily querulous because he himself had accepted an invitation to the wedding. There was always the possibility, of course, that as a married and family man himself he wished to present or appear to present a somewhat misogamistic front to a callow young bridegroom still in his forties. I don't know about that but I had to get home. The fishing boat was duly provided; I got home got to my wedding on time and so did the DO. The wedding and small reception passed off in the usual way as did the honeymoon which was 'doon sooth'. It had to be brief because I already sent out postcards for a round of tests in Stronsay the following week. Time in weeks was becoming none too plentiful.

I believe it could have been during that particular visit to North Ronaldsay or if not that one some other one early in the year that I was able to comply with a request from an English university The North Ronaldsay sheep are, as many people know, a special breed or at the very least a highly specialised variety. They are small, rather like the Soay sheep, and I should think noted more for their mutton than for their wool. I freely admit I know absolutely nothing about wool but those fleeces seemed to me to be really nothing in particular though I could be quite wrong about that. The above request which I shall explain later was in connection with these sheep. Right round the island following the beach head all the way is the famous wall of which more later and what the sheep see of that wall is almost exclusively the outer face of it. Outside the wall of the beach head or the shore they are and there they remain, season in season out. The only exceptions made are at those combinations of the weather, the tide and the positions of the sheep themselves which might place them in danger of drowning that and bringing the in-lamb ewes on to the grass to flush them a bit shortly before lambing. Apart from that all sheep are on a straight diet of seaweed of whatever species may occur there, plus the few morsels of grass they may find here and there close to the wall.

The lambs are rather quaint looking little creatures which somehow reminded me strongly of a small old fashioned type of fox terrier in their general conformation and the appearance of their coats. They seemed even more nimble than the lambs of other and mostly bigger breeds. Presumably because of the constant diet of seaweed the mutton from the sheep had a flavour which seemed to me quite different from the ordinary and quite like venison from the Arran Hills but with more fat in it than is generally found in venison. Deer in Arran or at least in the northern half of it are very commonly seen at night crossing the road on their way back from the shore where they have been presumably to feed on seaweed. Such visits to the shore are by no means confined to night time so that taking them all together it seems likely that large quantities of seaweed are eaten by them. How much effect this may have on the flavour of the venison is something I would not care to guess.

My recollections of that mutton is that along with boiled potatoes which were themselves probably grown in soil liberally fertilised with seaweed every year (you know perfectly well I do not mean that anybody grew boiled potatoes), the two together could appeal even to a poorly discerning palate and stimulate a poor appetite like mine. That was one place where one might taste and enjoy real mutton and real potatoes.

Whether a few weeks before that visit or at some other time which is not remembered and does not matter anyway, I received a letter from one department of the University of Bristol asking me could I provide to them a few blood samples from the North Ronaldsay sheep in containers which the Department would provide. They thought about ten samples would be suffice. In the event they asked for five of which I managed to provide three but those three I did get good and sterile. I was later told by the people concerned in that department that three samples were enough for the purposes anyway.

The arrival of the letter was fortunate in its timing because had it been a fortnight later I would by then have left North Ronladsay and would not have received any mail there before leaving it. Having once left it after the annual herd tests there might have been as much as a year go by before I had sufficient cause to visit again.

In due course I took the letter and sterile containers with me to North Ronaldsay, showed them to one or two of the flock owners there and got instant cooperation from them. It seemed to be no trouble at all to them to take in a few sheep from the shore to a grassy spot behind the wall and out of the wind. I got my blood samples and got them on their way the very next day. As things turned out had the samples not left the island when they did they would have been held up for about another fortnight after that.

A good many more weeks went past without word to me about the blood samples. Eventually I learned on inquiry that they did not reveal any significant differences from any other ordinary samples of sheep's blood. That was what I was told and have no reason to doubt it. Next time I was in North Ronaldsay I told the men who had helped me to get the samples as much as I knew about of their sheep and showed them what little the letter said.

Probably the most interesting feature of all about North Ronaldsay is the wall. Very likely any native of the island could tell the inquirer all that he or she might be commonly expected to ask about it. Some of the questions might be to ask what would be the length of the wall when was it first put there; was it all built in a continuous operation or was it put up in bits and pieces over a long period and the bits and pieces gradually joined up one with another; or what exactly did take place? Has there been a wall of some kind round the island since a time before records began and if so what does that make its minimum age? Is there some kind of system of labour for maintaining it and were the stones used for building it taken from the land or from the shore or, as seems more likely, some from both sources?

All these questions came crowding into my mind as I looked at the wall and the more I considered it the more remarkable it seemed. It is about three and a half miles from end to end, the southern tip of it incidentally being called Strom Ness. Like the other example of that name at the other side of Orkney, Stromness spelt as one word, both seem to be the name of headlands round which run ocean tides in full force. 'Strom' here seems to have the same meaning as in 'maelstrom', a stream. Speaking of placenames, about five miles SSE of Strom Ness in North Ronaldsay is a small headland, Start Point, exactly the same name as the other one in Devon which suggests that the word 'Start' here had another meaning. The Sanday one has a lighthouse on it and can be reached on foot at low tide. The shore near it is literally white with millions of sea shells in all stages of disintegration. Perhaps one day I shall see the other Start Point for comparison with the Sanday one. The latter is known locally mostly as 'The Start'.

North Ronaldsay is so curved and so indented with little bays that the maximum width might be debatable but the perimeter wall seems according to a rough estimate taken from a map to be about twelve miles long, give or take a mile or so for which all the little ins and outs might easily account.

At first sight it might seem to be real tough luck on the sheep that they are kept almost entirely outside the wall but the tough luck may be more apparent than real. If the sheep were on the inside of the wall there would always be some part of it or other which would give the shelter no matter from which direction the wind and the rain came. It follows the that sheep outside such a wall would similarly always have some part or parts of it which they could have between them and the wind, assuming of course that the tide always allowed them to reach those parts of the wall which would shelter them. But I have no doubt the flock owners know all the moves dictated by these and other considerations and act accordingly.

I know of no other island large or small anywhere which has a wall of any kind going completely round it or round any substantial part of it. And I know of no other wall which having got itself a complete perimeter wall of dry stone dyking uses it as a vital component in the management of its sheep in such a way that almost their entire nourishment is not merely perpetually renewed but also perpetually washed by the sea and all at no cost. In those two or three respects North Ronaldsay is surely unique, certainly unique in my own limited experience of islands wall and sheep.

CHAPTER 28

This story so far has kept fairly well to chronological order until it comes to my time in Orkney. After a few years in the North Isles, while very little of what took place has been forgotten the exact order of events was not necessarily the order in which they are related here.

That being the case, I am not at all sure when it was that I first began to feel the total burden of all the work, all the responsibility and of course fallibility which increased as the work became too heavy. The factors operating against satisfactory performance of the work took a dozen different forms acting in as many different ways.

To take but one situation: I might have got my postcards all delivered; I might rise fresh on the appointed morning and be ready for the round of test I had arranged. The telephone rings generally before or during breakfast thereby ensuring that that particular meal is one of the lightest. I may have to alter my timetable slightly or I may not. In either case my movements are just that little bit more hasty all through. Stomach muscles, back muscles or whatever group happen to be most susceptible to stress show response.

Again I might be, as I was on one occasion, right in the middle of a fair sized herd test, about 130, when there came an urgent call to go to another farm about four or five miles away to the bull. I was not told more than that. The owner had discovered with rather a shock that in the interval since the bull had last been let out he had either been chained too tightly on his return to his stall or his neck had grown considerably fatter or both. Whatever the cause or causes, his chain was embedded and overgrown with granulation tissue on the crest of his neck.

The owner, by no means an excitable man, was quite perturbed and spoke about cutting down the whole trevice, a wooden one to which the chain was attached. I did not see that that was going to help very much. I knew that the bull had been quiet in the past when I had him for hoof trimming, despite the discomfort caused to him on that job, and I decided to take a small risk.

He was standing in an end stall as bulls very often are if they are tied at all. I went quietly up between him and the wall, gently caught the two ends of the chain in my hands, unhooked it and let the free end fall.

No sooner did he hear the chain fall than he gave one toss of his head, yanked the chain clear of his neck, part turned, part backed out of his stall and was standing on the byre walk all in about three seconds and never so much as brushed against any part of me. That was remarkable because he was a big beast with little space for movement. He might easily have bumped my head with his and he would never have noticed the difference. Come to think of it, I might not have noticed a lot after that either but for quite a different reason. Or he might have squashed me flat against the wall whereas instead of doing either of these things he moved with the agility and precision of a ballet dancer.

After that all that remained was to give the owner some dry dressing to sprinkle or blow on to the neck and get back to my test but not before the owner had ensured that I did not leave without adequate refreshment, something which was not necessary but none the less welcome.

In all my time I had seen only two other cases of a chain embedded in a neck. None of the three seemed to turn out to be as bad as it looked at first sight.

By the time I resumed the test at the point where I had stopped one hour had passed. The afternoon job had become an evening finish. Luckily it was also the finish of that day's work.

The day might find me at a herd which from my point of view was seriously undermanned if the cattle were fractious in having only one man, the owner or his representative, to help me. Worse than that, was to have no man at all because the owner had gone to work somewhere leaving his wife in charge. Usually about the first thing the wife hastened to tell me was that she never took anything to do with the cattle and knew very little about them. (But hadn't I heard all that sad story many a weary time before.) The final variation was that the owner was a woman who was also the only attendant the cattle ever saw. The consequence was that when any man came into the byre they were a little perturbed. When it was a man in a black rubber coat and boots the were more perturbed and when that man found his way up between them and started jabbing their necks, however gently, with small sharp needles, their behaviour merited a much stronger description. I always managed to do the job in cases of that kind but only with a disproportionate expenditure of effort and nervous energy.

Dear old back in fact began to feel the burden of existence more and more as the weeks and months went by. For this gradual worsening of its state I blamed three types of experience it received. The first was in the type of stance I adopted for tuberculin testing in which I crouched as in the manner of a boxer to keep my head out of reach of the bovine head, especially if it had horns. There was some mild pleasure in discovering that the cattle with which I had to work were nearly all Aberdeen Angus or crosses of that breed which meant that they were polled.

The second factor affecting the old lumbar area was that when I was in that crouching position with feet in line ahead astern to avoid having my toes trampled with the quick side step of a fore foot there would often be a quick sidewise lunge of a hind foot. That movement had the effect of giving me a hard sidewise bump on one hip, a movement which when endlessly repeated had its own disastrous effect on the small of my back.

The third factor was that while sitting or reclining in an easy chair should have given and did give some relief, sitting writing at a desk or a table did not.

Still bad back or no bad back I was able to work on and keep the test lists from going too far into arrears but then another physical ailment appeared. I got one set of toes, i.e. one foot, trodden upon really heavily, one full value nothing stinted tread. I expect I hopped about a bit and uttered a few fervent words not commonly heard at garden parties but I was able to carry on. Then the other lot of toes got the same treatment. At that I began to feel that things were stacking up against me just a little bit more than I could sustain. However a short rest spell with a little judicious working – after all I had treated lameness in other domestic animals often enough, hadn't I? – and I should be all right and able to go again. And so I was. Then the whole bloody thing happened all over again. First the five right toes got it then the five left toes just as before. I believe I am literally correct in describing the second treading as bloody there were traces of blood just where chilblains commonly appear.

If getting a sharp hoof edge with a quarter of a ton of bovine animal on it placed on top of a soft wellington boot and sliding off it was agonizing the first time it was doubly so the second time on two sets of toes not fully recovered from the first. After it happened to the second foot for the second time not only were the feet painful all the time but because of them and the lumbar ache I was fairly completely immobilized.

The weeks flitted past with during them several abortive attempts by me to make up some of the leeway in herd tests. The situation was worrying me and it was deteriorating. In addition to my several aches, as if sheer physical duress was not hazard enough, there were herds here and there which most vets who had tested them quite frankly feared. One such herd was on the island of Eday. Eday is about eight miles long and varies in width from two miles to half a mile across the middle at which point what with a small land loch to the west side of it and a stretch of tidal sand directly east of the loch the island is nearly cut in two.

To the north-east of it and two or three hundred yards from it is the Calf of Eday, a tiny island. The narrow sea passage between them called Calf Sound always seemed to me uncommonly like a section of a big river, an impression much strengthened by seeing the tide racing through it in either direction and by the water being made to seem darker because of the high ground on both sides of it. On the west side the land to the north ends in a headland called the Red Head, the redness being that of a high red sandstone cliff with thousands of seabirds on it. Opposite it on the east side is the Grey Head, the northern extremity of the Calf of Eday which at about half the height of the Red Head never seemed to have as much attention nor as many cameras directed towards it as were directed towards its neighbour. Those two heads, one at 200 feet, the other about 100 feet high towering over the steamer comparatively tiny between them always seemed to me as if they were a small section of some other country placed there.

To the west of Eday and lying between it and Westray is the small island of Fara, or as the local people pronounce it 'Fairey', separated from Westray to the north of it and Eday to the south of it by narrow sounds, the south one about half a mile wide, the north one Weatherness Souns, perhaps one third of a mile. If the tide runs fast through Calf Sound it must run a great deal faster and more turbulently through Weatherness Sound. That at any rate is what I can only suppose because truth to tell

I never once found the time to get close enough to it to see for myself though I was often near it as when working in the south end of Westray.

I remember once asking in Divisional office if the Calf of Eday was an attested calf, finding all the staff very hesitant in answer. General opinion seemed to be that it was not. Finally someone timidly suggested that as the Calf of Eday could not be cattle because Eday was not a cow perhaps it did not really matter whether the Calf was attested or not. This new thought was a great help to all of us and saved us from having to decide what to enter under the heading 'Breed' for the calf. A suggestion that as it had a grey head it might be described as a Hereford cross was sternly overruled because the Head or rather the head had to be white and it was not. Ruthlessly overruled also was the suggestion that because it had not a tail the breed could be entered as Manx even though it was not the Calf of Man. The discussion was becoming far too complicated and was summarily abandoned before it could reach international level, probably starting with the EEC.

So far as I am aware no one had ever raided this weighty question before then and I would like to be able to claim here that a profound and breeding silence descended upon the company but in fact nothing at all like that occurred.

I think I started out a little way back when talking of certain herds being frightening to tell about a certain herd in Eday; this was a biggish herd of over100 head which although there was plenty of good housing for it on the farm premises was largely allowed to manage itself out of doors. It never seemed to be in any way lacking in nourishment if the vigour displayed by the cattle at the herd test was any clue. I do not know what arrangements there were for breeding but there never seemed to be any lack of calves nor vigour in those calves and their elder brothers and sisters. There is of course a thing called hybrid vigour. We had that. Above that level of energy I wonder what is the description applicable to that explosive type of activity which so greatly enlivened the proceedings at the annual herd tests.

There was a large, modern, well built byre which held 80 to 90 head. This would be filled in the usual way with two beasts per stall which was how I found it when I went into it in the course of the test. I was then invited to proceed alone between the pairs and apply the test but I, having seen the cattle and having heard about them long before I ever saw them, knew a trick worth two of that. So when someone suggested to me, 'Go on up tae their hieds. They're quiet, they'll nivver titch ye,' I was indeed hopeful that they would not touch me. But also I said to one of the owners who had spoken to me that if the cattle were all that quiet it should be no trouble to him to go up to their heads just to steady them and to hold the chains out of my way.

He certainly was able to hold the chains out of the way and the heads where held steady but only with a stout rope from each one the rope being led over the trevice through the slide ring in the adjacent stall and pulled tight; that way I did not get a single kick nor a knock from a horn yet we got round the whole byre with surprising ease and in reasonable time.

But it must be admitted in fairness to the herd that wild and all as they were not merely by reputation but in fact, after a few herd tests and particularly on the second day round each one, even the most fiery of the cattle, the most inveterately belligerent old cows, the senior matrons of the herd were less difficult to handle. There was one, however, not a bad looking beast she was at that, about seven years old which if she could not go over the top of the rail of the chute leading to the crush needed only the slightest weakness in the door of that structure or the merest split second lateness in closing it and she was out. Away. Gone like a black thunderbolt round the end of the house and up to the hill. Once free there was no hope of bringing her back again without bringing them all back and we could not do that for lack of time among other reasons. Fortunately I had got a fleeting touch of her neck skin before she jerked open both throttles and took off. We got her identity by a process of elimination.

There was a story, though which of the Eday herds it concerned I cannot now say, that a number of cattle were put on to the island of Fara and left to fend for themselves for rather a long time. Fara was at one time inhabited but had been evacuated long before those cattle were put there. Whatever way things went with them there seemed to be occasion for certain officials concerned with animal health and welfare to take some action in respect of the cattle, a job which was going to be best accomplished with rifles or long ropes, or so the officials thought.

According to the story which is probably not merely heavily embroidered but completely untrue the marksmanship was not good. Those animals took a strongly unfavourable view of things in general, the marksmen in particular, and the hunters became the hunted. Their salvation lay in the deserted buildings on the island. These the marksmen reached and in them gained height with remarkable celerity.

Whether they jumped for the joists or galloped up old staircases or got on top of hay racks or high walls and whether they completed their work from those points or not, I do not know. Nor could I say as to that when I do not even know if there is any truth in the story at all. But this I do venture to say: that if it is not a true story it might easily have been one. Animals of certain breeds in situations of that kind where, as in this case, the younger ones may have been totally unacquainted with man, are as likely as not to resent his presence, especially if he starts making them targets for rotten marksmanship with a rifle.

None of the herds one day ever produced anything like that in my time there, though there were two or three animals in that particular herd which showed from the very start that they wanted nothing to do with anybody and would not stand for anything they could repulse. One animal in particular I remember, not a bull nor a female, either of which might have been seen as being too much motivated by its own sex hormones, but a bullock. He may not have been wholly clear of the male hormone but at any rate he stood in the middle of the courtyard, scraped up dirt occasionally with his forefoot and bellowed defiance at the human beings around him. They were not going to clutter him with cattle crushes nor ropes nor any other lumber of that kind. He had other ideas and the human animals had best take note of that.

I repeatedly advised the animals not to get brave with him and they all seemed readily disposed to take my advice. But In the end when he had literally had time to cool down and did cool very rapidly by standing alone in a cold wind he came quietly enough, was handled in the crush and let out to the hill.

With herds such as that one which took a disproportionate length of time to test plus the ache in the forearms which I suppose was a type of writer's cramp and two twice trodden feet I was far behind with my timetable for the work. My wife, in an effort to reduce further risk to my feet, bought in my absence and without consulting me a pair of Wellingtons with steel toecaps guaranteed to resist up to half a ton weight. These would have defied any single bovine hoof unless the animal had got the edge of its hoof behind the edge of the steel toecap which might have been very unpleasant for me. But in any case they were three and a half pounds in weight each and so loose fitting as to be liable to be left behind by my feet especially in very sticky ground. Reluctantly, perhaps foolishly, I decided that they were not the answer. Maybe if I had had them before the injuries to my feet who knows what protection they might have given me for the rest of the work. But there it was, almost like the hand of fate. The way things turned out I got more injuries in two months than I had received in the preceding ten years just when I could least afford to be off work and the very year after cancelling a long held insurance policy against injuries which had never happened. 'That' as some folk might say 'is life'.

CHAPTER 29

Though so far to the north of the rest of the country we in Orkney got winter weather much less severe than might have been expected and certainly much less so than the weather in many parts far to the south of us. Perhaps not too many people realise if they ever think about it at all that latitude 59 deg. North passes south of the North Isles and just misses Kirkwall. Latitude 60 deg. North which cuts the southern end of Shetland just touches the southern tip of Greenland. Yet we get surprisingly little snow. In the eight and a half winters I spent between the Mainland and the North Isles I could recall only three occasions on which my progress was noticeably impeded by snow and though I cannot remember when each one occurred it seems likely that two of them were part of the same snowy spell.

One of them at any rate was on Papa Westray. During one week in that January I pedalled short distances for access to some of the places on some of the days and for the rest plunged through soft snow of varying depths. One of the furthest away places on the island was also the highest and I was somewhat astonished to find while I was struggling towards it as my starting point one morning a well grown lamb jumping through the snow heading towards its mother. (This was in January.) I had gone through an opening in a dry stone dyke and there they were, the two of them, on the upper and windward side of the dyke at that, the lamb big and in very good heart. I did not pause to look at the ewe because for her to be able to feed a lamb like that she must have been fairly well fleshed. What either of them got to eat was more than I could see. Perhaps there was some hand feeding being done.

That round would have been done, I think, on a Saturday. I got through all the herds I had to see that morning without being given cause to hesitate at any point otherwise I would never have got through in time to get as far as I got that day. My third round being thus completed, clear as were the previous two, and the island therefore clear for another year, there arose a suddenly developed race between me and the clock for connection with the ship. Not that the clock was trying to get aboard. I was.

She was sailing that afternoon, it must have been a Saturday, at the same little bay from which I had first boarded her at the end of my first visit to Papa Westray but this time without any of the accompaniments and diversions of the first time. The ship was waiting and the small boat had only just pushed off from the beach when the farmer's car conveying me came charging down the field and pulled up on the beach head. We both ran down to the boat, the farmer being far the stronger obligingly carrying my travelling case and getting it aboard the small boat. We had to do very little wading, hardly more than ankle depth, and in any case we were wearing wellingtons.

My landlady had assured me with unremitting assiduity from the moment I got back to the house that I would not make the connection with the steamer. It was therefore with the greatest satisfaction that I climbed into that dinghy and mentally cocked a king size snook at the gloomy prognostications and the scene on which I would not now be compelled to spend a lot of further and useless time unless I could hire a motorboat to take me across to Westray. With any half decent sort of luck I would from then be clear of Papa Westray for another year. To arrive in Westray late on a winter Saturday leaving behind me or in a sense taking with me a 'clear' Papa Westray was cause enough for mild elation and a very mild celebration. Once I had got myself comfortably installed as of yore in the hotel in Westray I duly observed the occasion in the true spirit of the evening within the meaning of the act and the true spirit of the evening entered into me. There was more work and more snow ahead as I well knew, but for the moment anyway I was making the most of my Saturday evening. I reckoned I had earned it. But before I settled down I had to get out the postcards arranging the next week's work. Notifying the owners was done by posting my postcards at the nearby post office to go out with the newly arrived mail. Resident in the island as I then was and with the use of the internal mail services the rest of the arranging would follow on as before. What arrangement I made about use of a car is now quite forgotten. I must have had my own shipped out from Stronsay.

The work did follow on. The only difference so far as I can recall was that I postcarded one or two places which in the event because of the snowfall I was unable to visit. Another black mark against me, I have no doubt. I do not know. I have no means of knowing but I suspect that when I balked at plunging through snow for some indefinite distance to start a biggish herd test which I might not be able to reach for a second visit to complete the test I would be deemed to be at fault and would be the subject of a complaint. There was at least one herd which I had programmed to start that did not start as planned and because of snow could not possibly have reached for second visit and readings if I had been so bold as to start it. By thus failing to render a test and give a verdict on it if I had started it I would have set back the date of its performance by at least two months.

That sort of thing might have been no great harm at any time in the months January, February and March or earlier. Between March and May it could be very inconvenient. The great rule seemed to be that unless the veterinary inspector could be reasonably sure of completing a test in the usual way he had better not start it.

There was only one time in Westray when although the weather had nothing to do with it I thought I was not going to be able to finish the job.

There we were in this big new byre containing 80 to 90 head which was the whole herd. It was a good byre, a little bit cold perhaps and with some echo in it but otherwise all right. Now I do not know whether it was on account of the cold, whether it was an inborn natural tendency in that herd of cattle or merely habit, but I would have been prepared to bet that at no time during my visit within that byre were fewer than five per cent of those animals bellowing at whatever volume they could produce. The men in charge seemed not to notice it at all while I in contrast seemed unable to take proper note of anything else. For the first eight or ten pairs I measured the skins, silently memorised my readings and booked them. In between pairs I replied in some manner to whatever I thought had been said to me. But somewhere about a quarter of the way through I had to break off, go outside and sit down. After a few minutes of quietness and easy breathing I was able to resume and finish the job.

It so happens that a headache from any cause whatever is something virtually unknown to me but the sheer dazing effect of that incessant torrent of noise was something of which a brief experience was worth any amount of description. How might have anyone felt with a headache and doing that job I do not attempt to imagine. Morning headaches are not entirely unknown among vets out stationed on work of one sort or another and while I cannot speak from experience I understand that on certain mornings the cranial cavity is temporarily occupied by a very small very temperamental blacksmith with big feet. Maybe I had nothing to talk about.

In the foregoing I have drawn some attention to a little mentioned but very real occupational hazard. People may think that because a vet in agricultural practice lives if not in deeply rural surroundings at least more in country than in town he is thereby automatically safe from the noise hazard. Not so. Even deeply rurally situated as on the outer isles he does sometimes find noise of a volume and character which outdoes any ordinary industrial process or processes combined. At the same time he is the recipient of some physical violence combined with a generous measure of smelly steamy atmosphere included as part of his programme, perhaps partly to help him to decide whether he is really settled on being a vet in agricultural practice or not.

As a matter of fact, in a majority of cases it seems he finds he is so set. Not only that but that the work is evoking in him a wonderful talent for fluency in modern languages that he never suspected he had. One likely result is that on being placed in the midst of a large number of cattle assembled for some purpose such as blood testing or tuberculin testing and finding himself being bumped, trodden upon, kicked, soiled and breathing warm humid smelly air he may find himself saying things like 'Dear me' and 'Oh my goodness' but he also uses a number of other and less usual expressions which come to him and which he never until then thought he knew. Many members of our profession are outstanding linguists though their talent is not so much in what they say as in the eloquence with which they say it.

Physical injury, noises and bad air are or were not the only physical hazards of the rural, in particular the island, vet. There is another one, namely cold, paralysing cold, in the form of wind, sometimes reinforced with rain if not with sea spray as well.

There was one morning when as by previous arrangement I was standing in the yard of a big farm ready to start the annual herd test. The cattle had all been gathered and either penned or stalled according to what they were. The first part of the job was to run about sixty of the young cattle through a crush where I had to stand and apply the test. And I did stand and apply it. I jabbed tuberculin into their necks for about half an hour more or less, then I got stuck.

The yard wherein the young cattle were assembled and presented for test was near the seashore not many yards from the high tide mark. There was a screaming onshore wind tearing in at me between two buildings of which the long walls ran at right angles to the sea shore. Between them was a perfect channel for the wind with or without rain or spray or both and in that channel I stood. Everyone was cold and getting colder because the weather and the season of the year did not allow of anything else. Latterly my hands, not so cold that they would not manipulate the syringes at all, will them as I might, using whatever warning devices were available. The entire test had to be abandoned as that site was the only one on which that part of the test could be done. There was no other sheltered enclosures for that purpose.

Another black mark for me, no doubt it was. The acquiring of that one, however, had the wry consolation that by the time I gave in I could not have cared what happened next to me to, the herd, to the owners, to the Ministry of Agriculture records, anybody, anything. The devil himself run off with them all and either keep them or return them as he might choose, dammit. This was a case for self preservation on my part, come what might.

But nobody should go off with the idea despite any impression I may have given here that winds of great strength were anything unusual in Orkney, far from it. I had not been long settled in Stronsay before I had evolved a new saying, a sort of local home made proverb: 'Orkney for wind but Arran for rain.' Not that either area could not put on a very respectable show in both departments. They could and they did but there was no doubt at all that Orkney had it for wind.

Before I ever reached Orkney I had read in the English press during my time in Wales of the two hurricanes that swept Orkney and many a story I heard about them after I got there.

There was one morning on the Mainland of Orkney before I had resumed practice. I was working at a farm well to the north of Finstown. On this farm the byre stood close to the sea, far enough above the high water mark but not many yards from it. The hurricane came on, did its worst and passed off again during the night. That was the first hurricane and it lasted from some time between midnight and 2.00 a.m. for most of the rest of that January night. The farmhouse was not damaged, the family and everybody else inside it were all right. In the dairy byre all the cows were quite all right. The only trouble was that there was no roof on the byre nor was there any sign of that roof about the place. With wind from the west of it and sea immediately to the east of it the entire roof slates, sarking couples, everything, had taken off, probably in one piece and was well on its way to Norway or Denmark before its absence was discovered.

On another place, this one fairly highly situated, where I had to call about some small matter, probably either a retest or a query the owner, who was a young man, told me how in the morning, this must have been during the second hurricane, we know because it started about 8.00 a.m., he waited for the wind to abate before he would cross the yard to feed his cattle. He waited and waited and latterly, seeing the wind force increasing rather than abating, he set out and managed but only just to cross the yard on his hands and knees, fodder the beasts and get back into the house.

There was a little place, again on fairly high ground, right at the south end of South Ronaldsay. To get there from Kirkwall one had to cross the three causeways, 'the Churchill barriers', as they were called, to get on to South Ronaldsay and then still had to drive a few miles south. The smallholder whom I was visiting showed me a spot where he had had three small corn stacks. One was in a slight hollow, perhaps six or eight feet lower than the other two, one on either side of the hollow, with not more than ten to twenty yards between any two of them.

What he found on inspection after the blast was that the corn stack in the hollow which was only a short recess not open at both ends had been neatly removed, leaving the ground behind it as if it had never been there. Those on either side of it on higher ground were hardly touched at all. That seemed to me to be one of the most striking examples of the freakish effects which those high velocity winds could produce.

Later on, a good few moments after that when I had been living in Stronsay for a time, I was told by a man who kept a relatively large number of poultry at the time of the hurricanes how he fared, first with the weather then with the governmental clerical attempts at compensating him for his heavy losses under the scheme which the government launched for the relief of those who had suffered any appreciable loss through storm damage.

His stock of poultry totalled not far off 2,000 head all told. The hurricane by removing his hens, hen houses, night arks and anything else that would take removing left him with a number of head which was but a small fraction of what he had owned the previous day. According to the man's story, the sum offered as total compensation to him was so niggardly, so absurdly and uselessly low, that it was declined with whatever politeness could be commanded at the time in the circumstances, probably not a great deal.

I did not hear of anywhere being driven before the wind hurricane and going over any cliff or cliffs. Perhaps there were no cattle out of doors on ground bearing that kind of hazard or maybe any cattle on such ground in such wind found sufficient shelter in the various sheltered spots they would know and were not inclined to drift before the wind. There was one such tale about Eday but whether it related to the hurricane or whether it even had a basis of truth I do not know.

CHAPTER 30

In the clerical work required in connection with the field work there was considerable if gradual elaboration. For such things as anti-abortion vaccinations and the Attested Herds Scheme there was a marked increase in the documentation required for each job we did. The systems in use before those changes were introduced seemed to me to be adequate and I for one never saw the need for elaboration nor any of the improvements it was presumably intended to effect. Of course it did create more work all round and probably created some new jobs.

Those jobs might have been totally unproductive as indeed they had every appearance of being; they might even have been counter productive by absorbing some of the working time of those people in 'the field' who did the real spadework. They were the ones who either produced something themselves or gave more or less arduous service to things produced or did both. By the time they had made their contribution to animal health or long before that if they were farmers, bred, reared the animals for their animal health to become the concern of anyone who what was strictly the minimum necessary.

However some people somewhere decide for some reasons unlikely to be good ones that more information such as more figures, no matter how repetitive, are desirable if not essential in themselves, beside helping to reduce the unemployment total. So those simple creatures in the field who imagine they are helping the nation along by producing something or giving a service in respect of some product despite what sometimes looks like sheer thinly concealed obstructionism by certain types of officialdom must jolly well pause and answer the man behind the desk. He is there, firmly planted behind his desk. He has a good job discovering all sorts of queries he can send out to people, all sorts of information he can ask of them and he does not intend to be shifted from his that desk except to a better one.

By those circumstances such as indicated above and earlier herein and by the consequences arising from them I was finding the going more and more difficult as time went on. The clerical duties considered by themselves were not too difficult though they could have been less so. The real headaches, the really disruptive attempts, I reckon came when one tried to apportion a selection of items from a sliding scale of fees according to rentals, a scale of mileage according to distances falling within certain specified brackets with very often the complication of Ministry work included. The Ministry was not at all concerned with rents of places visited but was concerned not to pay more than its strictly proper share of the joint mileages assuming that anybody ever knew what would be a proper share which nobody ever did. I myself never knew and was on the spot doing the work.

Although the Ministry work was what brought in the livelihood or at least the great bulk of it, practice i.e. doing clinical work as might be suddenly required by the stockowner, took priority if any question of priority should ever arise. This fact, as we have seen before, could and did lead to complications as in the case of a big strong heifer performing 'eversio uteri' before the day's work had begun. She has the vet called to her he reaches her and gets her fixed up before he does anything else thus leaving himself 'wabbit oot', i.e. quite tired before he has even started the day's work he had planned for himself.

Another time I was all set to go on a round of small herd tests and had got a fine spring morning for starting them too when the phone rang. Incidentally, if there was one time when I wanted less than at any other time to take a phone call it was on an occasion such as those few minutes just before I got away from the house. This time was from the owner of a sheep supposedly not lambing as she ought to have been doing. So I arrive at her, fortunately not very far off my way instead of at my first herd. I get my patient lambed and am about to make yet another vain attempt to make up lost time when the owner informs me with a light chuckle that, that was very good, a very good job I did, but it really was not the one for which he had called me.

I had already lost three quarters of an hour on his first sheep. By then I should have been heading for my second small herd. What was I to do? I longed to tell him something like 'Well bad luck for you and your next case too. You should have had her ready and presented her to me at the outset instead of as now not even got her caught. You cannot very well expect me to keep several other owners waiting for more than an hour past their times while you collect all the cases you want me to see, can you?'

That or something like it was what he deserved to be told and what he should have been told. To that I might have added, 'And it looks to me like though you have deliberately delayed me for reasons best known to yourself.' Yes, now long afterwards how easy it is to be with hindsight.

But remember, practice takes priority. Had I ignored his second sheep at the time by postponing it until I had some free time such as my dinner hour he would have felt he had grounds there for complaint to Divisional Office and might well have done so or else deemed himself mightily magnanimous if he did not.

Divisional Office, which seemed to be the recipient of all complaints about me would have heard only the client's side of it. Only once, this once being at a time when there was a question of four miles of Ministry business charged by me but not run in my own car, was the name of the informant even hinted at and even at that the actual name was avoided like unstable explosive. Apart from that the most confidential information imparted to me from Divisional Office or some other source at or above that level was that there had been 'numerous complaints' about me.

On the occasion above mentioned I would imagine that while the owner of the sheep did not complain the owners of the herds that were kept waiting probably did. I am not assured on that point but it is a reasonable assumption. I do know that at least one of them had turned his cattle out before I got to him and covered his displeasure more by his taciturn manner than by any speaking he did which was very little. My position seemed to be that whichever way I faced I was going to be shot. Events on that particular morning seemed to bring into sharp focus one particular aspect of what had hither to been a more or less blurred panorama filling the entire background of the new venture; in other words I was trying to fill a position which was well described as 'plain bloody impossible'. It occurs to me that the Ministry men could have seen very easily why I should have any notable difficulty with my work. They had no practice. The practitioners in Kirkwall may not have seen it either. Neither they nor the Ministry men were single handed.

But if I did nothing else I at least showed at that the day when one person could meet all the demands of practice and Ministry work in those six North Isles if there ever was such a day had long since passed.

In trying to please everybody or at least as many people as possible I most likely pleased nobody very well and wholly displeased others. All the same, those who had demands on my services or were dependant to some extent and in some respect on my own work were very ready to go running with a complaint not to me but to Divisional Office. How often I heard the cry, 'He should be reported!' not about me but about others. Hearing that about others what reason had I to suppose that I would be spared the same? One easily noticeable feature of that oft-recommended procedure was that those most ready to use it were seldom those who had themselves at any time attempted any form of public service except perhaps of the most undemanding kind. With a little reflection one could see the idea and a very attractive one it is. 'No, no, I cannot give a hand to push or pull the cart myself but I can sit on it, hit the horse and tell it what to do.'

Nevertheless to one who had put all his resources, physical, mental and material into the venture and expended his best effort as I had done, however inadequate and misguided it may have been for some or even all of the time, to have given them as I believed I had given more help veterinary wise than they had ever had before and then instead of receiving any mark of appreciation had complaints about me go over my head unknown to me and by persons unnamed to me was something which largely removed any motive I had still got left in me. I did not ask for the names of the 'numerous' complainants. How numerous they were, and I had only unsupported allegations that there were any at all, was of no consequence to me without the relevant names and addresses and these I would never have got.

That was near the end of my reign as uncrowned underpaid veterinary trail-blazer in the North Isles and I became somewhat depressed. In what might pass for the wording of a weather report: 'A deep depression has settled over that particular part of Orkney with some showers and a few bright intervals. This depression will be slow to clear but will gradually give place to brighter weather coming from the south.' Not quite authentic met.-man stuff but it will serve.

There happened also about that time something else which did nothing to lift the depression.

I had completed the work for my fourth winter and spring there. My financial year ended in late summer and my profit by chartered accountant's figures was my best to date, well up on any of my first three years. Income tax payable was virtually £444 which represented a fairly respectable taxable income for a one man practice and still a fairly new one at that in the year 1959-60.

That was all right. I paid it in two instalments of £222 each, less a penny or two. I have never felt I could afford to pay what the Income Tax man demanded of me but I managed it. Then a few weeks I got another demand for £50. I did not query it. I reckoned that by the time I would write back to HM. Inspector of taxes querying it, pointing that I had already paid two half yearly instalments, asking why should I pay this £50, write to my CA in Kirkwall and in the end possibly be advised to pay it, I might as well pay at the outset and have less trouble for the same ending.

'Besides,' I told myself gloomily, ' I can at best give only a fairly small part of my time to the cotes [?]and at that I am like a novice boxer versus a professional whose whole training and occupation it is. Climb into the ring with him and if he does not floor me immediately it will be only because he wished to amuse himself with my efforts at defence and counter attack.' I probably also had the feeling consciously or subconsciously that I was losing on all sides anyway: might as well let the tail go with the head.

A total payment of nearly £500 in 1959-60 was probably the equivalent of something like £2,000-£2,500 at the time off writing this some twenty years later. Still it was but one of a number of a number of things which together gradually dimmed the bright optimism and effort shown at the start of the venture.

One of these things was the problem of the car or rather replacement of the car.

I gradually came to understand about it that between running over long stretches of salt sands at low tides to reach certain somewhat inaccessible places and running often on shore roads with salt water on their surfaces my car, unless I washed its under parts after each journey simply did not stand a chance of long survival. To have attempted that much washing of it was not a practical proposition.

The outlook was blue merging into black. Once again I was in close sympathy with the Mayor and Corporation (of Hamelin town) in their deal with the Pied Piper. But their problem was comparatively simple: they had only rats and latterly the Piper himself to worry them. And if the Piper showed in his actions a degree of unpredictability perplexing to his employers, well, I reckoned I had learned something about unpredictability too.

Div. Office could not be as ready with a string of critical corrective comment on this occasion when the fault clearly lay with the livestock owner as the other times when the fault for something or other allegedly lay with me.

There must be innumerable people who finding they had not got satisfaction on some issue pursed it with one part or another of some government department only to give up in frustration after a prolonged effort which gained them nothing. How many of us setting out to obtain for ourselves or others if not justice, at least a ruling or an explanation of a bad decision, have come to the same conclusion as that cynical individual who declared that God seemed mostly to be on the side of the big battalions. Cynical perhaps but realistic too for so often it does seem that while might is not necessarily right (though it may be), might is generally what prevails.

There is an unmentioned but nonetheless well known technique for dealing with tiresome little people who want answers to awkward questions or perhaps something more than that such as correction of or explanation of anomalies, inconsistencies etc. especially if there is any question of further departmental expenditure or of saying anything and any way committal.

Your letter is under consideration; it has been passed to the department concerned; it is awaiting our receipt of the information you request; of course you raise some interesting points and these have been drawn to the attention of our Mr Blank/ Dash/ Stroke who will be replying to you in due course.

The reply when received is either irrelevant, non-committal about everything, a rebuttal of your main points, a combination of any two or more of these or not a letter at all but a phone call.

And how fearless the caller can be. The singlehanded principal of a small practice in his capacity as local veterinary inspector will be addressed and told things in tones no less authoritative and not more conciliatory than would be used to address say the president of the National Farmers' Union. The chances of the former being able to make a recording of the telephone conversation would be remote and even if he had one such a record would not be admissible anywhere as evidence. Receipt of a few such calls by me at times over the years did gradually produce some extension of experience and with it some change in outlook.

Of course it is well known to some people at any rate that one great advantage of a phone call whether in reply to written word or as a message delivered without warning is that it catches the recipient unaware and if he or she is inexperienced, unprepared for it. So the caller can spend whatever time may be desired beforehand to prepare a message which may be an apparently inane collection of rambling irrelevancies and any other such deadly devices as may be chosen for the purpose. That purpose may be the intended refutation of some point previously raised or to present fresh information or may be just barely disguised hectoring.

The recipient's best defence does not consist of saying that there is someone else present with him or her as that may only encourage the caller who then says that what he has to say will only take a minute and who may be very appreciative of any additional audience. The recipient had best have someone else knocking and ringing urgently at the door just at that moment or at latest just when the caller is launching into his main theme if he had one. Better than that of course if a pan of fat or even milk is boiling over or the room being set on fire by the baby, the electric radiator or even a spark from the fire. The next step, having gabbled one's explanation into the mouthpiece, is to tell the caller how terribly sorry you are to interrupt the call but will call back later. You don't need to say how much later.

Where such a call is received in a situation where none of the above happenings can be arranged (pans of boiling fat and toddling babies in busy offices being really not too credible) you can have a shockingly bad line full of static as with a matchbox in well practised hands at the mouthpiece. The recipient who is trying very hard to hear what is being said then shouts through all the static to the caller that he had better write whatever it is he wishes to say. Always keep two or three empty matchboxes near the telephone if you really must have one.

These then are some of the simpler ways of answering the less acceptable phone calls. The telephone being such a temperamental creature, one time all smooth cooperation the next time a quite unhelpful, downright obstructive opponent of easy rapid communication the caller would never establish evidence to match any base suspicious he might have.

Another course of action I might have adopted regarding the starving herd would have been to approach the Royal College of Veterinary Surgeons for a ruling as proper procedure on the matter of discovery during a visit of chronic maltreatment of an entire herd of cattle small though that herd might be. So why not? To give a ruling on a local matter of that kind would have been difficult if not impossible. To get one would take time. In this case there was no time to initiate this case and conduct a probably protracted correspondence and inquiry on it. A long phone call, perhaps more than one phone call, might have cleared up the matter. I did not know and was not keen to find out. The calls would of course have been between me in the North Isles and the Royal College in London.

This problem of procedure such as in the above case was but one of many which had cropped up as my new situation developed and for all I know now or ever knew it and the others may have had more effect on me than I realised at that time. It does not matter now. This much I did know: that things were going less and less well for me.

Labouring on and 'labouring' just about describes the heavier parts of my outside work to which I sometime alluded as 'high class navvying' and meant what I said, I seemed to find less and less opportunity for discussion with anyone who might be conceivably of some help or at least interested not so much in my affairs as in the difficulty I found in dealing with them.

So far from finding help there was one time when staying in the hotel in one of the islands I was taking part in what I thought was a quite inconsequent conversation. The others taking part in it were the local doctor his wife and one or both of the couple who had the hotel. During it and in line with the general run of the talk I happened to say that I thought I was probably taking too much whisky in the course of the day (nearly all drinking men and women express this same pious sentiment from time to time) and I thought no more about it. I believe I added that I would probably be better in lodgings where there was no supply of booze.

Now, at this point in the story I do not, could not, blame anyone if he or she should disbelieve what I am now going to tell even though what I tell is the unadorned undeniable truth.

That same day or the next day I was out on a round either on tuberculin testing or on clinical cases and duly got back to my hotel room. Blow me sky high if I did not find that my room had been stripped clean of all my effects. Immediate inquiry of the management by me as to the whereabouts of my stuff produced the information that it was not even in the hotel but they did tell me where it was. When I approached them I thought nothing else but that my room had been changed and that they had somehow forgotten to tell me. How wrong I was in my second surprise, how right with the first.

My room had certainly been changed. So in fact had my address. My stuff was not even within the hotel because the doctor had taken upon himself to arrange with the people in one of the local private houses to have me as a boarder for the remainder of my stay that time in that island. Without any discussion with me or warning of any kind to me he or others or perhaps with the help of others had entered my room, removed all my property and transferred it to the house he had selected for me. That to me was absolutely breathtaking yet one peculiar little feature I noticed about the transaction was that although I made plain both to the people in the private house and to the hoteliers that the move had neither my knowledge or approval, no one seemed to show any sense of outrage nor even surprise about it all.

Ah well what now? Although I had not exactly 'asked for it' I had certainly 'got it' and having got it decided to give it a trial. Although far from pleased by the incident and greatly puzzled by the behaviour of whoever created it I decided to stay on if I could in the house to which my stuff had been taken. The opportunity so oddly created seemed worth pursuing if against all indications and expectations it could be made to work. I have used the word breathtaking and I quite literally would have needed a better supply of breath to have asked all the questions I had in mind.

It was probably some time before that incident that the young doctor and his wife invited me over to their house for supper one evening shortly after we first met. I gladly accepted and duly fulfilled the invitation, for evening entertainments of any kind were all too few. When I got there I found a parking place for my car about twenty to thirty yards from their front door, reckoning that the evening might be a dry one which it was I had a modest tot on my own in the car. That tot carried the double purpose of making my own conversation flow more easily and making theirs seem more interesting.

Looking back on that evening as I have done many times since then I should have seen then what I saw later that one certain remark by the doctor might have warned me of something. We were exchanging our reminiscences: what we agreed was good and what was bad, what needed doing and what needed undoing, when out of the blue it came:

'I saw you having a drink in your car before you came in here.' Now I am not all that easily shocked or otherwise upset and to learn in that manner that my host had been spying on me was making no secret of the fact and was taxing me with it as if I had done something wrong did not stop my replying mildly, 'Yes, I had a spot of whisky before I came in.'

I forget what if any colourless rejoinder he or his wife made to that but I must have been finally resolved to stay polite at all costs for I managed to avoid adding any tailpiece out of several which sprang to mind. I might for instance have said but did not say, 'You see, I guessed that was more than I might be offered here and I seem to have been right about that idea.'

Conversation thereafter no doubt would have become a little strained and although I did not finish my visit immediately after that incredible gaffe by mine host I probably left earlier than was first intended.

After he had taken upon himself to change my lodging in such abrupt manner I felt strongly like taking action either at common law or by complaint to that body which governs the professional conduct of doctors even if only to save him from his own possible future unbalanced actions. It could happen, I reckoned, that he would equally offend and insult someone else who would not stop at there mere feeling of anger but would take action of some kind. In the end I did nothing, partly for lack of time but I judged my best plan to be 'masterly inactivity'.

How did his plan for my lodging work out anyway? It did not work out at all well as we were soon shown by a prime illustration of how awkward it could be. The owner of the hotel kept a small flock of sheep. One of those sheep was not merely trying to lamb but trying to do it in the middle of the night: at least it was about three o clock in the morning when the phone rang in the house where I was then staying. The man of the house came to my bedroom door and gave me the message.

The sheep were not kept at the hotel but at a smallholding which had on it unoccupied buildings two or three miles up the island. I was able to get fairly close to the place with my car and then on foot to follow the man with the Tilley lantern for the rest of the way. The patient was in very bad shape. Not only the owner but two other men as well had had a go at delivering the lamb or lambs. I never found out how many were there because when I tried to insert my hand which was slim compared with theirs I found the passage swollen and dry and the uterus at least dry, so much so that I could hardly brought out anything much bigger than a kitten so little scope was there for me to move my hand. Only with much lubrication did I gain entry at all but still could not manipulate anything.

There remained the question of a caesarean. Against the patient's chances of surviving that rather formidable operation was the presence of considerable toxaemia and quite probably septicaemia. I had medicine to counter both of these. The other main obstacle was her enfeebled state. The journey in some vehicle or other back to the village and the delay for the patient while we prepared for the operation, found a place, found a suitable table and sterilised everything to be used in the wound, etc., were going to reduce seriously any chances she might otherwise have had. The lamb or lambs were almost certainly dead: certain enough that they could be presumed dead. Even if I got a successful outcome to the case the value of the ewe the would probably be less than I would have had to charge for the operation and medication.

The owner may have had a pretty clear idea beforehand of what the outcome of the case was going to be because without further delay after I had discussed the case with him he produced a twelve bore shotgun and cartridges. I made the bang. We all arrived back at the hotel where we stopped until daylight came in, thus avoiding further disturbance of the residents in my new lodging. I found an opportunity to impress on the owner that if he ever had any more lambing cases which he thought I should attend, please, please to let me have the first of them. To be brought in at fourth hand, I told him, as happened in this case, did not give either the ewe or me much of a chance.

I lodged in the private house for a few days after that but what with the awkwardness of receiving messages with the unannounced change of address and phone number, lack of any notice to stock owners beforehand, the usual irregularity of meal hours, etc. it was soon decided that I was better placed in the hotel so back to the hotel I went. The precipitate and unbalanced action shown in moving all my effects from the hotel, whatever harm it may have done, certainly did no good at all.

Several times about then and many times since then I have wondered if every stranger who came to work in the North Isles was similarly liable to be the subject of unwanted attentions from somewhat irrational doctors or was I alone specially favoured in that respect? It seemed and seems a valid question.

Damn it all, I thought to myself, some folk might think that to be answerable to the Ministry of Agriculture on at least two of their schemes in those six North Isles, to the Highland and Islands Veterinary Service Schemes, to the Income Tax people and last and most important the livestock owners, made more than enough demands on my time and energy. If these islands were also to be, as they seemed to be in some cases, the last refuge of certain types of doctors, could at least be spared their unrequested, unwanted and unhelpful attentions. So far as I was concerned the difference between their attentions and the help of just one competent doctor had I been able to reach one when I wanted one could have been vital to the success or otherwise of my venture as I called it.

CHAPTER 32

When I first started in the North Isles one of my first jobs was the case of a flock of sheep in Westray. They were not thoroughly sick and they were certainly not thoroughly well. They ate but without zest, they could move but did not seem too sure about how to move nor if they decided where they wished to go or how to get there. They were not all equally affected and the trouble, if I remember rightly, seemed to be confined to the in-lamb ewes.

I had never before had experience of anything quite like it either in the sheep or in any other animal. All I could do was to note as much about the trouble as I could see at the time and find out more about it afterwards. Among the first information I received was that the trouble now affecting the sheep or one indistinguishable from it had been seen a few times in the past but had worn off gradually without anyone knowing the cause or why it went away.

I duly relayed all I could tell to the appropriate research station of the Animal Health Branch of the Ministry of Agriculture and got back word saying that the syndrome sounded more like cobalt deficiency than anything else. They added that while that was the one deficiency for which they could not test they suggested that a course of cobalt be administered. That was done, the symptoms disappeared and some years later had not returned.

That case was of interest partly because it seemed to be one in which we all learned together, the stock owners and myself, while presumably the research people were enabled to add to their maps of cobalt-deficiency areas another one which they had not known until then.

Another special area deficiency which seemed to come slowly to light was that of magnesium on the island of Sanday. More than once to my knowledge cattle which were most often cows in full milk were either found dead or died before help could be got to them. This seemed to happen rather oftener on Sanday than on the other islands though there may not have been a lot to choose between them in that respect.

There was the time when I did as I had unwittingly done at times before just as then. I fell in with a passing flu germ while I was on Sanday. That particular virus put me to bed with a temperature showing about three degrees of a rise. When as it happened I had pretty well finished emptying jugs of watery drinks and testing the absorbency of various towels on my skin and was thinking about hitting the deck again, I got a message. This one came from Divisional Office, to which the matter had been reported. Two cows had been found dead out of doors at a small place a mile or two up the island. The message was passed to me simply for me to decide whether I suspected notifiable disease or not.

One sudden death could be anything. Two like that in the absence of lightning or possibly poisoning which were both ruled out looked as if they might just possibly be due to anthrax: highly unlikely but of course no one could say definitely that it was not.

As things had turned out the steamer sailing for that week suited me for the purpose of having the microscope and the methylene blue stain sent over from Stronsay. They were sent and duly reached me in Sanday. I drove to the place where the two carcases were, made smears from both of them and my smears were good but as anticipated they showed no trace of *B. anthracis*. I knew what the little blighter would have looked like had he been there because I had seen him once newly fixed on a slide about twenty-five years earlier and pictures of him occasionally since then besides having seen him at college and I knew he did not change much with the passage of time.

So to the relief of everybody concerned the carcases were declared negative for anthrax but with everything to suggest that they were cases of magnesium deficiency. I mean, at least, cases which we commonly call grass staggers and which whatever the real trouble is respond to injections of a magnesium salt in solution. To be simply and solely deficiency of a magnesium salt or salts in the bloodstream they seem to develop and have fatal consequences in a terrifying short time.

For many years now it had seemed to me quite mysterious that a bovine animal at no particular age or stage can be apparently normal at one moment and within an hour or two of that moment be dead or dying of some ailment which is arrested by timely injection of a salt of magnesium, generally the sulphate. Because such dosage can and does to all appearances save the animal's life we call the ailment magnesium deficiency but can mineral deficiency by itself possibly develop from apparent normality sufficiently to cause and be the sole cause of the animal's death within an hour? Though to me this ailment remains a mystery, I daresay there is now a much greater understanding of it gained since those days when I was last confronted with cases of it.

At this point a really competent practitioner, having started a discussion of this kind when in the company of his colleagues and got it really going, will soon remember a really urgent appointment elsewhere which he really must keep. He then quietly and rapidly evaporates. Of course, the people who are most likely to know most about this trouble and who are best placed for finding out more are the research workers in laboratories and elsewhere sometimes likened to detectives in other professions.

But I did not need any detective to tell me that same evening that my little excursion up the island had been a trifle premature. I know that better next day when I was in bed again.

Whether it was on that same visit to Sanday or on some other one I cannot say but I recall that there was one time when doing the herd test of a biggish herd test in the north end of the island everything in the cow byre seemed normal as we worked our way through it. We carried on through some more cattle, stopped, had dinner, resumed work and were walking through the cow byre again when one of the cows was seen to be obviously ill. She was not near calving either past or to come and this dramatic collapse did not look like calcium deficiency in any case.

There was very likely a good fairy passing by just then who kindly dropped the idea in passing because suddenly I got it. How else I got it I cannot imagine for the case must have been one of the first if not the first of its kind that I had seen anywhere in the isles. Magnesium. Without a word of explanation I took off for the car followed by a astonished farmer's son who seeing me cantering briskly across the yard was no doubt that although all farm vets were somewhat mad some more than others I had at last gone quite, quite all the way. Gosh what a pity. And me such a nice chap too.

To the boot of the car. Bottle of magnesium, the flutter valve injection apparatus, into the house for hot water or if not hot as warm as could be had just then, to heat the injection. The flutter valve was already sterile in its container, normally kept ready for immediate use as at that moment. We got the stuff into the cow via the anterior abdominal vein commonly called the milk vein. I may have placed the last part of the injection subcutaneously somewhere near her backbone: I forget now but anyway we got a pleasingly rapid response. I may be wrong about this but I reckon that that cow just before that treatment did not have a great many more minutes to live.

There were sundry other cases which I did not see but which by what I was told of them during consultations by telephone seemed to support my idea about exceptional magnesium deficiency In that area. There was another case, not on Sanday this time but on Stronsay, to which I was called and though I got there in something like fifteen minutes the patient was quite dead. From what was said on the telephone I got the impression that the speaker thought the case might be already dead or dying even as he spoke. That case was again a milk cow, this time about four miles distant and I reckon that no matter how quickly I had got ready for take off and covered those miles the outcome would have been the same. It was just one of those cases for which the practitioner sadly writes opposite the note in the daybook DBA commonly used to mean Dead before Arrival.

That cow was a fair example of the sort of case which neither I nor anyone not close to it as it developed could hardly have expected to win. Many a time before and since then I have wondered how many other cases occurred to which I was called and of which I never even heard.

I still had the feeling that with something like 14,000 cattle in the six islands, no matter how clear of trouble they were when I set out to practice there (and at that time pretty clear of trouble myself), there were bound to be many more veterinary jobs among them all than I was ever told existed. That thought which amounted almost to a certainty emerged only very gradually.

One consequence, perhaps foreseeable by a very wise person, did eventually develop and was perhaps inevitable. It was that as the number of call out to cases from being nil at the start of my venture never rose above a thin trickle, probably fewer calls in a week than an ordinarily busy practice would take in a morning, my preparations for those few gradually diminished. Thus there came to be what could properly be described as a very mild slow downward spiral.

It was near the end of my third quarter of my seventh year there when the Ministry of Agriculture representative and about the same time the HIVSS spokesman told me that it was considered advisable that I resign from each appointment and so, acting in accordance with that advice, I gave each party my resignation. Only then did I discover that those two bodies were represented to me by the same individual, one who was well known to me though it seems now that I did not know him well. In all my years there he never once indicated that he represented both.

At the end of my appointments and for a little over a year following resignation I was pretty much free to do as I pleased so far as one very unreliable back permitted which was sometimes not very far at all before progress would be abruptly halted. But so far as dear old back allowed I was able to enjoy my surroundings. From where I lived in the village of Whitehall on the north shore of Stronsay the tiny island of Papa Stronsay lay only two or three hundred yards away to the north. In area it is less than half a square mile yet despite its smallness it has on it a fairly big farmhouse with all the usual outbuildings and a loch which is big in relation to the land area of the island. In former times the entire island was used and occupied as a farm and evidently a fertile one at that. And if the farm was a trifle isolated, at least the farmer would have no quarrels with his neighbours about fences or drains or water rights, things of that kind. His only neighbours were the seals which occasionally came ashore.

There were still a few cattle on it during some or all of the time I was in those parts and I sometimes had to go across to them though for what purpose is not now clear but it was probably for tuberculin testing. Papa Stronsay like Stronsay itself was used in bygone days for sites for much of the work connected with the herring industry.

Of this industry there are still many relics to be seen in both islands which between them form a natural shelter for small vessels. Stronsay itself still had two massive stone built piers about 80 to100 yards apart. When I was there the village still had one or two people who had walked across from pier to pier on the decks of the fishing boats moored side by side with many more tied between them and the shore. Stronsay was said to be the biggest centre for the herring industry between Fraserburgh and the Faroes until the war brought it to an abrupt halt in 1939.

Interesting as those comparatively recent developments were they were far less so to me than the archaeological remains to be found in the island much as the Pictish dwellings or what are said to be Pictish dwellings on Lamb Head. These are what seem to be simply two or three stone lined pits connected by narrow covered trenches also stone lined. I have leaned into them and peered in as far as I could without falling in but I learned little about them that way and what was their purpose and approximate age nobody could tell me. I doubt if even their existence is known to archaeologists. It did not seem to be when I was there. It has been claimed that the chambers and trenches communicate with the face of the sea cliff which is only a few yards away and that as well as being dwellings they may have been part of a defensive system, maybe as a look-out post and certainly for that purpose they would seem to have been admirably situated.

For myself I would just love to know what went on there not merely hundreds but thousands of years ago. Did those prehistoric people keep cattle and sheep and did prehistoric vets go round them trying to cure whatever ailments they had? There now is but one interesting line for further investigation. Maybe one day I shall go back and explore a little more than was done first time, then write a most learned thesis on it after giving it proper thought.

And I bet that any archaeologist reading this putative work would find in it such new information which he or she and colleagues never imagined existed until then (which it didn't anyway). And for sure any old Pict returning to that scene and whatever I might write about him would immediately and vigorously protest that he was not to be depicted in that manner. Meantime I reckon I must leave that and and other things thereabout as they are, for some little time yet, anyway.

Above: Machrie and part of the west side of Arran - about one mile from the author's birthplace.

Below: The Mull of Kintyre from Catacol.

Above: The Newton Shore at Lochranza

Below: Robert Sillars, July 2007 - A short distance from the road between Lochranza and Sannox.

Above: Sannox Beach - almost identical to the view my father had when he wrote this book.

Below: Brodick Bay - with the author's final home just about visible on the left.